THE IMPACT
OF THE UNION

EIGHT ECONOMIC THEORISTS

EVALUATE THE LABOR UNION MOVEMENT

Edited by David McCord Wright

John Maurice Clark

Gottfried Haberler

Frank H. Knight

Kenneth E. Boulding

Edward H. Chamberlin

Milton Friedman

David McCord Wright

Paul A. Samuelson

Essay Index Reprint Series

BOOKS FOR LIBRARIES PRESS
FREEPORT, NEW YORK

071843

STANDARD BOOK NUMBER:
8369-1116-4

LIBRARY OF CONGRESS CATALOG CARD NUMBER:
69-17596

PRINTED IN THE UNITED STATES OF AMERICA

Contents

Contents

INTRODUCTION

WE PRESENT in this book an edited report of the Institute on the Structure of the Labor Market held at the American University (Washington, D. C.) on May 12 and 13, 1950. Since this institute was unusual in several respects, it will help to explain something of its underlying philosophy.

People today are increasingly coming to realize that while specialization has great advantages it has disadvantages too. The specialist, often preoccupied with some particular technique, may lose sight of those parts of a problem which do not come within his special frame of reference. Theoretically, of course, the work of different specialists with different approaches may be correlated, but this does not necessarily happen. And even when it does, some of the basic problems may be lost amid the interstices of special disciplines.

Accordingly, the authorities of the American University felt that labor difficulties are so pervasive an element in the modern economy that academic specialization and compartmentalization, as useful as they are in other areas, might fail to do justice to them. The most fruitful discussion of labor issues, it was thought, might often be expected from those economists who combine with an intimate knowledge of empirical data the habit of thinking in terms of the economy *as a whole*. This statement is not intended to minimize in any way the value of the specialist. It was merely felt that a conference of general economic theorists might relate certain factors and bring to light certain problems that might prove to have been largely neglected in more specialized inquiries.

Following out this plan, eight outstanding general theorists, representing a wide variety of economic and political points of view, were invited to participate in the discussions.

It was decided to organize the institute as a sort of "conclave" in order to save time and to maximize results. Since every participant was familiarized in advance with the content of the papers submitted by the other conferees, time-consuming introductions could be spared. After listening to a relatively brief summary of every paper, the group was able to plunge into discussion.

A policy of privacy seemed preferable, furthermore, on the grounds that certain technical questions of economic analysis could be better clarified in a small intimate group. There was less temptation to deviate, and reconciliation of differences was made easier. In the absence of an audience, nobody would be tempted to speak *pour la galerie*.

The formal papers presented here have been carefully revised by their authors in the light of the discussions. In addition, a unique feature of the present volume is the inclusion, after each formal paper, of lengthy excerpts from the oral discussion which followed its first reading. While these excerpts have been edited in the interests of brevity, clarity, and coherence, a great effort has been made to preserve as much as possible the atmosphere of informal discussion and to stick as closely to the actual words and order of the dialogue as the standards named would permit.

The contributors have all, with one exception, been able to revise the edited discussions of their papers before the book went to press, and all have seen the complete galley proof of the book before the make-up of page proof. Because of the absence of several participants in Europe it was impossible to get transcripts to everyone as soon as we would have wished, but the co-operation of contributors has nevertheless enabled us to produce a satisfactory transcript. The reader should remember, however, that these are the "off-the-cuff" remarks of an informal discussion. They were not, and are not now, presented as authoritative. Nevertheless it was thought that the interchange of ideas in the excerpts would be of great interest to the general public and would serve to point up some of the outstanding issues. Final responsibility for the publication of this material must rest with the publishers and the editor.

The participants have had complete freedom in the preparation and revision of their papers. Occasionally, editorial footnotes have been added, but that is all. In some cases the participants varied so widely from their prepared statements as virtually to give new papers: in one instance, where the divergence was widest, both papers have been presented in full; in Professor Samuelson's case, the essential content of his remarks at the Institute, as distinguished from his formal paper, appears in his final comment. This comment, together with the final comments of some of the other participants, will be found at the end of the volume.

This book is not intended to achieve anything so grandiose as a "cure" for the labor problem. We do feel, however, that here are presented a number of vitally important questions which must be dealt with if a lasting solution is to be reached, and which are frequently overlooked. We present this discussion in the hope that it may contribute something toward a workable and democratic solution.

In conclusion, the participants and the editor wish to thank Dr. Fritz Karl Mann, Chairman of the Department of Economics, American University, who organized the conference and handled all the preliminary correspondence.

DAVID MC CORD WRIGHT

University of Virginia
Charlottesville, Virginia
March, 1951

CHAPTER I

Criteria of Sound Wage Adjustment, with Emphasis on the Question of Inflationary Effects

BY JOHN MAURICE CLARK

1. Revived Interest in Wage Theory of a New Sort

THE current revival of interest in wage theory involves an altered orientation in an altered setting, calling for a good deal of rethinking before applying familiar principles to existing conditions. One key element is a shift in emphasis among the various questions that theory may ask about wages. In particular, there seems to be a growing separation between the question of what determines wages, and the question as to what wages are economically sound.[1] In the days when the concept of competitive equilibrium was dominant, a single theory had some claim to answering both questions. But, with the growing power of unions, thinking about actual wage adjustments fell into the hands of labor specialists, increasingly absorbed in the strategy and tactics of collective bargaining. This bargaining appeared to consist of psychology, diplomacy, politics, and poker, backed by coercive pressures on occasion—the whole well fortified against pressures of supply and demand, and having little

---

[1] This is, of course, an oversimplification. Determinants may be examined under actual or hypothetical conditions; inquiry may be limited to the formal framework or pattern in which determinants act, or it may extend to the substantive levels and structures that result. Inquiry into soundness breaks up into effects—an objective question—and criteria by which their desirability will be judged.

to do with equilibrium or with competition as ordinarily understood by economists. Indeed, even its connections with the kinds of consideration customarily regarded as economic seem plentifully interwoven with other motifs.

Economic theorizing about wages, in making its necessary adaptations to this movement, has gone through various phases, to which Professor Chamberlin refers in his paper (chap. viii). Typical was the view that unions could not raise total wages above the competitive level, but might be useful in raising them up to this level if they were below it owing to employers' superior bargaining power. On the other side, unions might be harmful in distorting the relative adjustments in the wage structure and preventing salutary downward flexibility during recessions. Lord Keynes successfully challenged the usefulness of such flexibility and, in general, contributed to the decrease in theoretical thinking about wages.

But this decrease was only temporary. In the economics of total income, spending, and employment, wages cannot be permanently ignored, but the emphasis is now on effects of wages rather than on causal determinants of wage structures or wage levels, and old answers do not fit the new setting. As to the effect of general changes in the level of wages or prices on the volume of production or employment, it can no longer be simply assumed that general reductions will stimulate demand in the same way in which reductions of single prices or single wage rates increase the demand for a particular commodity or a particular kind of labor. In the single case, it is legitimate to ignore the fact that price is income as well as cost, since the spending of the income is diffused and not concentrated on the particular commodity. But for general movements exclusive concentration on the cost side becomes clearly incorrect; the income side is equally important, and a more comprehensive (and more complicated) treatment is called for. Such a treatment had to wait until economists, freed from the taboo of Say's law, were ready to undertake real analysis of the factors governing the total volume of spending.

Another orienting problem is the part wages play in inflation. Here a favoring circumstance is the fact that labor unions are now employing trained economists, who are concerned with rationalizing union objectives, including higher wages, with sound arguments; and who are at the same time concerned about the tendency of wage increases to be nullified, or partly nullified, by rising prices. Thus labor unions are beginning to think in terms of economic theories, as distinct from the arts of power and bargaining pressure, and to mix their cultivation of these arts with concern about external forces which set limits on what sheer bargaining power can accomplish. All these elements find expression in current theoretical thinking about wages.

2. *Some Basic Attitudes Toward the Market* [2]

The discussion at the conference revealed divergent attitudes on a number of underlying matters of the nature and behavior of the market and of market forces, making it highly advisable, in the interest of avoiding misunderstanding and waste motion, for each participant to explain where he stands on these basic matters. First, perhaps, may come the question of the precision and determinateness with which forces of supply and demand, and cognate forces, act in the market. Some of the members of the conference appear to hold that the equation of supply and demand determines both particular prices and general levels; that there is some level of wages that will "clear the market" (which must mean making supply and demand for labor equal); and that if the labor market is made competitive it will find that level. Some have indicated that the principle of marginal productivity dictates wage adjustments with

[2] Most of this section was inserted after the conference, to clarify my position on points raised in the oral discussion.

such precision that any material departure will have unfortunate economic consequences, including unemployment.

As against this view, I have elsewhere taken the position 'that most economic adjustments contain a substantial margin of indeterminateness, and that it is the part of science to recognize this.[3] For this purpose, "indeterminate" means "not precisely determined by the apparatus of demand curves, cost curves, or other determinants with which 'economic laws' have been constructed." Within this "indeterminate" range, other influences play upon the result. As more is learned about these other influences, uncertainty may be reduced, but discretionary action must presumably always leave a margin of indeterminateness for economists, and the growth of group organization tends to widen this margin. The idea that general levels of prices and wages are determinate, in the sense explained above, is a conjecture, and, in the face of the patent facts as to bargaining, elastic credit, managed money, and political intervention, bears a heavy burden of proof. The presumption is strongly against it.

More specifically, what makes the general level of prices? Differing concepts on this appear to underlie the divergence of view as to whether prices can be pushed up from the side of money costs, by wage increases, or whether this can happen only if there is an inflationary demand, in which case it will happen independently of any push from wages. This seems to be a problem about which economists can believe what they choose, and cannot be proved wrong. One school emphasizes monetary supply, the other income-flow as a determinant of total demand; one minimizes, the other stresses the facility with which businesses, forced to pay higher wages, can and will find ways to finance the outlay. They may use sluggishly moving bank balances more actively, or may get more credit and

[3] J. M. Clark, "Varieties of Economic Law and Their Limiting Factors," *Proceedings*, American Philosophical Society, Vol. 94 (1950), No. 2, pp. 121-126.

thus put more money, and more income, into circulation, possibly enough to sustain physical production undiminished at the increased cost rate. Probably no one regards the monetary supply and velocity as wholly inelastic and unresponsive to the "needs of trade," or as having unlimited capacity to expand in response to increased costs.

The view which explicitly or implicitly underlies typical attitudes would seem to be that, when total demand has an inflationary potential, prices may or may not rise by the full amount which this potential makes possible, depending on other conditions than the demand potential alone. It also seems to be implied that there can be conditions in which there is no *active* inflationary pressure from the side of demand, but in which demand is strong enough, and moods confident enough, to respond to increased money wages with increased credit and undiminished production. Short of this, there is presumably a condition in which monetary expansion will not offset the whole effect of a price increase, and therefore prices cannot be raised without some slight restriction of sales and some resulting unemployment, but in which unions may still push wages up, and thereby push prices up, not recognizing that increased wages can have any responsibility for increased unemployment—and indeed, in any particular case, the connection would be hard to prove. Existence of some unemployment does not as a practical matter veto a wage increase, though it may make it more difficult to secure.

This implies that unions can raise money wages—if that possibility is doubted—though it is consistent with Professor Friedman's contention (chap. x) that the power of unions in this matter is often overestimated. They can make larger gains when conditions of demand are favorable than when they are unfavorable, as Professor Friedman contends, but this does not prove that conditions of demand would have produced the same gains if there had been no unions. Unions consciously undertake to secure credit for gains that would have come without their efforts, but this does not prove that all such credit is 100 per cent fictitious. It seems rational to attribute to unions some influence toward the result that, over the nineteenth and twentieth centuries, gains in productivity in American industry have taken the form of a great increase in money wages, at a price level that showed no downward trend, rather than in reduced prices at stable levels of money wages. But monetary expansion would presumably have produced a good deal of this effect in any case.

The power of unions to raise real wages is probably subject to more reservations than their power to raise money wages. They could raise real wages if they increased productivity beyond what it would otherwise have been, or if they increased their proportionate share at the expense of other shares. They may, on balance, have reduced the proportionate share which employers would otherwise have kept; and insofar as this has happened, the results have probably been more favorable than unfavorable for total real production and income. They may have been able to do something equivalent to levying a tax on business profits, which could not be wholly shifted. But the share of business may be presumed to depend mainly on the effectiveness of competitive forces in limiting profits; and union activities have not been consistently on the side of stronger competition in the sale of business products. Moreover, the proportionate share of business has remained notably stable, in terms of long-run trends.

Those at whose expense organized labor has its principal chance to make gains are farmers, unorganized white-collar workers, some other workers on sluggishly adjusted salaries, and some recipients of long-term interest and derived incomes. Insofar as these gains come at the expense of previously more-favored groups, they may on balance be salutary, representing a hastening of an equalizing process which would otherwise have come in smaller degree and more slowly, through the effect of more equal educational opportunities.[4] The reverse is true of gains at the expense of less-favored groups.

The converse of the problem of general increases in prices is that of general reductions in prices, and especially of their efficacy in restoring shrunken demand. Earlier ideas as to their efficacy have been heavily deflated, and what remains applies more to the flexibility of particular prices than to general overall reductions.

The earlier ideas on this subject probably had some relation to the quantity theory of money. Under the most rigid form of this theory (which no one holds) the problem would be simple. If money, and its velocity of circulation, were both constant, or determined by factors independent of the volume of production and income, then a 10 per cent shortage of demand could be neutralized by a 10 per cent reduction of prices. Actually, the quantity of money shrinks, though less than the shrinkage of income, and velocity shrinks also. The upshot seems to be that it would need vastly more than a 10 per cent reduction of prices before the stagnant balances acquired such increased real buying power as to lure buyers into spending sufficiently more than a normal proportion of their shrunken incomes to overcome a 10 per cent shrinkage of demand. This is especially true because balances are likely to stagnate largely in the hands of businesses, which are unlikely to spend them unless demand from consumers is in sight. Thus it is natural that economists generally judge that, to be effective, a general reduction of prices would have to go so disproportionately far that other methods of supporting demand would appear less disturbing. On the other hand, economists generally agree that it is important that particular prices should be freely adjustable, and that reductions of single prices, which stand as

[4] *Comment by Wright:* But excessive pursuit of literal income-equality can involve several very undesirable consequences (see chap. xviii, "Concluding Summary").

obstacles to demand, can have a substantial effect on total real production and employment.

For the rest, I shall take the same basic attitude as in other recent writings: that powerful unions are not only inevitable, but indispensable; that their powers are necessarily monopolistic, in the simple sense of unified control of the fixing of the selling price of a factor of production; that some limit should be set on their powers, especially powers of coercion and restrictive powers which make them impervious to the forces of supply and demand; but that literal application of the antitrust laws is not warranted—the lines must be drawn in different places. This leaves unions with powers outside the contemplation of the competitive system, and this carries responsibility—recognized or not—for using these powers in ways consistent with the requirements of a healthy economy as a whole.

The alternatives seem to be: wage-induced inflation, or, if this is to be avoided, either voluntary restraint or compulsory control of prices and of wages. Professor Haberler suggests a further alternative (chap. ii): checking of inflation by fiscal and monetary restrictions and accepting the unemployment which would presumably result from limiting demand while wages and prices are maintained. Assuming that these last two methods are rejected as peacetime policies, we are driven to explore the remaining tolerable alternative, asking, granted that unions recognize that they have responsibilities (as, in general terms, they do), and further assuming that they are ready to let wage adjustments be governed by what is reasonable, instead of by sheer power, what standards might be formulated to give the needed definiteness to such a policy, how these standards might be implemented, what are some of the necessary conditions, and some of the difficulties that would have to be met; finally, granting that there will be shortcomings, how much in the way of shortcomings the economy can reasonably tolerate.

3. What Determines Wages?

This problem breaks up into the differential structure of wages as between industries, areas, jobs, and individuals, and the total level of wages, in money terms, in real terms, and as a fraction of the product of the industry in question, or of the product of the economy as a whole. The power of unions being what it is, these matters are, at least in the first instance, the playthings of bargaining forces—a term which to an increasing extent covers monopoly in the sale of labor. As to economic forces or laws, setting limits on the heights to which union bargaining power can force wages, I shall consider only one: the fact that the sum of real incomes is limited by total output, and total real wage income is limited by total output minus the minimum necessary allowance for the other shares. And, for the present purpose, we may concentrate on the share which it is necessary to allow to capital and enterprise.

This approach treats real wages as a residual share; and there is a good deal of reason in this view, always remembering that we are dealing with the share which has absorbed a larger total amount of the gains of technical progress than any other, and which has been very effectively administered on the principle of "more, without limit," and that we are asking what its inescapable limits are; also remembering that we are dealing with aggregates for the economy and not with the relation of wages and profits for a single enterprise where profits are the residual share.

For practical purposes, the trouble with this limit on wages is that it is ambiguous; it appears in at least two forms. In principle, there is the concept of the socially necessary minimum share of capital and enterprise, without which investment would be restricted, and total income would suffer, with the result that the attempt to force wages up would be self-defeating. If this kind of limit is self-enforcing, it must be so by trial and error—by transgressing it and taking the consequences. But if this goes on until error is demonstrated conclusively, it will mean transgressing substantially and for a considerable time, and the consequences might be fairly serious. Before these consequences are incurred, there is a more practical kind of limit likely to be encountered: namely, the power of business to protect profits by raising prices.

If competitive and other conditions were as an economic theorist would like to have them, these two limits might coincide closely enough so that the limit set by price inflation could be accepted as a warning that we were reaching the other, more fundamental limit, and as a safety valve to prevent us from exceeding it. Prices would not be raised as a result of a wage increase, unless the genuinely necessary minimum of profits was being encroached on; and prices would rise only enough to neutralize the excessive portion of the encroachment. The trouble is that there is no guarantee that prices will not rise before profits have been squeezed down to the genuinely necessary minimum, or that they will rise as soon as profits reach that minimum. And, since workers and employers are not likely to agree as to whether profits are or are not larger than necessary— or for that matter, as to how large profits actually are—neither are they likely to agree as to whether the rise in price that neutralizes the rise in money wages is the effect of an overruling economic law, setting limits on real wages, or is a case of arbitrary profiteering, which need not and should not be acquiesced in. The nature of the limit may be undeniable in principle, but the question of whether it has been reached in any given case bids fair to remain subject to dispute, at least until methods of proof have developed far beyond their present state.

The test may be made under different conditions, with corresponding differences in the results. It may happen when demand is strong enough to be inflationary. In that case, it is theoretically plausible that prices should take the lead, and wages should follow with a lag. That is the traditional picture, still spoken of as if it were an invariable "law"; but it is far too simple. It is likely to be true of raw materials; but under present conditions of union power and alertness, it is very likely to be more misleading than true in strongly organized manufacturing and other industries, where prices move sluggishly, especially when demand is not actively inflationary but is strong enough to permit a rise in prices if the push comes from the side of costs.

On the other hand, a wage increase may be forced when demand is insufficient and unemployment exists. Union economists have equally vigorous arguments ready for this case, urging that demand needs to be strengthened by the increased diffusion of purchasing power that would result. But while the arguments may be just as vigorous, the resistance will be stronger; the wage increases will be harder to bring about, and harder to pass on to the customer. If they are passed on, the result may be a restriction of demand that would neutralize the effect of increased diffusion of dollar purchasing power. And if they are not passed on, the intensified restriction of profits might intensify the shrinkage of capital outlays; and these effects might counteract any increase in consumer demand.

Another way in which high wages might limit employment is by stimulating the use of labor-saving devices, or the substitution of capital for high-priced labor. This would be opposite to the effect just considered, in that it operates via increasing investment rather than decreasing it. It has been pointed out that, if it is a question of a general rise in wages, the wage increase should increase the cost of capital goods as well as the labor cost of processing. The effect might then be limited to industries in which wages or wage costs had risen more than they had in the capital goods industries, or to industries in which wage cost is a larger fraction of total cost of the value-adding process than it is in capital goods industries. Or it might be simply that productivity has increased in the capital goods industries more than in many other industries, so that unit cost has not increased, though wage rates have; or that the capital goods have become more efficient in their performance. Then the real reason for introducing them would be the technical advance, not the increase in wages.

But when labor-saving equipment is installed, the immediate effect might be an increase of employment in the capital goods industries preceding the decrease in the industries where the equipment is to be used. If the process goes on continuously, in an expanding economy, it seems that the net effect on employment might be plus for a considerable period, though presumably not indefinitely. This consideration, for what it may be worth, reinforces the arguments of those who claim that higher wages make for more jobs, rather than fewer. We shall have to look further into this question.

Wages can be too low as well as too high, even—it seems reasonably clear—by the test of maximum employment. But in such a case, even more than with too-high wages, the economic consequences are likely to be postponed, and their causes disguised, so that they could not be depended on to act as automatic correctives. High profits, if gained at the expense of low real wages, are likely to stimulate a temporary investment boom, on too narrow a consumption base to be enduring. Ultimately, the boom would outrun the openings created by technical advance, plus consumer demand, but only after an interval.

The upshot of all these cases seems to be that the natural limits on wages, money or real, maxima or minima, cannot be depended on to bring about a determinate result, or to obviate controversy as to whether the natural limit has been reached or not. If the monopoly power of unions were destroyed, and single workers left bargaining competitively with employers, many of whom would still have a measure of local buyer monopoly power in their labor market, there seems ample ground for holding that wages would be too low for maximum employment, and profit rates too high for maximum continuing total profits. With monopolistic unions, pursuing the goal of "more, without limit" and using their power to the full, wages seem certain to be forced too high, with the kinds of consequences just sketched.

It seems that wages can only be kept more or less dependably within their natural economic limits by the conscious and intelligent pursuit of correct standards. There does not seem to be any devisable system under which the blind play of irresponsibly conflicting interests will bring such a result. I shall have more to say about this in connection with the contrary position taken by Professor Friedman (chap. x), who rejects both this proposition and the conclusion which seems to follow from it: that it is necessary to look beyond bargaining institutions to the end result, and ask what is an economically sound wage at which these institutions must aim if they are to bring tolerable results.

4. *What Is an Economically Sound Wage?*

This question may, if one likes, be restated in terms of two objective criteria, on which this discussion will concentrate. What wage will be noninflationary, and what noninflationary wage will be consistent with the closest practicable approach to full employment? The fact that people do not want inflation and do want high-level employment may, if one likes, be considered a coincidence in this objectively neutral inquiry. It is not stipulated that the wage shall actually bring about full employment, because it is not certain that any wage structure can do this; a good wage structure may be necessary but not sufficient. And of course an economy may be in an inflationary condition for reasons other than the behavior of wages; the suggested criterion means simply that wages shall not push prices up, or aggravate an excess of demand that may be pulling them up. As to wage differentials, the discussion will build on the concept of the kind of adjustment that would result from a dynamic, competitive process, one in which differentials are continually being created as well as ironed out. It will not assume the imaginary end result of abstract equilibrium, in which competitive processes would have to come to an end, along with all other processes of social life and change.

The requirements of a noninflationary wage have been discussed a good deal lately, and it is probably not necessary to dwell on them or to elaborate them.[5] The idea presupposes that prices can be pushed up by wage increases, as indicated earlier, whether or not this leads to unemployment. The basic requirement is that, in a long-term trend, money wages—probably best measured for this purpose by average hourly earnings—for the economy as a whole, should not rise faster than average productivity per worker-hour in the economy as a whole. Increased productivity is not the only possible source of wage increases; but it is the only thing that can enable a long-continued and substantial wage increase to be absorbed without pushing prices up.

At any given starting point there may or may not be some slack in profits out of which some wage increases in excess of increases in productivity might be absorbed. This is a question of fact, and at present a highly controversial one. It is also possible, as S. H. Slichter has suggested, that there is a long-run trend toward a very slow decrease in the percentage of total product going to property, and a corresponding increase in the percentage share going to labor.[6] In that case, if over-all productivity increased, for example, 2 per cent per year, it might

[5] Cf. S. H. Slichter, *The American Economy* (Knopf, 1948), pp. 37-39, 42-44; also "Productivity and Wages," *Review of Economics and Statistics*, November, 1949, pp. 292-311, by several authors. S. E. Harris, in an introductory note to the latter, credits Will Lissner with starting the present phase of the discussion.

[6] See Charlotte Knight, ed., *The Economics of Collective Bargaining* (University of California Institute of Industrial Relations, 1950), pp. 36-38.

be practicable for wages to increase very slightly more, but the excess would be of the order of magnitude of a very small fraction of 1 per cent. As for other shares than the employer's profits, opportunities for continuous wage gains at their expense also appear so small as to be negligible in the very rough approximations and crude adjustments we are dealing with.[7]

This principle does not mean that wages in particular industries should follow the course of productivity in these industries and their resulting ability to pay, promptly absorbing the whole of any gain. Still less does it mean doing this for single enterprises. Where productivity has increased in one industry more than the average for the economy as a whole, a mobile and competitive system would cause the gains to be diffused with a moderate lag, and the process of diffusion could most usefully begin at once, via a reduction of prices. This would tend to expand sales (unless demand was quite inelastic) and would help to prevent the improvement from leading to technological unemployment. If the wage structure were governed by impossibly perfect competition, wages would be no higher in this industry than in other industries in which productivity had lagged behind the over-all average, but in which the character of the work called for labor of equally high or scarce quality, and made equally exacting demands on it. If wages rose in all industries by the average rate of increase in productivity, money costs of production would rise in these lagging industries, and their prices would have to rise, while prices in the more rapidly progressing industries would be falling.

The nearest practicable approach to this theoretical standard is presumably a compromise, in which the gains from better-than-average advances in productivity would be divided between the employer, the customer, and the worker, with the customer's share increasing and the employer's share (from this particular improvement) dwindling as this improvement became standard

[7] Cf. Slichter, *op. cit.*, pp. 32-36.

practice, so that it set the general competitive pace. Most of the gain might go to increase the employer's profits at first; but as other concerns caught up, their competition would pass the gain on to the customer in lower prices.[8] And an employer with foresight would start giving the customer a substantial share at once, figuring that the resulting increase in sales would be likely to be more enduring than an extra-high rate of profit per unit, and therefore be a sounder form in which to take his gains.[9] The accompanying avoidance or mitigation of technological unemployment is something that should have a high place in any employer's scheme of objectives, in its own right; but it should also help to reduce the workers' distrust of improvements, and make them more willing to co-operate in their adoption.

As to wages, some differential would also serve a useful purpose in giving the workers an incentive to co-operate in the adoption of improvements. And it is natural that workers in the especially progressive industries would try to keep their special gains as long as possible. But if they got the whole gain, beyond the minimum share the employer needed to induce him to make the improvement, and if they kept it indefinitely, adding to it whenever a further above-average improvement was made, and if this became the general rule in the economy, wage differentials would become intolerably inequitable, as some industries maintained for a long time a rate of increase of productivity above the average, perhaps merely because they possessed greater natural opportunities, while others fell behind this rate, perhaps through no fault of their own. And employment in the more progressive industries would suffer, because the existing labor force would be capable of producing more,

---

[8] This whole process, I take it, is the one which Professor Wright speaks of as a "race between innovation and imputation."

[9] This might be regarded as a rough application of the "minimax" principle, complicated by incommensurable considerations.

but there would be no room for reducing prices, to enable the market to take the increased output.

A more reasonable practice would be to give a smaller wage differential, with the expectation that other groups would catch up in a few years, unless some fresh improvement kept the rate of advance in the leading industries ahead of the average. In this way, the temporary differentials could be ironed out upward, without the necessity of wage reductions.

Wage differentials due to a permanent decline in demand in some industries, and long-continued rapid growth of demand in others, might be more enduring and more likely to necessitate some reductions. But if the economy maintained its expanding quality, these reductions would not affect more than a minor fraction of the working population.

As to the requirements of a wage that would be consistent with maximum employment, it should presumably represent a division of the total national income, such that for any given income the total amount spent, for consumption plus investment, would be a maximum over a long trend. (It is assumed that the wage adjustment would not substantially alter the fraction spent by government, or the balance of imports and exports.) If an increase in wages came out of profits, without affecting in the first instance either prices or productivity, the optimum would be reached when the increase in consumer spending due to a wage increase was offset by a reduction of investment spending, due to the reduced share of profits. But this optimum seems likely to be the high point of a gently rounded curve, so that there would be a range—narrow or wide—within which a change in distribution would have only a very small effect on total spending.[10] This concept of a total-spending function probably has some indicative value for long-run trends, but for shorter movements the behavior of invest-

[10] This curve is apparently involved in one of the sections through one of Professor Boulding's contour maps (chap. vi).

ment is a more complex function of time, expectations (or moods of optimism and pessimism), and backlogs and surpluses left over from previous periods. In the latter respect, consumers' durable goods share the quality of investment, differing in being bought for use and not to produce a product for sale in an uncertain future market. It has already been suggested that without unions, the fraction going to wages would be below the optimum, and that with very strong unions, it tends to be pushed above the optimum.[11]

If profits are protected by raising prices to cover increased wage costs, then it may be that an increase in money wages has no power to raise real wages. In that case, the effects on the distribution of income, and the resulting effects on total spending, would be those resulting from inflation of the sort that is pushed up from the side of costs, as distinct from that in which the active force is an excess of demand over supply. In general, though one can hardly be certain, it seems that inflation of this cost-induced sort is likely to be unfavorable to a high total-spending function, even in a country as nearly self-sufficient as the United States is at present. To the extent that prices merely rise enough to protect the minimum necessary margin of profit, the effect is more favorable than if prices had not risen. In place of a transfer of essential income from employers to workers, there is a transfer from recipients of fixed or sluggishly moving incomes; however, this involves the need for an expanded total flow of dollar income and spending, which may or may not be forthcoming.

In a country that depends more heavily on foreign trade, the unfavorable effects of price inflation are greater. Conversely, the favorable effects of price reductions would be greater also,

[11] Professor S. H. Slichter has taken this position in various recent writings, especially "Wage-Price Policy and Employment," *Amer. Econ. Rev.*, May, 1946, pp. 304, 309-311; *The Challenge of Industrial Relations* (Cornell University Press, 1947), pp. 77-95; *The American Economy*, pp. 42-44.

though in any careful appraisal of the probabilities it would be necessary to take account of the stage of the business cycle at which the price movement occurs, and of the bearing of this on the responsiveness or unresponsiveness of demand.

The argument so far has gone on the assumption that the total-spending function is in no danger of becoming too large, and that any increase in it will take effect in increased production and employment. If the total-spending function is already so high as to be actively inflationary from the side of demand, then this assumption would be reversed, and the optimum wage would be one leading to a reduced total-spending function. Actually, as there is probably no need to argue, there is a wide range within which the effects of increased total spending are divided between more employment and higher prices.

Another requirement for maximum employment is that the structure of differential wages should not do such substantial violence to the relative productivities of different workers, at similar work, as to make some relatively unprofitable to employ, and therefore handicap them in seeking employment. This adjustment to relative productivity does not need to be precise. Even a cursory examination of the general character of prevailing methods of wage payment serves to indicate that they cannot possibly be closely adjusted to the relative productivities of workers of different productivity, who nevertheless are employed side by side. Perhaps the most important group of cases are the inferior workers who have to be hired as "full employment" is approached, but who are not worth the standard wage, unless the better workers are worth more. This suggests that these inferior workers—Slichter speaks of them as the last 5 per cent—do not become employable unless total demand has become inflationary. If so, that would seem to be a defect in the differential wage structure, putting an obstacle in the way of maximum employment.

5. *Does Full Employment Require an Inflationary Demand?*

Leaving the role of wage costs to be taken up later, we may consider the relation between full employment and excessive demand for goods. There seems to be a growing tendency, in planned economies, to seek full employment by building up an inflationary excess of demand. This may be reinforced by the view that full employment cannot be secured except in this kind of a market. This view has a good deal to support it, in spite of being less pleasant than the older theoretical Keynesian view that inflation (or "true inflation") could not or would not come about unless full employment was reached or exceeded. This was always too good to be true, for various reasons, some of which could be classed as monopolistic elements or other defects in the market structure, while others seemed, in effect, natural and unavoidable, though of course they would have more effect in proportion as the market was more seriously imperfect. We may look at the more natural causes first.

There are bound to be different relations of supply and demand in different parts of the economy at any one time: scarcities of some products and surpluses of others. This is inevitable in any growing and changing economy. Then, from one standpoint, if the shortages equal the surpluses, total demand may be said to be adequate, or sufficient for full employment; but this will not bring full employment, so long as the inequalities persist. Perhaps, in a theoretically perfect market, these inequalities would not persist; prices and wages would fall in the surplus sectors and rise in the shortage sectors, and resources would move from one to the other until an equal balance was restored. But this kind of perfect mobility and flexibility is out of the question.

Mobility of labor is obviously desirable, and much can be done to promote it, by better organization of the labor market;

but it can never be perfectly costless, frictionless, or unattended with risk or uncertainty. The resistances will be greatly reduced by a high level of demand; workers will move if they have fairly definite job openings to move to. But this still calls for time, and facilitating arrangements; also, if the openings require a worker to learn a new occupation, he may still fail to respond.

As to two-way flexibility of prices and wages, it operates within increasingly narrow limits. The freest flexibility, of course, is that which is natural to agriculture and some other extractive industries; but here downward flexibility is limited by the system of price supports. These supports included that of bituminous coal for a short time before the war, and may include it again. In manufacturing and trade, prices are characteristically sticky. Downward flexibility does exist, but it operates within limits which seem to be growing narrower. In manufacturing, price flexibility cannot go very far unless wages are also flexible; and the resistance of wages to reduction seems to be getting close to an absolute and accepted veto.

Under these circumstances, even a situation in which there is not excess of total demand, but in which surpluses and shortages are equal, would have a net balance of inflationary effect on prices, which would rise in the shortage sectors more readily than they would decline in the surplus areas. And this is for reasons, some of which it would be idle to dismiss as defects of the market structure; they are too nearly inevitable. This upward bias of the wage-price structure is probably not in itself large enough to be important, but it may be worth keeping in mind in connection with other upward pressures that are at work. It does furnish a reason why upward price pressures should appear while there is still some unemployment. If this unemployment is reduced by a general over-all expansion of demand without any improvement in the fluidity of the market structure, then before the last pools of unemployment are mopped up there will be an inflationary excess of demand everywhere else in the economy, or at least a net inflationary balance.

And it seems inherently probable that, if a high standard of full employment is reached, the accompanying inflationary pressure will drive prices up faster than the economy can safely endure.

This might lead different people to different policy conclusions, according to whether or not they set a high standard of full employment as an unconditional "must"; whether or not they object strenuously to direct controls of prices or wages, or both; whether or not they are prepared to do a good deal to assist and facilitate mobility in the labor market, or perhaps to use authority, ordering workers to stay in one job or to move to another, or holding this power in reserve for occasional use; and finally, whether or not they regard a creeping inflation as a lesser evil than any of the various things it is necessary to do to avoid it or to repress it.

Taking for granted at this point the necessary level of total demand, an economy that is willing to give workers orders as to what they are to work at and where, and can do this successfully, can handle a condition of very full employment without the necessity of inflationary pressure. If the authorities are unwilling or unable to go this far, but are willing to undertake direct controls of prices and wages, and able to make them work tolerably, they can handle a high level of full employment, and repress the accompanying inflationary pressures. If neither kind of regimentation is in their outfit of available or acceptable tools, then they must pin their faith on a highly mobile labor market, in which workers will move if jobs are open, without waiting for a shortage of labor to build up inflationary wage premiums. Even so, they can hardly hope to handle, without inflation, as high a level of employment as the regimenting types of economy can. But if they can keep labor highly mobile, they can probably handle a satisfactorily high level of total demand without a serious degree of inflation from the causes so far considered.

6. *The Push from Increased Wage Costs*

Money wages push up costs if they rise faster than average productivity per man-hour. The over-all increase in man-hour productivity for the economy as a whole is probably of the order of 2 per cent per year. But it appears that unions are under pressure to produce gains for their members amounting to a good deal more than this, in the form of money wages or allowances having an equivalent effect on costs. This pressure appears to be felt as compulsory—a necessity of survival for the union, or at least for the leaders, if they are to hold their jobs. Here lies one of the most deep-rooted dilemmas of unionism.

The forces working toward such an excess are formidable. While the large unions are keenly aware that wage increases matched by price increases are futile for labor as a whole, single increases are not futile for the particular union that gets them; the gain comes to its members and the price is paid mostly by others. One union can gain in this way, or it can lose if it neglects to keep up with the others. And 2 per cent a year is not a spectacular gain, though it becomes spectacular if it goes on indefinitely: it means doubling in about thirty-five years (and that would look rather munificent to professors, a class whose real income has not increased in the past fifty years—some would say it has decreased).

In any case, the war and postwar experience of this country went far to establish, in organized labor, a confirmed habit of getting much bigger gains than this modest 2 per cent. This has built up something very like a vested interest. During most of this period, wages were freed from normal peacetime dependence on the productivity of labor in terms of normal peacetime goods, while productivity in terms of munitions had no comparable meaning, and even the concept of "real wages" lost a good deal of its normal meaning (command over goods) when it included an abnormally large quota of savings which were, for consumers as a whole, compulsory.

The end of the war brought the drive to raise hourly wage rates so that the peacetime working week would earn as much as the longer wartime working week had earned with overtime. This called for a great increase of wage rates, not correlated with any commensurate increase in productivity. An inexorable drive to make this good, in real terms, would be bound to maintain an inflationary wage-price spiral, until such time as productivity could catch up with the increased real-wage target (minus whatever could be gained at the expense of other groups). This condition is temporary, but the habit of getting wage increases a good deal in excess of increases in over-all productivity may persist and make trouble over a longer period.

7. *How Much Inflation Is Tolerable?*

If the inflationary forces are as strong as this suggests, it may be overly optimistic to assume that they can be completely contained or neutralized. A more realistic objective may contemplate some long-term upward drift of prices, but may hope to keep it slow enough to avoid substantial harm. Some have contended that a spot of inflation has a salutary stimulative effect on the economy, shifting income from the passive saver and *rentier* to the active, promotional, risk-taking elements. Inflation means that the interest on loans is reduced by the shrinking buying power of the principal, and thus can be one form of "euthanasia of the *rentier*."

One possible standard might be that real interest might be reduced to little more than a nominal return, but not to zero or a minus quantity. On this basis, the limit might be set at 2 per cent per year, or even a fraction more. But the real yield of 2½ per cent government bonds would be wiped out by a 2½ per cent rate of inflation, and the Series E war savings bonds would be turned into a losing investment by an inflation of 3 per cent per year. I have been told that it is a weak argument that rests on such a degree of tenderness for recipients of interest. But when one considers the long-run effects on retirement annuities and funded pensions, the argument seems stronger. At 2 per cent annual inflation, a man who at age thirty contributes to a retirement contract destined to yield a stipulated income at age sixty-five will find that this income has lost half its value when he begins to receive it. That appears to be too much shrinkage.[12] Considering these long-run shrinkages and their impact, it seems that the rate of continued inflation that can be regarded as relatively harmless must be put at less than 2 per cent a year, not more.

Two per cent a year of increased productivity, plus less than 2 per cent as a tolerable margin of inflation, adds up to less than 4 per cent a year of over-all wage increase which the economy could permit without substantial harmful effects. This is an average for different occupations in the economy, and for the whole economy is an average long-term rate, which might cover considerable fluctuations between periods of expansion and recession. It might be economically sound to concentrate the increase of wages in periods of expansion, provided that labor would put up with getting no money-wage increase in times of contraction, during which a decline in the cost of living might still afford some increase of real wages and wages relative to efficiency might be going down, as Professor Haberler's paper notes (chap. ii). To assume that workers would put up with this may be somewhat optimistic. To assume continued economic fluctuations is hardly too pessimistic, in the present state of thought and policy on economic stabilization. Allowing for the likelihood that periods of recognized contraction may be shorter on the average than periods of expansion, and that

---

[12] Rising interest rates can offset the effect of a steady inflation on current payments; but inflation is seldom steady. Conversion of all fixed claims to terms of constant purchasing power would involve complications which are not here considered.

some wage increases may be made during contractions, one comes out with a very rough estimate of the average wage increase, during active or expanding times, which could be regarded as noninflationary—perhaps 3 per cent per year, with 5½ to 6 per cent representing the limit of tolerable inflation. The more successful the country is in maintaining a high rate of activity and in confining recessions and depressions to short periods, the lower these figures would stand; and if depressions should be completely conquered, the noninflationary rate of wage increase would come down to the annual average increase in productivity—here tentatively estimated at 2 per cent per year.

From this standpoint, the early postwar "pattern" of wage increases, approximately 10 per cent in the leading industries, but averaging much less for industry as a whole, appears to have represented a gain for some groups at the expense of others, while the average effect was inflationary. It could be justified as a way of compromising the vexed question of the immediate transition from a wartime to a peacetime working week, provided that it does not become a habit, and that productivity is given a chance to catch up. Whether this will happen remains to be seen.

8. What Are the Chances for a Noninflationary Wage Policy?

Professor Haberler suggests that the American public will not tolerate continued inflation, but will restrict it by fiscal-monetary means, even at the price of unemployment (chap. ii), and others have expressed the view that a limited number of years of inflation, even of the creeping sort, would drive us to resume direct controls of prices and wages. To Americans, this would be a most unwelcome choice, accepted only because the alternative of inflation was even more unwelcome. Are there other possibilities? One suggestion is to break all monopoly powers, those of unions as well as those of business, and establish a thoroughgoing competitive system, under which prices and wages would be fixed that would "clear the markets." I will discuss this later (chap. xvii), in connection with Professor Friedman's paper (chap. x), presenting reasons why the policy appears unavailable.[13] I shall consider another possibility, which will seem utopian to some, but is less drastic and less improbable: namely, voluntary adoption or acceptance of a noninflationary wage policy as a goal, with the hope that, despite departures in practice, the actual outcome might be within the limits of tolerable inflation.

Even Professor Friedman's suggestion rests on the hope that unions might be persuaded of the futility of their bargaining activities.[14] I do not believe these bargaining activities are futile, and accordingly would not expect them to concede it, or to surrender the powers they deem essential, without a violent struggle. But unions do realize, at least "in principle," the futility of wage increases that are offset by price increases. And if they also became persuaded that the public will ultimately respond to continuous inflation with drastic action, it is not inconceivable that they might be farsighted enough to make a virtue of discretion before the actual necessity materializes.

If such a noninflationary wage policy is to be put in practice by voluntary adoption, a number of difficult requirements will have to be met. First come the basic attitudes that underlie

[13] Compare page 12 where I have contended that, if workers competed fully in the sale of labor, wages would probably be below the maximum employment level or range.

[14] *Comment by Friedman:* I do not accept this interpretation of my position. I have no hope that unions can be persuaded to commit suicide deliberately. My suggestion rests on the hope that the community at large can be persuaded of the virtues of competition; and the belief that, if they are so persuaded, there is no serious technical obstacle to the attainment of effective competition. (See chap. x.)

willingness to co-operate. Second come various implementing means, especially data in form to bear on various disputed questions of relevant fact, and authoritative enough to command acceptance. Third come procedures, and probably some minimum of formal or informal organization. Incidentally, these would all be needed, in some form or other, if compulsory controls were resorted to. Data and organization are obvious needs, but without an attitude of acceptance compulsory controls could not succeed in any free country.

But first it may be pertinent to name a few requirements that would *not* have to be met. It would not be necessary to get a precise measure of changes in productivity in different industries, because no attempt would be made to adjust wage differentials to the movements of productivity in particular industries—quite the contrary. To give the workers in a particular industry the whole benefit of any more-than-average increase in productivity that might have occurred in that industry, would be contrary to the purpose in view; and if some fractional concessions were made, the amount would be dictated by other factors than the precise increase in productivity in this industry. It would not be necessary to follow the year-to-year fluctuations of productivity, even for the economy as a whole, since there is no need for cyclical changes in wages to follow the cyclical changes in productivity with any precision.[15] If cyclical wage adjustments were ultimately found useful, they would presumably not be governed solely by cyclical changes in productivity.

The suggested standard does not require determination of a precise pattern of wage differentials between industries or areas—still less freezing that pattern once it is determined. Patterns of differentials are not static, though spectacular

[15] For example, the data adduced by Clark Kerr, in "Productivity and Wages," *Review of Economics and Statistics*, November, 1949, pp. 299-309, do not constitute an objection to the form of productivity standard here suggested, which is similar to that outlined by Davis and Hitch in the same article, pp. 292-298.

deviations, like the gain of coal miners in recent years, are exceptional. There will be departures from any voluntary "pattern"; and it is conservative to assume that most of them will be upward. If the "pattern" were set at 2 per cent increase per year, there would be room for deviations that would nearly double this average, before the margin of tolerable inflation was exceeded.

As to attitudes, the first requirement is that wage negotiators, on both sides, should accept the idea that the basic pattern of wages should be governed by reason more than by sheer force, political or economic. Between accepting this "in principle"—which may mean no more than lip service—and a working meeting of minds there is a stony road to travel. But the promising fact is that actual negotiations seem to have moved an appreciable distance in this direction. The reasoning may be largely rationalization of interest and power; but it is possible to hope that there is more reasonableness in the underlying attitudes of the parties than often appears in their propaganda statements or bargaining contentions, for obvious reasons. At any rate, the process of argument as to what is fair affords a basis on which to build toward standards of fairness that may ultimately command general acceptance.

A second requirement is that the attitudes of bargainers should reflect the interests of consumers. It has been suggested that this would be promoted if the great federations would exert an active influence over the wage policy embodied in the bargaining of their constituent unions, in order to bring to bear on wage bargaining the interest of a group, the majority of whose members are interested as consumers in any one wage adjustment. This is not the same thing as economy-wide bargaining, of which Professor Haberler speaks in his paper (chap. ii). It may be, as he contends, that literal economy-wide bargaining would have more inflationary power than industry-wide bargaining—if it chose to use its power in that way. But unions appear to have quite sufficient power to produce an inflationary result, bargaining as autonomous units, and the suggestion of federation influence does not bear directly on the extent of their power, but on whether they would choose to use their power in that way.

One major obstacle to a noninflationary wage adjustment is the conflict over the reasonableness of the level of profits. As long as business succeeds in protecting, by price increases if necessary, a level of profits that labor regards as grossly swollen, strong unions may be expected to take an attitude like the following: "We don't think you have any proper business to raise your prices to compensate for this wage increase we're demanding. If you do it, we'll blame you. But if we know you're going to do it, we still want the increase in wages." If the dispute over profits were cleared up, possibly the wage demands would merely be rationalized differently, but they would be harder to justify. An important step would be taken if the level of profits that labor is willing to acquiesce in, and the level business will protect by price increases, became approximately equal. And it seems that the only route to such a meeting of minds is via a thorough airing of the facts and figures, including the thorny question of depreciation reserves in a time when prices have been rising rapidly.

It seems likely that both unions and employers have gone at this question wrong end to: unions prejudging arguable questions bearing on the justification of profits, and employers insisting that prices are none of labor's business, thus by-passing the relevant fact that labor's attitude on wages is affected, among other things, by its ideas and attitudes about profits. It seems that a fresh start is needed on this issue, with a more open-minded attitude on both sides.

I have deliberately put this question of profits ahead of the more obvious question of measuring gains in productivity. It is, of course, important to have the best data possible on this question, but the most pertinent index, at least as a point of departure, is probably an index of national income per worker-hour, deflated by an appropriate price index, as suggested by Davis and Hitch.[16] But such figures for the past are, of course, important only as indications of what may be expected for the future, and this is always subject to possible change, though the presumption is against sudden and radical departures from long-established past trends.

The proper role of economists in this matter is probably, in the main, the furnishing of the best possible data, rather than attempts at authoritative pronouncements as to what is economically practicable or sound. Economists have an unfortunate record of proving that things are impossible or unsound which afterward came to pass, without all the disastrous consequences that had been foretold. Wages have increased, during the past century and a quarter, more than most economists would, in general, have regarded as sound; and over most of this period the results have probably on balance been favorable, even to the long-run interests of business. At present, some economists lean too far toward supporting any and all wage increases. The views of economists deserve weight, but are not the final word.

Given the necessary attitudes and data, procedures for giving them effect still need to be developed. Here the next step may grow out of the method of intergroup conferences, toward which the President's Council of Economic Advisers is feeling its way, trying first to prepare the ground and afford a basis on which such conferences may progress toward more operational effectiveness than they have had in the past. Progress in this direction is more important than many other matters that are more prominent and spectacular.

[16] "Productivity and Wages," *op. cit.*, pp. 292, 295-296.

9. *Obstacles to Be Overcome*

One objection to the kind of approach here discussed is based on the contention that actual wage changes and differentials do not follow any such simple pattern as is contemplated, but respond to a multitude of factors, hardly reducible to any manageable pattern. It should go without saying that the mere fact that wages do not now behave in the way suggested is not proof that they can never alter this behavior. The practical student, familiar with the momentum of existing ways of doing things, may tend to underestimate the possibilities of rational change, just as the theorist, on his side, may underestimate the factor of inertia. Back of this factor lies the fact that negotiators have developed techniques, which they know how to employ, and in which they have a vested interest. Some individuals might be incapable of adopting successfully any far-reaching changes. Their minds are not exactly open to argument that these methods are not producing fully satisfactory results, and that other methods might work better.

One obstacle, already mentioned, is the need of unions, and of their leaders, to justify themselves to their members by substantial and tangible gains, in excess of what over-all productivity affords for them all, taken together. Contributory to this is the fiction that all the wage gains are wholly the result of union action, and also an unwarranted emphasis on wage gains as the most tangible and measurable form of benefit. If the suggested changes came to pass, unions and their leaders might feel that their importance to their members had been dangerously reduced—dangerously from the standpoint of their continued ability to hold their place and importance.

A truer perspective would, I believe, largely do away with this danger. As to wages, once unions are well established, and both sides have developed adult attitudes, it should not be necessary for unions to claim credit for all the gains that are made, in order to gain acceptance of the view that the contribution they do make is of strategic importance. Also, unions are vitally needed for other purposes, connected with the protection of the human rights of workers on the job; in fact, their contribution on this score is probably more important than the contribution they have made in securing larger wage gains than would have been made in any case, important as this contribution may be. Incidentally, their human rights contribution equally with their wage contribution may be in need of being put on a basis of equity and sound principle, as opposed to arbitrary exercise of power. But that is another story.

To sum up, progress toward rational and noninflationary wage adjustments is not an easy matter, but it does not appear hopeless. Movement in this direction will surely be worth whatever effort it may cost.[17]

[17] *Editor's note:* Since Professor Clark's and Professor Haberler's papers were discussed jointly, the report of the discussion will be found at the end of Professor Haberler's paper (see chap. iii).

CHAPTER II

Wage Policy, Employment, and Economic Stability

BY GOTTFRIED HABERLER

AN increasing number of economists have become alarmed by recent trends in wage policy. The view has gained ground that economic stability is dangerously threatened and economic progress seriously retarded by the action of powerful trade unions. The thesis has been advanced and has been widely accepted that the power of labor organizations has grown to the point where unions are beginning to be incompatible with the free enterprise economy (cf. C. E. Lindblom, *Unions and Capitalism* [Yale University Press, 1949]). Even those who find these fears exaggerated [1] do not deny that current trends push wage policies close toward the danger line beyond which they would be positively disruptive and intolerable, although they voice confidence that that line will not actually be transgressed.

This growing emphasis on the wage question is undoubtedly partly to be explained as a reaction against the neglect of the wage-price problem by the Keynesians. It is, however, also solidly based upon the undeniable fact of the growing power of organized labor.[2] I do not think it can be denied that for better

[1] E.g., J. Dunlop's review of Lindblom's book in *Amer. Econ. Rev.*, June, 1950; and W. A. Morton, "Trade Unionism, Full Employment and Inflation," *Amer. Econ. Rev.*, March, 1950.

[2] The question has been much debated whether it is justified to speak of labor monopolies. This is, however, a rather unimportant issue. Surely the classical theory of monopoly cannot be applied to trade unions with-

or for worse we have here a potent new factor. One may welcome the change or one may hold the view that the change wrought by this new factor is not as yet so powerful as to obstruct the working of the free enterprise economy. But to argue that unions have very little influence either on the wage structure or on the real-wage level or even on the money-wage level sounds rather implausible.[3]

Industry-wide collective bargaining under the threat of prolonged work stoppages is only one part of the new wage policy. Numerous governmental policies work in the same direction, directly by pushing up wages, and indirectly through strengthening the bargaining power of the unions. The most important of these measures are minimum wage legislation, social security schemes, and more liberal unemployment benefits.

The most important net effect of all these measures and policies is to make money wages rigid downward and to exert a constant upward pressure upon money-wage rates and even more so upon efficiency wages and the wage cost of output. The influence on real-wage rates depends also on price changes and is therefore a more complicated story. The effect on average

---

out important modification, because they do not maximize their members' income in the sense in which a monopolist maximizes profits. But it is equally certain that unions try to, and in many cases actually do, concentrate, i.e., "monopolize" the supply of labor in their hands. They surely do not act competitively. The precise rules of their conduct and strategy is, of course, a most interesting and important problem. But the debate whether unions can be called "labor monopolies" has not contributed to the solution of that problem.

[3] See J. Dunlop's suggestive review of Lindblom's book, *op. cit.* He there argues and cites evidence for the proposition that unions have very little influence on the wage structure. But he seems also to be inclined to assert that they have little influence on the wage level. That unions cannot affect the real-wage level sounds less improbable than that they cannot push up the money-wage level. In fact, the proposition that real wages cannot be influenced by labor organization is an old classical tenet which has been largely abandoned or severely modified by many neoclassical writers.

annual labor income is a still more complex question, because it depends, in addition to the factors mentioned, upon the average length of the work week and upon the unemployment percentage. Apart from these effects on over-all averages, it is difficult to believe that unionization and union policies do not also change the wage structure, especially in the United States where only a fraction of the total labor force is organized in unions and where the labor movement still lacks an over-all country-wide organization and policy.

2

I am going to deal with only one of the many economic aspects of the problem—not to mention noneconomic (political and sociological) implications—namely, with the bearing of the new wage policy upon employment, unemployment, and economic stability. This question itself is rather complex; it has many facets and must be broken down into subquestions.

There is first the question of cyclical fluctuations in employment. How are wage rigidity and constant upward pressure on money wages likely to influence length and amplitude of the business cycle? Is it to be expected that the cycle will be intensified or is the opposite likely to be true?

It is possible that the question has to be again subdivided according to the type of cycle. It seems to be necessary at any rate to deal separately with the role of the new wage policy in the inflationary postwar boom and its possible aftermath, postwar depression.

A different question is that of long-run effects on employment. It is not impossible to hold that the new factors in wage determination are not likely to intensify cyclical instability, although they make the maintenance of long-run full or high employment difficult; in other words, that they may produce symptoms of "secular stagnation," although cyclical fluctuations may remain unaffected or even be damped down.

A different matter altogether—which may have, however, serious indirect effects on the problem of maintaining long-run high employment and the trade cycle—is the severely adverse effect which compartmentalization of the labor market, reduction in labor mobility, maintenance of large, economically unjustified wage differentials between different labor groups, excessive shortening of the work week—not to mention featherbedding and similar activities of trade unions—must have upon long-run efficiency and output of the economy as a whole.

The first question, the influence of downward wage rigidity and upward wage pressure on the business cycle, is the most difficult of all. We have here, by almost general consent, one of the unsettled questions on which recent business cycle theory has thrown little light. The currently fashionable cycle theories, based more or less on Keynesian economics, largely ignore the problem. Prices and wages are largely assumed constant. This is true also of the last word in this field: viz., of Hicks's *Contribution to the Theory of the Trade Cycle* (Clarendon Press, 1950). What happens usually is that the problem of wage-price relationships in its bearing on the business cycle is at first consciously ignored and set aside. But then the authors get enraptured with their cyclical models based on the assumption of constant prices and wages and impressed by their own ingenuity which has gone into the construction of these models. They become impatient to apply these models and imperceptibly they are led to draw from the lack of knowledge about how wage and price changes affect the cycle the conclusion that changes in wage-price relationships really do not matter at all. Once that conviction is reached, it is not hard to rationalize it by more or less plausible reasons.

This is a rather unsatisfactory state of affairs. Surely it is better to recognize frankly these defects in our theoretical knowledge, even if they cannot be completely remedied, than to gloss over the difficulties in the way I have indicated. In this attitude of caution, I feel greatly strengthened by Professor J. M.

Clark's cautious remarks on this subject in his addendum to the U.N. *Report on Full Employment Policies* [*National and International Measures for Full Employment* (Lake Success, 1949), pp. 100-104].

I shall return to the cyclical aspect later—and propose to discuss first the long-run employment problem. In other words, I shall first abstract from cyclical complications partly because this procedure is simpler and partly because, in view of full-employment policies which are being pursued now everywhere, it is quite likely that the full employment assumption will prove to be more useful and appropriate today and in the future than it was in former periods.

3

Many economists have come to the conclusion that the wage policies pursued today by labor unions are in the long run incompatible with the maintenance of full employment at stable prices. This proposition has recently been christened Lewis's Law, not after the name of its discoverer but, as Dr. Morton, the inventor of the term, puts it, "after its most eminent practitioner, Mr. John L. Lewis of the United Mine Workers." [4] Among the economists who have expressed this view recently are Pigou, Slichter, Bronfenbrenner, Reder, and the present writer.[5] This view is, of course, held by the different writers mentioned with varying degrees of confidence and conviction and with a varying number of qualifications.

It will be advisable to state clearly the premises from which

[4] W. A. Morton, *op. cit.*, p. 26.

[5] See Morton, *loc. cit.*, for references. Pigou's latest pronouncement is in *Lapses from Full Employment* (Macmillan, 1945). Professor J. M. Clark's paper in the present volume (chap. i) seems to put him into the same group, although his wisdom would never permit him to make a very apodictic assertion on questions which like the one under consideration depend *inter alia* on political and social imponderabilia.

the proposition in question is derived. We may distinguish one theoretical and two factual premises from which the conclusion follows: (1) There is under any given set of circumstances a certain limit beyond which the money-wage level cannot be pushed without either a rise in prices or the appearance of unemployment. (2) Our society will not tolerate an indefinite rise in prices. Sooner or later, steps will be taken through monetary or fiscal policy, or direct control, to counteract further price rises. (3) Labor unions are not satisfied with wage increases on this side of the critical limit; they tend to push beyond it. Conclusion: Unemployment is inevitable.

The three propositions are not of equal plausibility. Evidently only the first one is a purely economic proposition, and in the cautious form in which I have stated it above its validity can hardly be questioned, although one may hold very different opinions about the exact location of the critical limit in any concrete situation.

The second proposition is of a very different nature. With how much inflation society is willing to put up is evidently not a purely economic question, and no precise answer is possible. I would be prepared, however, to argue that in a country like the United States in peacetime inflation would not be allowed to continue very long. There are many millions of bondholders, insurance policy holders, owners of deposits and mortgages, etc., whose progressive expropriation by a fall in the purchasing power of money could not proceed very far without meeting with increasingly determined resistance. I think that an inflationary price rise of not more than 5 per cent a year would bring on effective countermeasures either of a fiscal and monetary kind or of attempts to introduce more thoroughgoing controls within two or three years at the latest—in peacetime, of course, not during war or immediate postwar periods.

But there may be reactions against a rise in prices before deliberate decisions on the part of the central monetary and fiscal authorities to take anti-inflationary measures are put into effect.

Depending upon the existing monetary arrangements, the deflationary or anti-inflationary reactions may come "automatically" without explicit decision at the top. Under any sort of a gold standard prices cannot go on rising. And when the brake on further credit expansion is applied while wages continue to be pushed up, unemployment necessarily follows.

In the United States of today this kind of automatism is hardly operative in its pure form. But it does not follow that the price level is entirely flexible upward in the absence of a conscious anti-inflationary policy from the top. There is a kind of subtle resistance against price rises which makes itself felt, even if the general liquidity position would seem to put no impediment in the way of a further expansion of credit: price rises lead to speculative inventory accumulation which cannot go on indefinitely, especially with the generally cautious attitude which has now prevailed for several years. The banks become apprehensive when prices rise and put on gentle resistance against further expansion. Demand for investment goods is likely to be elastic and this demand elasticity is easily reinforced by a negative elasticity of price expectations; that is to say, price rises may be regarded as transitory and induce postponement of investment decisions. Reactions of this sort are highly deflationary.[6]

Moreover, there is the following circumstance to be considered. The upward pressure on wages is not applied continuously and uniformly at all points at the same time. It comes here and there, intermittently and spasmodically as wage con-

[6] See Hicks's interesting remarks in his *Contribution to the Theory of the Trade Cycle, op. cit.*, pp. 130-131. A word of caution ought to be added, however: arguments assuming particular kinds of expectations are notoriously slippery and subject to sudden reversal. The trouble is that it is hard to see how such arguments can be avoided. But in the present context the situation is not so serious, because even if expectations were not as assumed in the text, we could fall back on conscious credit restriction.

tracts expire. Now for any one group of workers it is easy to price some of its members out of the market. If wages were raised all around at the same time, resistance would be less and price rises due to the rise in wage costs would follow more easily. The futility and dangers of the procedure would, of course, be quickly revealed, and reactions by monetary and fiscal policy would come into play sooner or later. (Other political reactions through control of unions perhaps combined with price control and related measures are also likely.)

Let us elaborate that point a little more. If wages for particular groups of workers are pushed up, the resistance against the wage increase by the industries concerned is likely to be greater and the "automatic" deflationary reaction (apart from deliberate policies) of the economy as a whole will be stronger than if the general wage level is raised, because it will not be possible for any one industry fully to pass on a rise in labor cost by raising prices to the consumer. Similarly, any particular firm in an industry is not in a good position to raise its price, even if for the product of industry as a whole demand is fairly inelastic. It follows that industry-wide bargaining strengthens the bargaining power of labor. This latter fact is, of course, well known. What is not so generally realized is that economy-wide bargaining for wages would tend to break down employer resistance to wage demands even more and would facilitate the development of a wage-price spiral. For industry as a whole or large groups of industries could better afford a rise in wage costs, because in view of the higher labor income resulting from higher wage rates and the consequent rise in consumer demand, it would be easier to raise prices. (In other words, just as demand for the product of an industry is less elastic than that for an individual firm, so demand for the product of industry as a whole is less elastic than that for the product of any particular industry in isolation—the demand curve for the single industry (or firm) being drawn under the assumption that other industries (or firms) will not have their cost curve changed in the same manner as the given one.)

This is, I think, overlooked by those economists who, like Lord Beveridge, recommend economy-wide collective bargaining in the hope thereby of preventing wage-price spirals from upsetting full-employment policies.[7]

To sum up, my thesis is that there is likely to be increasing fiscal and monetary resistance if price inflation continues at a rate of, say, 5 per cent for, say, two years or longer.

Many will find this view too optimistic (some may say too pessimistic!). I may, of course, be wrong. In that case, the result of present wage trends will be inflation rather than unemployment. Also some combination of the two, unemployment in the face of inflation, is by no means impossible or even unlikely.

What is perhaps most likely to happen is that attempts to resist inflation will alternate with attempts to combat deficiencies in effective demand and unemployment, thus reinforcing the natural tendency of our economy to fluctuate in cycles. But to that aspect of the problem I shall turn a little later.

The third premise mentioned above, that unions tend to push their wage demands beyond the point that is compatible with full employment and stable prices, is, it is true, not more than a guess. But in view of recent experience here, and current as well as earlier experience abroad, it seems to me a good guess. It is plausible in view of past behavior as well as of the theories prevalent in union circles and among labor economists. I am thinking especially of the "purchasing power theory of wages" which states that wages must be raised in order to raise or main-

[7] They may be right, however, in the sense that economy-wide collective bargaining would bring the issue to a head—precisely for the reason that it would tend to accentuate instability—and thus lead to the adoption of a system under which the government would more or less decree the wage level. But such a system could no longer be called "collective bargaining." It could at best be political bargaining.

tain "purchasing power." (More will be said about this theory below.)

It seems to be also a well-established fact that the existence of unemployment and the threat of more unemployment is the most effective, and in democratic countries perhaps the only effective, restraint of union power. The reason for this is fairly obvious, notwithstanding the fact that from the point of view of the purchasing power theory wage increases would be especially beneficial in periods of heavy unemployment.

This suggests the picture of an underemployment equilibrium with that level of unemployment which is needed to neutralize union pressure for wage increases incompatible with a stable price level. Such a picture seems to be clearly in the mind of Pigou [8] and Myrdal.[9] Is the underemployment equilibrium visualized by Pigou and Myrdal different from the Keynesian view? Good Keynesians will surely say as different as anything can be. I am not so sure, however. But one thing seems certain: reality does not or only rarely does present the picture of a stable underemployment equilibrium. What we find is cyclical fluctuations and the underemployment equilibrium must therefore somehow be regarded as a trend value around which cyclical fluctuations take place. But before I discuss the cyclical aspects, I should like to say a few more words about premise (1) listed above.

4

That in any given situation there is a limit beyond which wages cannot be raised without producing either a rise in prices or unemployment should be obvious. But where that limit is and how it changes over time is not easy to say.

It is now widely assumed that equilibrium can be maintained,

[8] *Lapses from Full Employment, op. cit.*
[9] *Monetary Equilibrium* (W. Hodge, 1939), pp. 143 ff.

provided wages rise in proportion to the rise in average productivity. If output per man hour rises by, say, 2 per cent per year, average hourly wages (or earnings) too can go up by 2 per cent without causing unemployment or a rise in prices.

Brief reflection will make it clear that this proposition cannot be regarded as more than a very rough and unprecise rule of thumb. If output per man hour rises by roughly 2 per cent a year, wages cannot go up year after year by, say, 10 per cent. That much is certain. But it would be very unsafe to assume that a rise of 2 per cent, no more, no less, would be exactly what equilibrium requires.

The productivity rule is meant to hold for industry as a whole. It does not say that in each industry wages should be adjusted to average output per man hour in that industry. Such an interpretation would lead to absurd results, for example, in the case where an industry is mechanized by the installation of machinery.

Professor Hansen [10] has emphasized that ideally (allowing for some minor modification), in industries where productivity advances slower than the average as well as in those where it increases faster, wages should be kept in line with *average* productivity, although that means that temporarily, in the former case, wages will rise above productivity in that industry and, in the latter, will fall short of it. As a long-run proposition, assuming mobility of labor, this rule may be all right. But in the short run, with imperfect mobility, it would cause unnecessary unemployment in the slowly advancing industries. If wages are allowed to fall in the slowly advancing industries and to rise in the rapidly progressing industries, a better inducement for migration will be provided and output in the lagging industries will be better maintained. If wages are rigid downward, the inducement for labor to leave a declining in-

[10] Alvin Hansen, *Economic Policy and Full Employment* (McGraw-Hill, 1947), pp. 244-47.

dustry is provided by lack of job opportunities. Experience seems to show, however, that this is insufficient; if wages are good, many unemployed, instead of going elsewhere, prefer to wait in the hope that an opportunity for employment will present itself in the future.

But there are other difficulties apart from those caused by the dispersion around the average. Suppose dispersion is nil, we have a uniform average increase in man-hour output of 2 per cent. It does not follow that the *marginal* productivity of labor rises also by 2 per cent. It may have gone up by more or by less. The increase in average productivity may be due to accumulation of capital or to a change in the production function. Inventions, i.e., the change in the production function, may be of the labor-saving or capital-saving type. I do not think that there is a presumption that marginal productivity of labor rises always as much as average productivity. Moreover, there is no possibility of finding out statistically, beforehand or currently, how it has changed. Hence a mechanical application of the average productivity rule would be very unwise.

Moreover, a mechanical application is excluded by other, more pragmatic considerations. Statistics of average productivity are of limited accuracy and subject to divergent interpretations. Any extrapolation, as for example the famous 2 or 3 per cent per annum, is of very doubtful value. Furthermore, what is the area over which the averaging process should extend? Manufacturing industry? Manufacturing plus mining and services? Should agriculture be included? How about the government component of output, which has grown to large proportions? How about the international terms of trade? This last item is of little importance for the United States but cannot be ignored for most other countries.

Obviously not only wages but also social security benefits and perhaps items of collective consumption such as free education and the like should be taken into consideration.

A thorough consideration of these questions cannot be undertaken here. But a mere enumeration of the points mentioned should throw doubt upon the usefulness of the productivity formula.

The upshot of the matter is simply this, that there does not exist a good substitute for the competitive price mechanism of demand and supply. The competitive price mechanism would assure full employment (cyclical complications I shall discuss later), but not necessarily at stable prices. If we want both full employment and stable prices, the price mechanism must be combined with an appropriate monetary policy. If monetary policy is hamstrung by the necessity of holding interest rates down, the automatism cannot work, and some trial-and-error process of fixing wages must be substituted. But no formula based on average productivity can do more than indicate very roughly the order of magnitude of tolerable wage increases.

5

Before discussing the cyclical aspects of the problem, let me say a word about the postwar boom. The proposition that trade unionism of the aggressive contemporary type is incompatible with full employment at stable prices was, as far as this country is concerned, strongly suggested by the experience of the last five years. (It would not be hard to find earlier periods in other countries which would seem to support the generalization under review, say, Great Britain in the 1920's and Germany for some years during the same period.)

It has been argued (in an especially forceful manner by W. A. Morton, *op. cit.*) that the experience of 1945-1950 is inconclusive, because there exists another, better explanation for the price rise which took place. Even if there had been perfect competition in the labor market, wages and prices would have risen just as much, perhaps faster or more. The causes of the price and wage rise which would have happened in any case, unions or no unions, can be put either in terms of the quantity theory or in terms of the Keynesian income-expenditure approach. I agree with Professor Morton that it does not matter very much which one of the two approaches is used. I would argue that if fully and correctly stated the two types of analysis come pretty much to the same result. Through the liquidity preference schedule the quantity of money enters the Keynesian system and a reasonable quantity theory must pay attention to the possibility that V may undergo changes. But that is a side issue here, and we need not pursue it any further.

I grant that inflation was in the cards. Given the inflated volume of money and the monetary policy which refused to do anything about it (because government bond prices had to be kept stable), a sharp price rise was inevitable, and it would have come even more quickly with perfect competition all around. There was, as Professor Morton points out, a similar inflation after World War I, when labor unions were weak or non-existent.

I submit, however, that this in itself does not prove anything against the proposition under consideration. Suppose monetary and fiscal policy had been more vigorous, in other words, that inflation had been counteracted with greater energy, as Professor Morton recommends. Is it not certain that unemployment would have appeared? Professor Morton denies that because he thinks that labor unions would have meekly given up, or modified sufficiently, their drive for higher wages. My guess is they would not have sufficiently moderated their demands for higher wages unless a considerable volume of unemployment had restrained them. Surely the coal industry is not in good shape. But that does not prevent John L. Lewis from imposing higher wages, even if he has to flout the law and force the government of the United States into submission. Yet Professor Morton believes that Lewis would bow before the Federal

Reserve Board! [11] On the next page, he says, "There is little evidence . . . that labor has either the determination or the power to destroy price stability." I wish I could share Professor Morton's confidence, but I am afraid I cannot. Our economic system is a delicate mechanism which can be easily deranged by misguided actions without the intention of doing so.

6

I come now to the influence of wage policies on business cycles. For reasons which were indicated earlier, what I shall have to say on this subject is very tentative, at least as far as an uncontrolled system is concerned. Much more can be said, however, if certain plausible assumptions concerning monetary and fiscal policies are made.

A large part of modern cycle theory—concretely all the many models derived from, or related to, the Keynesian system, up to and including Hicks's last book—ignore wage and price changes, or pay only very cursory attention to them. This is in contrast to earlier theories which stressed, perhaps overstressed, price factors. No completely satisfactory combination of price *and* income analyses has yet been presented.

I take it for granted that there would be a business cycle, substantially as the one that we actually experience, even if wage policy were very different from what it is. The business cycle is, after all, a phenomenon of long standing. It has persisted over more than a hundred and fifty years, in all sorts of economic and social environments, and under very different wage and price structures and policies.

Let me try to approach the problem of the impact of recent

[11] "The central bank will resist inflationism and labor and business will be obliged to act accordingly" (*op. cit.*, p. 34). In the next few sentences Morton gives away his whole case. "Such resistance may provoke an immediate downturn in business but the alternative of continued inflation is worse." I agree, except that I would say "will" instead of "may."

trends of wage policy on the business cycle in the following way: I assume that there is a cycle and ask how it will be modified, when the following two forces impinge upon it: (1) During the upswing wages are pushed up by union pressure faster than they otherwise would rise; and (2) during the downswing of the cycle wages are prevented from falling or are perhaps even raised here and there.

Every business cycle upswing has been characterized up to now not only by a growing volume of output and employment but also by rising prices. The price rise is usually regarded as a factor which is calculated to intensify the cumulative force of the expansion and make its continuance precarious. This will be so (1) if inventory speculation and other anticipatory actions are induced and (2) if the expansion begins to press against monetary restraints, which may be the case either under a gold standard or similar arrangement by which the expansion of the currency is limited, or, in the absence of automatic restraints, if rising prices induce the monetary authorities to take restrictive measures.

From all this, it would seem to follow that a wage policy which leads to a rise in the wage and price level as soon as unemployment diminishes is likely to intensify and to accelerate the cumulative process of expansion and thus to shorten the prosperity phase of the cycle.

Of this result we cannot be quite sure, however, in a free, uncontrolled system, because it is possible that the upswing may have been slowed down and may have finally petered out, short of "full employment." [12] If that has been the case, it is conceivable (still not necessary) that its life has been prolonged by a rise in the wage level. In my opinion, however, most booms

[12] "Full employment" must, of course, be taken *cum grano salis*. An untractable bottleneck situation (and what is qualitatively though perhaps not quantitatively the same, unemployment even on a substantial scale in depressed areas which lie outside the expansionary stream) has to be classed as "full employment."

"hit the ceiling" of "full employment." [13] This is especially the case if the upswing has been helped along by vigorous monetary and fiscal policy measures, as is likely to be the case nowadays.

If that is so, a policy which pushes up the general wage and price level is definitely likely to shorten the upswing and to cause a more violent reaction. If the price rise is violent, deflationary reaction (through policy or through automatic reactions as explained earlier) may lead to a setback before full employment is reached. [14] On the other hand, if full employment (or an equivalent bottleneck situation) is reached, the depressive reaction will be more violent, if at that time prices are rising fast. There are two reasons: (1) If the system hits the ceiling with greater force, it will bounce back more violently; and (2) if prices have been rising until recently and the price level is at a higher level, expansionary policy measures are more difficult to justify as well as to implement.

I come now to the contraction phase of the cycle. Suppose the downswing of the business cycle has started. How will it be influenced by a wage policy which makes wages rigid downward, prevents them from falling or perhaps pushes them up in some places?

The problem of the proper wage policy in a depression has been much discussed in recent years in connection with the so-called "Pigou-effect" and what might be called the "Keynes-effect."

By the Keynes-effect I mean the influence of a fall of the wage and price level upon employment via the liquidity preference and the rate of interest. When wages and prices fall, the real value of the quantity of money increases. This depresses the rate of interest and stimulates investment, provided that the

---

[13] This is also the opinion of Hicks. See his *Theory of the Trade Cycle, passim.* "Full employment" must not be taken literally. A "bottleneck situation" is sufficient.

[14] The downturn of 1937 was probably a good example.

liquidity preference curve is not entirely elastic (in other words, provided that the propensity to hoard is so strong that the rate of interest does not fall), and provided the marginal efficiency of capital is not inelastic with respect to the rate of interest.

Most Keynesians have overlooked that this is only one of several avenues by which a fall in wages and in prices can affect the level of output and employment. Another way by which under a free competitive system full employment would be restored is indicated by the Pigou-effect, whose operation is not limited by the two conditions concerning the liquidity preference schedule and the marginal efficiency of capital mentioned above.

The Pigou-effect consists of the upward shift of the consumption function induced by the increased liquidity resulting from a fall in the wage and price level. In other words, if there is competition, and wages and prices are flexible, the wage and price level will fall so long as there is unemployment; as a consequence, the real value of the money stock will rise beyond all limits and sooner or later the point must be reached where the level of current saving falls to the level of net new investment (even if the latter is zero or negative). From there on the system will move back to full employment.

In my opinion, the propositions constituting the Pigou-effect are incontrovertible and effectively dispose of the Keynesian notion of a static, competitive underemployment equilibrium.

But I shall refrain from using the Keynes- or Pigou-effects in what follows, not so much because I have had my say on that subject in various places, but rather because I have always felt and still believe that the Keynesian framework within which the two effects operate is too static and too narrow to be of much use for the problem at hand. The Pigou-effect does explain why unemployment could not exist indefinitely with flexible wages and prices, but I think it would be very unwise to rely on it to terminate a depression. In the short run the appreciation of money debts would cause very serious troubles, and the inducement to invest might be temporarily sharply reduced. Hence, although full employment would be restored eventually, the situation might easily become much worse before it gets better. For some time the result might be full employment with a low real wage or even with low real national income. (Such a situation could be described as one of "disguised" unemployment, although I am not sure that it is the same thing which Mrs. Joan Robinson had in mind when she coined the concept of disguised unemployment.)

There are better methods available for raising the level of liquidity than reducing the wage and price level: namely, monetary and fiscal policy including deficit spending by tax reduction. (These policies may, of course, be of a more or less automatic character.) I think Keynes was right when he urged that monetary policy should be left to the monetary authorities and not be put on the shoulders of those responsible for wage policy.[15]

However, from the decision not to rely on the Keynes- and Pigou-effects it does not follow that wage rigidity is the best wage policy for depressions. Surely relative wages (i.e., the wage structure) should not be frozen but should remain flexible to adjust themselves to changing conditions. The incidence of depression is not uniform; some industries are hit harder than others. Nor must it be assumed that these changes are entirely temporary.

I think it is a great mistake to assume that no change in wages of certain groups of workers (apart from the effect of a change in the wage *level* via the rate of interest or the propensity to

---

[15] While I agree with him on that from a practical standpoint, it must be pointed out that he overlooked that—barring temporary setbacks of a dynamic nature—"monetary management by the trade unions" [*General Theory* (Harcourt, Brace & Co., 1936), p. 267] operates not only via reducing the rate of interest but also through raising the consumption function and the inducement to invest. In other words, he considered only what I called the Keynes-effect, but not the Pigou-effect.

consume, i.e., apart from the Keynes-effect and the Pigou-effect) can have an influence on total employment and aggregate output. The theory that there is no such direct influence (apart from the Keynes- and Pigou-effects) is very widely accepted today. This theory follows from the uncritical acceptance of a simplified Keynesian theory implying that consumption is a function exclusively of income, and that investment is a function exclusively of the rate of interest.[16]

But that is surely not so. Is it not obvious that price changes may directly influence aggregate consumption or investment? Is it not clearly possible that, say, a sharp rise in construction cost may unfavorably affect the volume of construction without any automatic compensation elsewhere? Or that service industries, say, the railroads or the theater, may price themselves out of the market? Some railroad workers and actors will become unemployed, when their wages rise. If this is accepted, it follows that in case there is unemployment in those industries, it will decrease, if wages are reduced. But is it not true that if construction activity increases, we shall have to say that the marginal efficiency of capital has gone up, and that if people go more to the theater or ride busses and railroads for pleasure that the consumption function of the community has shifted upward? My answer is simply this: Certainly it is true, but what of it? Such shifts are clearly possible and in many cases likely. If there is anything awkward about them, it can be only the theory which is unable to cope with such possibilities. Or should we say with Hegel, "The worse for the facts"?

My conclusion is that a freezing of relative wages and a refusal to permit selective wage reductions in a depression is bound to increase unemployment. It might be objected that by such selective wage reductions the wage level will be brought down unless there are compensatory wage increases elsewhere,

[16] Keynes himself was well aware, at least in principle, that this is at best a preliminary simplification, subject to exceptions and modifications.

while above the view was expressed that deliberate changes in the wage level were not good policy. The answer is that I would not recommend wholesale reductions of the wage level for the purpose of influencing employment and output through the operation of the Keynes- and Pigou-effects. But if selective wage reductions, apart from increasing employment in particular areas, should also bring the *level* of wages down, as a by-product as it were, I cannot see why that would be detrimental.[17]

I cannot take seriously the argument that a fall in wages is bad because it may create the expectation of further reductions and so discourage employment. What may happen, however, is that the elasticity of demand for labor in particular employments or industries is less than unity so that the payroll falls and demand of workers for wage goods declines. Hence, although employment in the industry where wages have been reduced is higher than it otherwise would be, a deflationary spiral may be set up elsewhere.[18] Thus a series of selective wage reductions may create deflation and so eventually defeat itself, although each of these reductions taken separately has served to raise employment at the point where it has been applied.

This kind of unfavorable effect that may (but need not) result from selective wage reductions can be easily forestalled by combining the policy of selective wage reductions with expansionary fiscal and monetary policies. Once again, the analysis is simpler and the results are much more definite if we can assume a vigorous monetary and fiscal policy of expansion.

[17] Efficiency wages will fall anyway in a depression, even if money-wage rates remain entirely unchanged. The reason is that less efficient workers will be dismissed first, and those remaining employed will make a greater effort to work efficiently when they are threatened with losing their jobs. That is certainly all to the good, but it is not enough.

[18] This is, however, not necessarily so. If buyers spend less on commodity A, the price of which has been reduced, they may spend more on B. Hence, if the income of A-producers has fallen, that of B-producers has gone up.

One more word ought to be said about the so-called "purchasing power theory" of wages, which can be regarded almost as the exact opposite to the view which has been expounded in the preceding pages. As mentioned before, this theory states, if applied to depression conditions, that wages should be raised for the purpose of strengthening purchasing power or effective demand, which is especially needed in depressions. I regard this reasoning as a most pernicious fallacy. But it is widely accepted not only by union leaders but by politicians and government officials.[19]

Many of those who recommend wage increases for the purpose of increasing purchasing power and effective demand do not carefully distinguish between wage rates and wage income. Purchasing power of workers and their effective demand are determined by payroll and labor income. These may or may not go up when wage rates are raised, depending upon the elasticity of demand for labor, which may well be unity or greater in a depression. Hence, a boost to wage rates is not a sure means of increasing workers' purchasing power, even in the narrow monetary sense. Monetary and fiscal measures of expansion are safer and more efficient methods for the strengthening of effective demand than wage increases. The early New Deal in the United States, and still more the French New Deal (Blum Experiment, 1934), were so unsuccessful as recovery policies because they overlooked this elementary distinction.

But even in those cases where the elasticity of demand for labor is less than unity it would be inadvisable to raise wages in a depression. First, if consumers spend more on commodity A, they may well spend less on commodity B, so that an increase

[19] During the recession in 1949, according to newspaper reports, Leon Keyserling, of the Council of Economic Advisers, made speeches to union leaders advising and urging them to press for higher wages on the ground that this would help to strengthen purchasing power and effective demand and so counteract deflation.

in purchasing power of A-workers may be wholly or partly off-set by a decrease in income of B-workers.

Secondly, employment in A will be reduced in any case (un-less demand for labor is entirely inelastic, which we may regard as very unlikely).

Thirdly, a policy of raising wages in depressions would result in higher prices or at least prevent a fall of the price level. This would not permit any favorable Keynes- or Pigou-effects. Even if we are not sanguine about the effectiveness of the Keynes- and Pigou-effects, we should not deliberately work against it. Such a policy would go against the natural grain of economic expectations and might well lead to unfavorable psychological reactions on the part of the business community.

Moreover, there are long-run considerations against it. Since prices invariably rise during the upswing of the cycle, it is desirable that they fall during the downswing. Many economists believe that it is desirable that prices should have a secular trend downward; they believe, in other words, that it is healthier if the fruits of progress are distributed by falling prices and constant (or only slowly rising) money incomes than through more sharply rising money incomes at constant prices.

I think a good case can be made for some such proposition. (It is evidently a matter of degree.) [20] But I shall not base my argument on this theory. I put forward the weaker proposition that there are serious objections on economic and especially on social grounds against an ever-rising price level. I do not refer here to the destabilizing effects of inflation in the short

[20] The only really serious objection is, it seems to me, that with the present temper of organized labor (and the same holds true of organized agriculture) such a policy is politically impossible. I do not see any difficulties in adverse expectations, because it is a matter of a slowly falling price *level*, which does not imply that any particular price must fall. In poor countries there may be serious objections against even a slow rise of real income of fixed interest receivers, but this is hardly an overriding consideration in the United States.

run. The question now under consideration is one of a long-run increase in the price level resulting from price rises during business upswings which are not completely offset by price falls in depressions.

The main disadvantage is that the fruits of progress are in this case unequally distributed. Fixed income receivers, bond-holders, insurance policy owners, pensioners, the proverbial widows and orphans, and the like are hurt. The existence of institutions such as universities and hospitals, whose real income depends on the purchasing power of money, is undermined. In the long run saving habits will be affected and saving will be unfavorably rechanneled; if the operation of the capital market is impeded and curtailed and if, as a consequence, provision for investment is mainly confined to self-financing, the distribution of capital will deviate more and more from the optimum.

Summary and Outlook

The growth of powerful and aggressive labor organizations confronts the United States society and economy with a new situation. Only one of the several economic problems raised by this development has been analyzed in the present paper: namely, the consequence for the volume of employment and economic stability of two basic results of the rise of powerful trade unions: the continuous upward pressure on wages, and the almost complete downward rigidity of money-wage rates. (Real-wage rates, average earnings in real and money terms, and efficiency wages have still a certain though surely much reduced measure of flexibility.)

Turning for a moment from cyclical fluctuations and war-induced inflation, the consequence of this new situation is that it becomes virtually impossible to maintain full employment at stable prices. When full employment is approached, unions are likely to press for wage increases in excess of the rate at which, in view of slowly advancing average productivity, wages can rise without necessitating a rise in the price level. Nobody can foretell with precision how fast the average wage level can, in fact, be increased without causing unemployment or inflation. But judging from past experience, Professor Clark (chap. i) estimates that it is in the neighborhood of 2 per cent per year.

It does not seem likely that unions will be satisfied with that rate of progress, which in view of their successes in recent years must look tantalizingly slow to them. If wages are pushed up faster, society will have to choose between unemployment and inflation. And if labor insists, as seems likely, on an annual advance in excess of average productivity, not only in money, but also in real terms (this could take the form of automatic cost-of-living adjustments of wages, or of price controls), the consequence must eventually be unemployment; for in the long run the possibility of increasing the income of labor as a whole at the expense of that of other classes of society is very limited, especially in view of the fact that the farmers know only too well how to protect their interests.[21]

In my opinion, an economic society like the American one is not likely to permit inflation to go very far in peacetime. This view is not shared by other members of the present symposium. They believe that few people are afraid of inflation nowadays. But let us not forget that this is an election year. It may be that few people foresee inflation, but I still believe that if it comes, if the cost of living rises by only as much as, say, 5-10 per cent a year, it will not take long, not longer, say, than a year or two, before steps are taken to check the price rise. If wages and labor cost are pushed up by trade unions and at the same time prices are held down by monetary and fiscal measures, unemployment is the unavoidable and immediate consequence.

---

[21] For small segments of the labor class the possibility of maintaining a high monopoly price for their services is, of course, much greater.

In a competitive economy the existence of unemployment would lead to a fall in money wages. It is true that wages were sticky though not quite rigid even before the period of unionization, but there can be no doubt that the downward rigidity has been greatly increased by union resistance to any wage reductions. But even now the existence of unemployment and the danger of more unemployment are very effective checks on demands for higher wages. How much unemployment is required in any given situation to maintain a stable equilibrium is an exceedingly complex question. The answer depends on the whole temper of the labor movement; the outlook, statesmanship, and strategy of union leaders; public policies; and other factors which I cannot even start to enumerate at this point.

The basic issues are, however, much complicated and obscured by the fact that downward rigidity and upward pressure on wage rates produced by labor unions impinge upon an economic system which is subject to cyclical fluctuations.

How in a free and uncontrolled system the cycle would be influenced by these two forces is not easy to say. Concretely we cannot be quite sure, on the one hand, whether greater downward rigidity of wages will always deepen or shorten depressions (even though under a completely flexible and competitive price and wage system involuntary unemployment could not exist), or, on the other side, whether upward pressure on wage rates will prolong or shorten the upswing. But if we can assume a vigorous full employment policy by means of monetary and fiscal measures, our results become much more definite.

The assumption which we make is not that the full employment policy is so effective as to eliminate the cycle altogether. If that were the case, the full employment analysis of the first part of the paper, where abstraction was made of cyclical complications, would apply, and the situation would be much simpler. What I here assume is more modest. On the upgrade of the cycle I assume that the full employment policy prevents the upswing from petering out before it has reached the ceiling of full employment (or an equivalent bottleneck situation), or before the boom has degenerated, short of full employment, into an intolerable price inflation. On the downgrade of the cycle I simply assume a mild cushioning effect which will effectively eliminate the danger of a temporary downward spiral of deflation being started by a policy of wage reduction.

Under this setup, which closely resembles the present situation in the United States, we can definitely say that upward pressure with downward rigidity of wages will result over the long period in a lower level of employment, or a rising price level, or, perhaps most likely, in some combination of the two. The reason is the following: the upswing will be always in danger of being interrupted short of full employment because of sharply rising prices. Furthermore, segmentation of the labor force into noncompeting groups, and reduction of labor mobility, which is greatly intensified by union activity, favor the emergence of intractable bottleneck situations and thus make the attainment of full employment impossible. The price rise which occurs during the upswing will be not or only insufficiently compensated by a price fall in the downswing. Moreover, wage rigidity downward will also result in a more or less complete freezing of relative wages, of the wage structure, which must still further impede labor mobility and reduce the adaptability of the whole economy.

The results of the new trend in wage policy in a world which is subject to cyclical fluctuations are, therefore, in the end not greatly different from those which we would expect in a stationary or smoothly progressing economy—with one possible exception, however: the resistance to the long-run increase in the price level will be weaker if periods of rising prices alternate with depressions or recessions during which the price movement is slightly downward. Hence the chances that the long-run price trend will be decidedly in the upward direction (in other words, the danger of a creeping long-run inflation) are greater in a world which is subject to cyclical swings than they would be in the absence of cyclical complications.

What conclusions must be drawn from this analysis? If the free enterprise system is to be preserved and drastic controls are to be avoided, it will be necessary, in my opinion, to change present wage policies and to reduce the monopolistic power of labor unions, because we can be sure that neither unemployment on a considerable scale nor inflation will be tolerated indefinitely.

How to bring about such a change in wage policy is a question which requires expert knowledge in the labor field, which I do not possess. I am inclined, however, to agree with Professor Friedman (chap. x)—and I certainly do hope that he is right— that comparatively mild measures would be sufficient to reduce monopoly power of labor unions sufficiently to make the smooth functioning of the free enterprise economy possible. Concretely, prohibition of violence and coercion, especially of picketing, protection of those willing to work, prohibition of closed shop agreements and application of the Sherman Act to trade unions, or, to put it briefly, a mild stiffening of the Taft-Hartley Act, may be sufficient to bring about the desired results. Whether there is any chance that such reform measures will be taken before an emergency (widespread strikes, unemployment, intolerable inflation) has arisen, and whether in the face of such an emergency reasonable and moderate reforms could be enacted, is open to legitimate doubt; but that question will not be discussed here.

I am unable, however, to share the optimism of those who almost deny that the growth of powerful labor unions during the last fifteen years or so has created serious difficulties for the maintenance of full employment at stable prices [22] on the ground that the inflation that has taken place must be explained entirely in monetary terms, war expenditure, and the like, and that it cannot be blamed, not even partially as is often done,

---

[22] Morton, *op. cit.*, comes perilously close to that position.

on union policies of high wages. I agree that given the repressed inflation inherited from the war and from the monetary policy (or rather lack of monetary policy) which we have had during the postwar period, prices and wages would have risen just as much or perhaps even faster if no unions had existed and the economy had been freely competitive all around. Moreover, it is undoubtedly true that inflation has greatly contributed to the vigorous growth of trade unions and that in a noninflationary (let alone deflationary) climate unions will find the going much harder. But it seems to me equally obvious that there is a strong trend factor in the growth of labor unions, and it is an illusion to assume that the adoption of noninflationary monetary and fiscal policies would dispose of the labor problem. Inflation has facilitated the growth of labor unions and has at the same time concealed the implications of that growth for employment policies.[23] But unions and their wage policies are not simply a transitory inflation phenomenon; they are here to stay. If anyone doubts that, let him reflect on the developments abroad, in Great Britain, Germany, and elsewhere.

[23] To make the latter remark clear, imagine what would have happened during the postwar years if by monetary policy the price level had been prevented from rising or if it had risen, say, only half as much as it actually did. There can be no doubt, it seems to me, that the consequence would have been immediate depression, unless we assume that union policy would have been entirely different. This assumption seems to me entirely unrealistic, although some slight modification of wage demands could have been expected if prices had been more nearly stable.

CHAPTER III

Selections from the Discussion
of the Clark and Haberler Papers

KNIGHT. I would like to start with a question to Professor Clark suggested by one of the last remarks he made. He talks all the way through about prices being "pushed up." I don't believe that happens much if at all.

CLARK. I suppose what I contemplate is the existence of a condition in our society in which there are a number of what are called administered prices together with a considerable range of flexibility in the amount of total purchasing power furnished by a flexible credit system. With these conditions there would be a considerable range within which the total level of prices might be affected by what happens in the labor market—pushing costs up.[1]

KNIGHT. Well, I should have said I was even more disturbed by manufacturers' and sellers' actions to protect their profit margins by raising prices, and that isn't quite the same thing. If they raise prices beyond what there is potential demand to take off, they certainly reduce their sales. And if they aren't in a monopoly position I don't see how they can do it. Of course, if they all acted as a unit they could.

CHAMBERLIN. If wages all go up pretty much together over an area, then manufacturers and sellers would naturally assume

[1] *Comment by Clark:* This position is amplified above in the section, "Some Basic Attitudes Toward the Market," of my paper (chap. i), largely written after the conference to clarify the points raised here.

everybody else was doing the same thing, and it would be very natural to have an upward adjustment.

KNIGHT. It can't happen without a monetary expansion, as I think Professor Haberler was suggesting.

SAMUELSON. May I raise a question? Assume, first, that you have rather flat supply curves for competitive industries, and that for many industries there aren't any important existing stocks which have to be sold at any price: in short, assume that things are, to a first approximation, produced almost to order. Then it is no doubt true that an increase in wage costs and price cannot be combined with the same volume of employment unless demand has changed. But even in that case you can have the effect absorbed by a falling off in production and employment.

My point, therefore, is this. It is, to a reasonable approximation, correct to say that at this partial equilibrium level costs do push up prices. However, they don't do it without penalties.

KNIGHT. And cause unemployment.

FRIEDMAN. You don't mean costs "do." You mean costs "can."

SAMUELSON. In such cases costs "do."

CLARK. I think there might be monetary expansion.

KNIGHT. Forced by this action? I remember hearing Senator Paul H. Douglas years ago when he was a Professor say, or advocate, as a cure for the depression, forcing wages up. Employers will go then to the banks and borrow—"They'll have to," he said.

It seemed to me you were almost committed to such a theory of general policy in your paper.

CLARK. Well, the whole purport of the paper was in the other direction.[2]

HABERLER. I thought so too. I didn't see anything of that sort.

[2] *Comment by Clark:* That is, it rejected the wage-boost theory of how to bring on a revival, and sought for ways to avoid imposing the above dilemma on the economy.

CHAMBERLIN. I was struck at one point by the possibility that Clark's level of economically sound wages wasn't so far from the familiar competitive level of wages after all. "Money wages shouldn't go up so fast as to force inflation"—but that is consistent with the conception of the competitive level of wages. "Maximum possible employment" is also consistent with the older idea of a competitive level of wages.

I was going to ask in just what way is it really different, or are we working back here toward that idea?

KNIGHT. I raised the prior question of whether forcing up of wages can force inflation; if so, how. I don't get it. Unless the cards were set to have inflation anyway. And I actually believe, as I think your paper said, that we had less rapid inflation because of trade unions in this postwar period than we would have had.

HABERLER. In this particular period. But if we take, say, in a normal period, when there is no such overhanging mass of purchasing power from the war, wouldn't you agree that there is usually a certain flexibility, that entrepreneurs can borrow from the banks, and then if they are forced to pay higher wages that may make them borrow?

KNIGHT. I don't believe they'd do it. I believe they'd do the opposite. If you haven't a setting for inflation, they will borrow less from the banks.

SAMUELSON. What would be the effect on prices of a million-fold increase in wages?

KNIGHT. Complete unemployment—things would all stop—there wouldn't be any production. No production or distribution or any business.

FRIEDMAN. Sure there would be, but you'd use a different kind of medium of exchange.

KNIGHT. I mean you have got to tell me how you are going to bring about a millionfold increase before I can answer such a question as that. It's impossible without a revolutionary change in the monetary standard.

HABERLER. If prices are pushed up and that leads to unemployment, then I think it's likely the public would demand that the government—by monetary and fiscal policies—push up the money supply to support the new price level.

KNIGHT. By political action. That's the only possible answer. Automatically it wouldn't happen.

HABERLER. But I say isn't there a possibility at least that for a short while the same result may come about without political action?

FRIEDMAN. You can of course have a combination of higher prices and unemployment in any particular line.

KNIGHT. Yes, I mean the fact there would be unemployment rather than sales at higher prices.

FRIEDMAN. I want to take the discussion back to the problem of policy. As I understand the position that both Haberler and Clark take, both start with a fundamental presumption that I shall accept for the moment though I don't really believe it to be valid—that a very significant fraction of wage rates in the economy today are fixed by organized groups bargaining one with another on an oligopolistic level rather than by the forces of competition.

Given that situation, they say, "Well, there are two ways society can do something about that. One way is to try to undermine the importance of these organized groups so as to get something which more closely approximates a competitive level." And they both—or at least Professor Clark, if I understand him—reject that as not feasible.[3] They then say there is a second alternative, and the second alternative is that society can establish some rules or step in as an umpire to arbitrate or to organize or to control somehow the bargaining among different groups and in the process establish reasonable rules in accordance with

---

[3] *Comment by Clark:* I don't reject a move in that direction, but do reject Friedman's apparent goal of a fully competitive seller's market for labor, as not only nonfeasible, but undesirable.

which the contentions of the different groups will be reconciled in the light of some very general principles.

Now, the point I would like to see us discuss is the implicit assumption that this second alternative is feasible. I want to argue that, if anything, it is less feasible than the first, unless you are willing to go all the way toward a completely regimented and controlled economy. And that is what I would like to see us turn to—whether in fact there is a feasible way in which society can enter into these particular bargains alone, in the wage bargains alone, without being forced to go very much further. If it is effective in controlling the wage bargains, that means it's effective in determining employment in different industries and outputs in different industries. Doesn't that mean it has to step in to do something at these various levels?

Given that you can determine the wage rate arbitrarily, it doesn't follow that employment in the particular occupation is arbitrary. And if a whole structure of relative wage rates is determined by negotiation and wage-fixing, which is essentially what is implied in the adoption of "reasonable" standards, why then the number of people employed in each of these occupations is also determined. Is there any way at all under those circumstances to assure that the total adds up to the sum you want, or, more important, to make the total number of people demanded in each occupation equal to the number of people who would like to get such jobs?

If we have wage rates fixed all over the lot, what is it that determines which people get which jobs, or which employers hire the number of people they want to? Can you set wages by criteria other than the equalization of demand and supply, unless you substitute some other mechanism to perform the latter function?

CLARK. Well, I'm not suggesting wage rates fixed in any more political sense than they are fixed now by bargaining.[4]

---

[4] *Comment by Clark:* The spirit of my paper was a search for standards that might be voluntarily followed by bargainers anxious to avoid provok-

FRIEDMAN. But either that bargaining is dominated by the economic conditions of demand and supply of labor or it is dominated by some general rules of the sort you suggested. It can't be dominated by both.

CLARK. Well, I am suspicious of any rigid, 100 per cent "either/or" position on a thing like that. I tend to think in terms of rather flexible limits.

HABERLER. I interpret Professor Clark differently from Dr. Friedman. I don't know what Clark would like to have, but he says in any case we can't have the system which we would like to have, free market and letting the wages find their level. That's practically out of the question. Wages have to be set by bargaining. And now he says, "What can we do?" Is it perhaps the safest thing to let wages rise as much as productivity, allowing some adjustment on the price side so that wage rises in proportion to productivity, if that turns out to be too much—I mean at constant prices—that then you would just let prices go up?

FRIEDMAN. Who is the "you" in each of these? "You" let prices go up. That implies there is somebody who can control.

HABERLER. That's monetary policy I imagine and—

FRIEDMAN. You said should these negotiators be limited to rises in wages equal to average productivity? Then somebody has to limit them. Who does it?

HABERLER. Union negotiators and the industry negotiators.

FRIEDMAN. But who tells them?

HABERLER. Clark tells them.

FRIEDMAN. But what is the sanction that leads them to follow his advice?

HABERLER. If they go a little too far nothing terrible will happen, except some unemployment will appear and then prices will go up a little bit.

FRIEDMAN. I agree that might well be the case. But it seems to me that Professor Clark is going beyond that.

---

ing compulsory political intervention. In its present form it has been revised to make this clearer than may originally have been the case.

SAMUELSON. Isn't Professor Clark saying no more than that these, shall we call them "crimes," are being committed, and that there are "criminals" who are committing these "crimes" and doing this in a matrix of public opinion, and that he wants them to consider what the effects of their "criminal" actions are and to moderate the degrees of their excesses in terms of what will happen if they do it? Is he saying something different from that?

CLARK. I would be willing to contemplate the possibility of doing things that would reduce some of the bargaining leverages, compulsory leverages that labor has at its disposal. I am not particularly optimistic, however, about how far it would be politically practicable to go on that.

Now, as to Friedman's second point, that goes a good deal further than anything I raised in my paper. I was, I think, raising the question in this form: If there are certain objective limits on what the unions can do in the way of grabbing off increased real income for their members, starting with the assumption that as things are there are established tendencies to go further than is economically desirable in that direction, to go to lengths that produce effects that we would agree I think are undesirable—

FRIEDMAN. Sure.

CLARK. —and if people in the business on the side of organized labor as well as of employers and maybe government can be persuaded that that is the case and can be persuaded to work at the further question of how far and how fast wages can move without these undesirable effects, you might get some very general approximate standards of economically desirable policy out of it.

And then the further question is whether there are any voluntary mechanisms through which those ideas might conceivably have an influence moderating the results of the actual process in action.

BOULDING. I was in a big meeting of the garment workers in New York in 1944 when the boys knew they could get a wage increase, and the union leaders had to explain why they couldn't have it, because of the "little steel formula." They had a perfect alibi. What the union leader wants more than anything else is an alibi. And this I think essentially is what Professor Clark is talking about. Granted that in the organized labor market wage negotiations are conducted in an atmosphere of the football field, do you have any standards for judging the results? And if you do have accepted standards for judging the results, does that then give the union leaders a greater ability to withstand the demands of the membership?

FRIEDMAN. Who is the "you"? You say, "Do 'you' have any standards?"

BOULDING. Union leaders.

FRIEDMAN. But then you'd better change the whole discussion. Let's not discuss the issue of what kind of standards would be economically desirable. For now we are on a different level. We say that what unions will do depends upon public opinion and public pressure. And now the appropriate question is to ask by what standards public pressure is likely to be guided or can be persuaded to let itself be guided.

SAMUELSON. That's the discussion.

FRIEDMAN. That's an altogether different issue from what standards are socially desirable.

It seems to me that to analyze the latter we ought to take Clark's proposal as essentially one that there should be some stated system of guides for administrative bodies that are going to fix wages and that we ought to consider the implications of such a plan for a moment independently of the particular guise that it takes.

HABERLER. Why can't we just say suppose wages did go up by 4 per cent on the average. Would that lead either to inflation or deflation? That's a perfectly economic problem. Professor Clark's guess is that we could maintain fairly full employment at stable prices. Now, is that true or is it not? How far might we try to bring that about?

FRIEDMAN. But as I think Professor Clark quite properly said in his paper, economists must still guess as to whether 4 per cent or 6 or 1 per cent would be right. I think he is absolutely right that they have been notoriously bad on that.

WRIGHT. If we are to begin to talk of productivity I am a little worried about two things. First of all, the idea that wages should rise with productivity seems to me something that has to be taken with a great many grains of salt, because you have the question of incentive for risk-bearing. Extensions of output, not necessarily but frequently, are accompanied by higher risks. And if the union is going to push up the wages bingo, right away, then there will not be the extra-high profit needed to compensate for those risks. There will be no reward for the risk, and nobody will make the extension. In other words, there may have to be a lag here in wage increases, a considerable lag I should say, to get venture capital, because otherwise there will not be enough incentive—I don't believe there is such a thing as some definite "reasonable" profit, say 10 per cent. Profits are reasonable with reference to the particular venture involved and the risks which it contains.

Now, though productivity may have gone up I think that for a while a chap would be justified in collecting considerable gravy. If you don't allow it you won't get *net* risky investment.

CLARK. That's why I was definitely opposed to the idea of wages being determined by the course of productivity or capacity to pay in the particular enterprise or the particular industry.

SAMUELSON. We don't want to get confused on the arithmetic of this problem. For wages to go up with productivity does not mean that wages will get the full marginal increment. It simply means that the same fraction of the total sales value or value added will go to labor.

WRIGHT. That still wouldn't meet my objection though, because since the extension may involve more risk than what you have been doing, if you only give the operator the same fraction it may not be enough inducement for him to bear the increased risk.

BOULDING. What we are saying is it is pernicious for wages to go up with productivity in particular industries, and that the proposition that the average wages go up with productivity has nothing to do with the proposition that wages in particular industries should go up with productivity.

WRIGHT. Of course, I saw Dr. Clark did not mean that particular wages should necessarily go up with the average.

HABERLER. There can be any lag you like in any particular industry or firm, but no lag for the economy as a whole. But I don't know that that is so serious.

WRIGHT. Suppose a regular union organizer—not an economist—had read this paper. I wonder if he wouldn't go off with the idea that every wage—his wage for example—ought to rise by 2 per cent a year?

I had one other thing I wanted to say. This assumption that a 2 per cent rise will continue under a strong labor movement is another proposition which seems to me highly debatable in view of the attitude of many unions which consciously or unconsciously leads to sabotage. For instance, we all had to come here by plane or automobile because of the strike to keep firemen on diesel engines.

I discuss this issue in my paper, but I think it altogether optimistic to say that present productivity trends will necessarily continue.

CHAMBERLIN. I would like to say a word about productivity in a particular vein. It seems clear to me that this is a simple example of where, because some industry has become much more productive through some improvement or innovation, the marginal productivity of labor may not be affected in the slightest. The change in productivity could all be intramarginal. And it's a very good example of the general proposition that Haberler developed a while ago which seems to me of prime importance, criticizing the general tendency now to speak in a very sloppy way about general productivity and marginal productivity and to confuse the two.

This proposition that wages should go up every year in accord with the increase in general productivity gives in fact no indication whatever as to the relationship of labor to the other factors of production and therefore as to the marginal productivity of labor and the amount by which labor should go up by the marginal productivity criterion. The point could hardly be more elementary.

KNIGHT. I wondered which you meant more than half the time when you used the word "productivity." Did you mean the specific product of labor or—

CLARK. I don't think anybody knows what the marginal productivity of labor is.

KNIGHT. I know, but you must have meant one or the other.

CLARK. I was talking about aggregate or average per capita productivity, with the proviso that at least we don't know that that kind of an adjustment would be inconsistent with the marginal productivity principle.

SAMUELSON. I would like to address a remark to Professor Haberler's analytical point about relative prices as they affect investment. It is fairly clear that there is now being worked out a kind of synthesis, a new aggregate of demand approach. "Neoclassical," I have suggested in my paper, is I think the word for it. I would like to second his suggestion that we don't want that to be an oversimplified thing. We don't want it to be something that can be put on a few diagrams and a few dimensions but one that takes everything into consideration.

In this connection it is interesting to note that a decade ago Professor Bergson and Professor Bissel addressed themselves to just this question, and they did come out with exactly your conclusion that relative price—this is published in *Econometrica* and the *Quarterly Journal of Economics*—that relative price changes can have substantive effects upon investment—substan-

tive effects both for good and evil, namely, that a raising of the
price of construction can under certain not implausible elasticities of demand actually increase the real "propensity to invest" and the real level of employment, and that is worked out
in some considerable detail.

Now, I don't know that that particular result is more plausible
than its opposite, but most of the examples given in the paper
were of the sort where a reduction in wages would benefit,
whereas there are also opposite cases.

Now, it is, of course, a very delicate problem of judgment
as to where the quantitative truth lies in that situation.

HABERLER. I think in principle I would agree with that. You
might get the opposite effect. Without introducing some sort
of expectations? [5]

SAMUELSON. Yes.

WRIGHT. Would this increase in investment be over-all investment or investment in that particular line?

SAMUELSON. It's an increase in investment in that line which
need not be accompanied by any compensating decline elsewhere.

[5] *Comment by Haberler:* Barring fancy *ad hoc* assumptions about expectations, a reduction in wages will always lead to an increase in output
and employment in the industry where it occurs, whether it is an investment goods industry or consumption goods industry. In his writings on
the Ricardo effect, Professor Hayek has made much of the possibility that
a fall in wages may lead to a substitution of labor for capital and thus
entail a reduction in the volume of investment. Without going into the
extreme intricacies of the theory of the Ricardo effect, it is safe to say
that most economists will very seriously doubt whether such a substitution
will happen on a substantial scale in the short run during a depression.
The only possible danger to employment which may result from wage
reductions in a depression is, in my opinion, a fall in the wage bill (demand
for labor being inelastic in the short run) which would lead to a fall
in demand for wage goods and may intensify a spiral of deflation. This
possible adverse effect can, however, easily be forestalled by simultaneous
expansionary monetary and fiscal policies, as explained in my paper (chap.
ii) and in my *Prosperity and Depression.*

BOULDING. If you can assume that a lot of different elasticities coexist (and this is something that bothers me a little), it's obvious that a change in the structure of relative wages, with wages increasing where demands are inelastic, and decreasing where demands are elastic, will have favorable effects on employment and output.

SAMUELSON. That's the point.

BOULDING. Of course, the thing that bothers me is the validity of this kind of economics of elasticity.

SAMUELSON. In the Bergson paper these are not superficial surface elasticities. They are elasticities rooted in some specific analysis. You can easily beg the employment question by always saying wherever the demand is inelastic raising wages will increase the wage bill. You haven't answered anything. You have simply stated how the wage bill moves when it moves.

CLARK. That sort of analysis bothers me somewhat on account of the consideration that where demand is highly elastic it's likely to be on account of a substitutionary relation between that and some other thing, so that if the price of that thing is raised people buy less of something else in order to spend a greater amount for that thing. And the same thing, reversed, in the case of inelastic demand.

SAMUELSON. There's no law of conservation of purchasing power that—

CLARK. No, but I'm bothered about the simple attempt to answer that question of effect on aggregate demand simply from examining the elasticity of demand for that particular thing.

SAMUELSON. Yes. And I reinforce your point. Let's have no simple theories on this.

FRIEDMAN. There certainly is something left of Say's Law. It certainly is true that if a price rise induces people to spend more on one commodity, that will tend to have the effect that they will spend less on others. I don't contend the two effects are necessarily numerically equal—which is Professor Clark's point.

BOULDING. If they all spend more on one commodity they all have more to spend.[6]

FRIEDMAN. It depends whether they spend more on the one commodity by spending less on others.

SAMUELSON. Professor Friedman's point is that if you take the schedule and consider broad categories of goods, and let's suppose you have a relative price change which is a substantial change, and suppose you think that this one large category has inelastic demand—then there is no law which tells us that the total spent remains quantitatively equal, but he says there is a *qualitative* presumption that the remaining effects are at least offsetting.

FRIEDMAN. Let me put it differently—that you want to take into account not only elasticities but also cross-elasticities. And on balance you would expect cross-elasticities to have some offsetting effect.

SAMUELSON. Or reinforcing.

FRIEDMAN. No, because of the initial limitation of total income—which introduces negative correlation between the expenditures on various categories—on balance I think you would expect that there is a limit to the extent to which expenditures can go up on one category without reduction in others.

SAMUELSON. The question is how savings behave.

FRIEDMAN. There is a limitation to savings. The question is whether you can support indefinite increase.

[6] *Comment by Wright:* This would be true only in very special cases. See the discussion of Mr. Boulding's paper (chap. vii).

Comment by Boulding: If everybody spends more on one commodity without spending less on others it is *always* true that the total of money receipts (which is the same as the total of expenditures) must increase. This does not mean, however, that the total of purchasing power is increased, because there may be offsetting price changes.

SAMUELSON. Let's put it in the record that it would be good to have inductive and deductive study of this sort of thing.

FRIEDMAN. Elasticity but also cross-elasticity.

KNIGHT. To keep things going, there is another point about Dr. Clark's paper that bothers me. I think it is one of the most sinister things in the whole social situation that an inflation creates so many fictitious profits that the laborers are demanding wages out of profits which aren't there at all except as an expression of an inflated price level.

CLARK. That's implicit in the point I made here near the end of the paper—that the question of fact as to whether there is an excess profit that labor can tap is one of the things that needs to be factually aired, including the question of fictitious profits due to general price changes.

KNIGHT. I suppose you saw an article by Jones of Yale purporting to prove by published accounts that the United States steel industry as a whole had been paying taxes and dividends out of capital during this period when the workers were insisting on more wages out of profits without a price rise.

FRIEDMAN. But if they didn't have that excuse they'd have some other excuse. Once again it seems to me we want to avoid paying much attention to what union leaders say. These attempts to interpret union behavior by what they say are like trying to figure out what causes longevity by going around asking old people how they happened to live so long.

SAMUELSON. There is one element of agreement which should go in the record. Everybody here seems to think a psychology pattern based on a 10 per cent per annum wage increase is untenable on any economic theory, and if a 10 per cent per annum—

KNIGHT. You mean without inflation?

SAMUELSON. Yes.

KNIGHT. Real wages?

SAMUELSON. Labor leaders as a whole are kidding themselves and they know it if they think they can get 10 per cent money increases all around per annum, which will eventually result in 10 per cent real-wage increases per annum all around.

FRIEDMAN. What does "all around" mean?

SAMUELSON. That's the pattern.

FRIEDMAN. You mean that we all agree that as a matter of prediction it is not conceivable that wage rates can go up in real terms 10 per cent per annum without creating unemployment?

SAMUELSON. Yes.

FRIEDMAN. I think we agree on that as a matter of prediction.

SAMUELSON. And as a matter of prediction we think attempts to bring it about by collective bargaining will cause a price increase and possibly unemployment.

FRIEDMAN. Well, that's another question, a much more difficult question. If you had a monetary system that was otherwise stable, it seems to me the main effect of an attempt to bring it about by unions would be the breakdown of the unions.

KNIGHT. We all know if you had three increases in annual wages of 10 per cent and production was maintained there wouldn't be enough product to pay it. They're getting more than that proportion of the product now. I mean labor on the whole gets somewhere around 70 or 80 per cent of the total product.

FRIEDMAN. That's the catch in the "all around." If by the "they" you mean unionized people, they aren't. They aren't. They're getting not more than at the outside a quarter of the national product. So that if the "they" means the union people it seems to me the two parts of Professor Samuelson's statement don't fit together. In the first place, you talk about prediction of what would happen if all labor were to get this. Then you say could unionized labor bring it about?

SAMUELSON. I didn't say that. I said "general pattern." Union leaders today profess to speak for the whole labor movement.

But if you speak to them they allege they are not getting gains at the expense of other workers, but are setting the standards for all.

I think we should view with alarm the notion that was prevalent for a few postwar years that a set of increases of 10 per cent a year is fair and possible—a pattern, by the way, which was broken, I hope for some time, by the recent recession.

BOULDING. That's where all these pension plans come from.

SAMUELSON. It's coming back in the back door, of course.

BOULDING. It's a fact they realize they can't get wages now. They have to get something.

SAMUELSON. I think that private pension plan increases are more pernicious than straight wage demands.

BOULDING. Far more pernicious.

Professor Boulding summarized the results of the latter parts of the session as follows:

We all (or nearly all) consent
If wages rise by ten per cent
It puts a choice before the nation
Of unemployment or inflation.

CHAPTER IV

Economics and Ethics of the Wage Problem

BY FRANK H. KNIGHT

THE wage problem, as our society confronts it, must be understood as a feature of the "modern economic order," and of "modern civilization" as a whole. Poverty and insecurity are age-old; they now arise in an economic system in which the bulk of the working population, no longer slaves or serfs, get their livelihood by the sale of personal services in the open market. Moreover, these evils have come to be felt acutely, in a sense not true of earlier types of culture, particularly as imperatively demanding that something be done about them by intelligent, organized action. This awareness and urge to act are not, to be sure, due only to more humane feelings, plus a general "activistic" attitude toward life and a faith in intelligence—novel as these are, in contrast with fatalism, or a faith that evils are somehow unreal or will be made right, somewhere and somehow, without planned human action. An important factor is the "awakening of the masses" and particularly the organization of large wage-earning groups, giving them *power*, economic and political, under a moral and legal order of personal liberty, to insist on their "rights" and to cause much loss to society at large if their demands are not met.

To analyze and explain the economic organization is primarily the task of *economics*. This new branch of knowledge labors under a serious psychological handicap in that it requires imaginative separation of different elements in human conduct and social relations, through use of abstract concepts. This type of thinking is clearly repugnant to deep "instincts" of most people, while in contrast with physics, for example, its results can be made effective through democratic processes only if generally understood by the electorate. The economic factor must in particular be brought into as clear a relation as possible with two others from which no sharp separation can be made. These are ethics and play. This is by no means all. Economics, ethics, and play are forms of *motivated* behavior (along with many others), and we know that such phenomena distinguish man categorically from inert physical things subject only to the ordinary laws of cause and effect as studied in the various natural sciences. (Intermediate "orders," plant and animal, complicate the problem but must here be simply left out of account.) The fact of motivation, with its accompaniments of striving, success, and failure or *error* in numerous meanings, implies that a strictly "scientific" treatment of human conduct in contrast with mechanical response (in nature or in man) is subject to sweeping limitations. We must further keep in mind that man is a social being, in a sense very different from the colonial insects or the herds of higher animals, where instinct mechanisms control behavior. Men co-operate, in a way inseparable from conflict; and they have social interests, likes and dislikes, which seem to have no ends beyond the "interestingness" of the activities in which they are expressed. Further, men have complex obligatory customs and laws, and last of all moral ideals; they judge acts and attitudes, their own and those of others, with approval and disapproval, implying norms distinct from mere subjective desire.[1]

Economics, distinguished from other human and social "sciences," has for its subject matter that aspect of the phenomena

[1] Men also, of course, pass *aesthetic* judgments, distinct from individual liking, not liking, disliking. In this sketch we can only note that in economics the distinction is ignored; matters of taste are treated as matters of desire merely.

which is referred to by the term "economy," or the verb, "to economize." This latter means the use, or more or less successful effort to use, of *means* to achieve *ends,* and to do it *economically,* or effectively, so as to achieve the maximum desirable result on the whole that is possible with the given means. Economy applies to the activity of any "unit," but in free society primarily to "the" unit, which we speak of as the individual while meaning in general the family. This may be "represented," more or less accurately, by its "head," but the family in some form is the smallest real unit in any society veiwed as historically continuing. The state, minor political divisions, and numerous "voluntary" organizations also function in various ways as economic units. We must note at once that people use means not only to achieve final ends, but also in considerable part to increase the stock of means itself, the main fact underlying economic *progress;* however, the ends are also constantly evolving or changing, spontaneously or more or less subject to complex conscious direction.

Perhaps the first distinction to be stressed is the separation of economic activity from play. In play, the value is in the activity itself, not in some end to which it is instrumental: or, the instrumental relation is reversed; the objective in play is not "real," but is set up to make the activity interesting. Part of the interest centers in *curiosity;* people act (also are spectators to action, further motivated by a social interest in entertaining, or receiving approving attention) in order to see what will come of it, in contrast with realizing a predetermined result. The end, beyond "scoring," is "to win"; but even this motive operates only during the game and when achieved (or when the chance is past) ceases to exist. Play may be solitary as well as social, and either competitive or ritualistic. But what must be said here is that economics deals with activity as instrumental to ends more substantive and permanent than mere symbols of victory or success. Yet, in everyday reality, both economic activity and the political action which controls or regulates and supplements it

partake of the nature of play as well as that of achieving desired
ends, "satisfying wants," through consumption.

Economic analysis must *abstract* from other aspects of pur-
posive action, but valid conclusions for policy cannot be drawn
in economic terms alone. Economic analysis not only has no
clear boundaries; it must be built up by successive stages of decreasing abstractness and generality, proceeding from propositions describing or defining all economic behavior to others that
apply in more limited circumstances. Hence, "principles" or
"theory" cannot be used to "prescribe," to guide policy, in contrast with abstractly describing what happens (describing a
general element or aspect of events); account must be taken of
many details of situations that fluctuate from case to case
and must be learned from empirical observation at the scene of
action. There is a rough analogy here with the study of theoretical mechanics, which starts with "frictionless" conditions
and other arbitrary standards and proceeds step by step through
the testing laboratory to engineering decisions made on the
ground. In a general way, the economic analogue of friction in
mechanics is *error*. Theoretical principles state what people try
to do rather than what they actually do; they describe "perfectly
economic" behavior, while in reality, of course, many forms of
error, ignorance, prejudice, etc., prevent men from achieving
the maximum results which might be had from the resources at
their command. And always, maximum efficiency in want-satis-
faction is a most incomplete and even distorted conception
of "the good life," the general goal of human thinking and
striving.

A further essential point by way of definition is that economics
does not consider the technical or technological side of efficiency
in the use of means. This is left to the various natural (or
psychological) sciences and applications of science. Economics
deals with the *allocation* of means among alternative ends or
modes of use. The whole science is developed out of, or applies,
a few simple principles that are "axiomatic" in the sense of being

matter of common knowledge and beyond dispute. The main principle is that of the satiability of particular wants, or diminishing utility; this accounts for apportionment in general. Use of means to gratify any single want is carried to the point where the means yield only as much as they would afford in some other use; there further expenditure is divided between the two uses. The general result is that the maximum utilization of means (any one or all) is secured by carrying the various lines of satisfaction to the point where the last final small increment of means (of the total supply) yields an equal "addition to total satisfaction" in all uses. This may be dignified by the name of "the economic principle." Cavils or hairsplitting about the nature of psychological quantities or measurement, and the logical possibility of deducing many of the conclusions from more general and abstract but less realistic assumptions will not be in question here. At a more empirical or physical level a second principle, parallel in form, holds for the use of physical means in achieving any physical end. If any one "factor of production" in a combination is increased, the others being held constant—e.g., if more labor is used with the same land and capital in raising wheat (passing for the moment over serious questions as to the meaning of these magnitudes)—it will be subject to "diminishing returns." And the producer of any good will strive to economize by apportioning his expenditures among the different factors (at given prices) so as to secure equal increments of (physical) product from equal increments of outlay (finally, or "at the margin").

As a device for clarifying these analytical distinctions— especially for separating the economic factor from the play interest, and from ethics and other social interests (subjective wants from more objective values)—it is useful to begin the discussion by considering the economic situation and problems of an isolated individual—the famous and mistakenly abused notion of a "Crusoe economy." We may be somewhat less unrealistic by postulating a society in which each *unit* (individual or "family" of some sort) is economically self-sufficient. There is no exchange or other form of "co-operation"; each unit entirely produces all it consumes or enjoys, using exclusively its own resources, human and external. (The Crusoe device also eliminates all special problems due to the use of money.) After pointing out that the more fundamental economic concepts have the same meaning for a Crusoe, if he seriously strives to practice "economic rationality," that they have for a member of our complex economic order, and also that the social-ethical problem is formally similar in a society regardless of its economic organization, we may consider briefly a social economy organized through the exchange of products alone (no buying and selling of productive services, or intermediate agents) and then turn to an economy of the form we mainly see around us. This of course is characterized precisely by such buying and selling, hence by the presence of the income distribution problem as we know it, with wages, rent, interest, and profit accruing largely to different persons, groups, or classes who thus find their interests conflicting in a special way.

2

A Crusoe (or Swiss Family Robinson) living on an otherwise uninhabited island, or a self-sufficient unit with otherwise "normal" social relations, would carry on production for consumption, economizing means in the satisfaction of wants. It is assumed to have the kinds of means universal in human life: personal capacities (natural and artificial qualities inseparably commingled); external resources (similarly characterized— a point to be stressed); and a "technology," based on a store of explicit or implicit "science." This last is only analytically separable from the personal capacities of human beings as "workers" but often has to be treated as an independent variable. The concepts here involved need to be defined with some care, in view of confusions in everyday use of terms and even in those of economists. In economics, production is a means to consumption as an end. The active human being has to be recognized as both a "productive agent" and a consumer, though no clear separation of these roles is possible. Most, if not all, productive agents require some maintenance and eventual replacement—again a more or less arbitrary distinction. This is as true of the "laborer" as of other agents; those called "natural" and "artificial" differ in degree and in detail, perhaps as much within each "class" as between the two. It is especially hard or unrealistic to distinguished between the maintenance of a laborer and his consumption that is an end, but conceptually the distinction is important (cf. Ricardo and Mill on "productive consumption").

Consumption is subjective enjoyment. What is consumed is the *services* of productive agents. Both enjoyment and service, as magnitudes, are flows, with a time dimension, and are "measured" as intensities (like light or electric current). They can not be thought of as block-magnitudes or stocks. Consumption of a service may involve in any degree the using up of the agent, from food or fuel at one extreme to "indestructible" things at the other (but with intermediate types as well as degrees). It is services that are directly *valued*. The value of an agent is simply the value of its expected future stream of service, but this is not merely an intensity times a time; the relation involves the *discounting* process, one of the worst sources of confusion in economic theory. (Services may also be valued at a time-point after any interval of flow, the discounting being reversed; house rent paid at the end of the month would be higher than if paid at the beginning, with payment at very short intervals intermediary in cost.) The fact that agents require maintenance (including any replacement) is connected with the fact that "current productive capacity" can be used to increase the stock of agents, instead of satisfying current wants. To be realistic, we assume that our Crusoe (self-sufficient unit) maintains and increases his stock-of-agents, meaning his "capital"—properly including himself and his family as far as they are in fact productive—also, as far as pertinent, his "technology." These relations also imply that all types of productive agents are finally interconvertible, and form a common "fund." (Qualifications necessary for complete empirical accuracy are too complex to take up here.)

Crusoe's choices, as a consumer, and as a producer (1) using given agents to maximize satisfaction and (2) apportioning productive capacity between consumption and capital maintenance or increase, will compel him to reduce both services and goods to a common denominator of "value." The value of a good relative to its service is the *capitalization* of the future service-stream at a rate equal to the rate (the highest rate) at which capital grows in the economy when all its yield (service) and no more is *invested*. The capitalization (discounting) rate reflects the growth rate, which is essentially a technological fact. But investment in technology—and most or all investment contains some of that element—precludes treating this rate as a "given" over any considerable period of time. And, since investment in technology is problem-solving, and advance prediction of the solution of a problem is self-contradictory, it is impossible to assert whether capital accumulation in the aggregate will decrease or increase the rate of yield.[2]

It is clear that Crusoe would need some unit for comparing and computing values, "money" in the sense used above. His comparisons would result in a virtual price system. And he would have to *impute* product among the agents used jointly in producing it, giving rise to "rent" and "wages" as concepts required in accounting and for managerial decisions.[3]

[2] Eliminating invention and exploration, and all discovery of techniques or resources, accumulation would presumably be subject to "diminishing returns" to the extent that there would be particular forms of capital not subject to equally free increase through investment. But it is wholly unrealistic to postulate any particular (final, historical) equilibrium rate of return, particularly the zero rate.

[3] Use of different terms for the yield of human and nonhuman agents is a source of confusion, though sometimes useful. Analytically, it would

Further, as just suggested, he will be forced to recognize · the amount of investment (sacrificed consumption) in his various productive agents, logically including himself and, perhaps separately, his store of scientific knowledge and technical skill. He will have to do this because of the continuous necessity of deciding whether just to maintain his "productive capacity" in each embodiment, or increase or decrease it, as contrasted with enjoying a somewhat smaller or larger current flow of consumption.

Recognition of capital instruments as embodying a certain quantity of investment involves the notion of a *rate* of yield, as distinguished from the rent of the agent itself. (It is perhaps better not to call it "interest" where there is no borrowing and lending, and no money.) Moreover, due to *errors* in decisions, the actual yield of our agent, its rent, will typically turn out somewhat more or less than expected or than what the investment would have yielded in some other use. Hence, rigorous accounting and accurate planning call for recognition of return on investment separate from rents. The difference could be an excess either way, and would constitute a *profit* (always including loss, negative profit), the fourth traditional form of income. It is also a profit when any concrete agent turns out to yield more or less than *that agent* might have produced in another use. This might be called "operating profit," in contrast with "promoter's" or "investment" profit, the form just mentioned. Thus there are really five functionally distinct types of income, if we separate wages and rent, though analytically it would be more accurate to use such a term as "hire" for both. But our point here is simply that, apart from social relations, the elementary concepts would have the same meaning for a Crusoe as for a mem-

---

be better to imagine our Crusoe as a slaveholder, doing no work himself and regarding his labor force as capital goods merely, yielding a rent (or, alternatively, interest on his investment—see text). But this would seem more "unrealistic"; in our age it is hard to picture human beings treated simply as inert instruments by "owners."

ber of pecuniary society—and would all have to be clearly conceived as a condition of making any practical decision "correctly."

We now briefly note that in a society made up of many self-sufficient units (Robinson Families of any scope) the same problems of economic ethics would arise that we are painfully familiar with. There would in all realism be wealth and poverty, superfluity and distress—in the absence of relief, "charity," voluntary or enforced. Naturally, being realistic, we assume that people would strive to improve their condition through saving and investment in the various forms of capital: ordinary implements and supplies, personal capacities, exploring for natural resources, scientific investigation, and invention. For, differences in ability and in "luck" (not objectively distinguishable in the case of decision-making) would at once produce inequality if the system started without inequality. (Economic equality cannot be accurately defined even where an established monetary system affords a suitable unit; it certainly does not mean equality of money income, per individual, or per family.) And, given the least start, inequality naturally tends to increase cumulatively, if people try to get ahead. Those who have more are always in a better position to get still more; "to him that hath shall be given." And this tendency goes on beyond the individual life, generation after generation (more or less counteracted by other tendencies, as tendencies always are). The inheritance of advantage or encumbrance strikes the modern liberal individualist as especially "unjust." We shall return to the question of moral obligation of the strong or fortunate to help the weak or unlucky. Only the facts are to the point here, especially the fact that these obligations are not in principle affected by the complete absence of economic organization of any form on a social scale—no exchange, no one in any sense "working for" anyone else, or being paid by anyone else. We note too that "property" is not peculiar, since any form of power or means can be used to get more of the same form or of other forms.

3

Organized co-operation of the form prevalent today may be thought of as a development in two stages from the society previously considered. The first stage would be an exchange economy in the proper, literal sense. Each family unit would produce a single final commodity, "from start to finish," or render a personal service, and these end-products would be exchanged in markets.[4]

The intermediate stage, the production and exchange of products, need not detain us long. The main facts needing to be brought out are the same negations that were obtained before. The same income forms would be potential, if not explicitly recognized, in the managerial decisions and accounting of the family unit. But there would still be no payment or receipt of wages, rents, interest, or profit, between persons, hence no "real" separation of such incomes. The economic problem of each unit would be somewhat altered. Instead of apportioning its resources among all the products desired for consumption it would try to select that product which would yield the largest return (in money and "psychic" values) and produce and sell this, and

[4] More realistically, they would be bought and sold against "money" of some form. In this sketch, we must assume that money is "neutral," thus separating it from the disturbances that arise from its use: specifically, from its changes in "value," and speculation on its future value—the primary cause of "business cycles" with all their attendant evils. We also "assume" a perfect market, with a definite uniform price of every product to all buyers and sellers, and, for simplicity, exclude middlemen and all speculation.

The idea of a two-stage development has some historical reality, in that a "handicraft economy" intervened between the medieval system of relatively self-sufficient manors and the modern age. But the idea is to be taken as an analytical device. It is nearer the truth, in general, to say that individualism developed through disintegration of a social matrix of custom and authority, not the progressive organization ("contract theory") of previously discrete persons.

would then apportion the proceeds of its sale in buying the chosen variety of goods from others. However, it would not be quite so unmistakable that each unit was simply working for himself or itself, using his own resources to satisfy his own wants (and to maintain or increase capital, or not). We might expect activities reflecting awareness of conflicting interests of producers and consumers of particular products. There might be efforts to negotiate or "bargain" over prices (presupposing not-quite-perfect markets), to exert "pressure," or to "monopolize"—unless we explicitly frame our assumptions to exclude such antics. Assuming ordinary conditions, there would as before be rich and poor, for the same reasons, and there would be the same "tendency" for inequality to increase (by differential growth, not actual depression of those low in the scale—ignoring the possibility of going into debt). And the same questions would be raised about the ethical obligation (and/or social necessity) of succor of the disadvantaged by (or at the cost of) those better off, through voluntary individual action or through social organization, using more or less compulsion.

4

Our modern economic order is not, typically and properly, an "exchange" economy. Specialization has been extended beyond the level at which the social unit produces and sells a product. People typically get their living by selling *productive capacity* to a *productive unit* or *enterprise* which carries on production and sells the product (or products, in reality often partial products). With the money received from some productive service or services the individual (social unit) buys his assortment of products for consumption, from whatever producers he finds to offer what he most wants on the best terms. Besides these typical individuals there are, of course, some—in part the same persons—who perform the new function of conducting enterprises, i.e., acting as *entrepreneurs*. Today, they are characteristically organized in groups as "corporations," meaning roughly the holders of voting common stock. The entrepreneur function is twofold: (1) to take the initiative in production by hiring resources and committing them to a particular product and mode of production; and (2) to take the "risk" or chance of being able to sell the product for enough to cover costs, including the market value of whatever services of person or property the owners furnish to the business (in addition to abstract "deciding"—but this is another separation that can only in part be carried through).

Under this organization, the four or five forms of income are to a large extent (far from completely) separated, going into the pockets of different persons performing the different functions: wage earners, lessors of various kinds of property, lenders of liquid capital, and entrepreneurs of the operating or the investing species. The income of the latter functionaries, called "profit," is in any one case as likely to be negative as positive, depending on his foresight and luck. The expectation or hope of a positive excess of receipts for products over outlays for productive services is the *incentive* to take the "risk" of loss, but it is misleading to call profit, when it occurs, the "reward" of risk-taking. We should not use this term for gambling gains, though business risk-taking has affinities with gambling which are in point here. Analytically, it is desirable to restrict entrepreneurial "risk" to that which cannot be insured against or eliminated by grouping cases; it is commonly thought better to call it by the different term, "uncertainty."

It is the entrepreneur who immediately pays the other three forms of income which to him are the costs of production. (Virtually always he himself receives some revenue from both labor and property; the latter may, in this case, be called either rent or interest.) To bring out the nature of the profit system (better called profit and loss system) and the relation between entrepreneur and wage-worker (and, presently, the receiver of rent or interest), it will be useful to proceed, as usual, by considering a hypothetical simple case. To get rid of the common confusion of profit with ownership income, we begin with a case where no property is involved. Let us think of a number of persons who wish to "co-operate" in such an activity as farming a piece of land where the land itself is a "free good," and other agents, tools, etc., are also free or negligible in cost. They must somehow agree on numerous technical details of the operation, their roles, etc., and on the division of the product. They could, of course, argue out or "negotiate" these matters as they go along, or negotiate contracts ahead of time. But they might also agree that one of the men is to take charge and the others simply to follow his instructions. Even then the division of the product might be made in any manner by agreement. As things typically work out in human affairs, the most effective and satisfactory arrangement is that some person or limited group "hires" the others to work under his (or their) direction, assigns to each a specified amount of the product income created, and himself takes "what is left," if anything, or takes the loss if there is a deficit. The fixed share of product is the meaning of wages, the "residual" share is that of "profit," and the directive function, coupled with responsibility for the result to the other parties, is "entrepreneurship." It is assumed that the laborers will work for the would-be entrepreneur who offers the best terms, and that he is "responsible." The qualification implies that the entrepreneur must have some resources as a surety for performing according to agreement. This does not necessarily mean that he must own property (other than personal capacity or labor-power), but property is the usual form of security. Insofar as the wage-workers are not actually made secure, they share in the entrepreneur function, regardless of how far they know what they are doing. It is because human beings do not completely "know what they are doing"—particularly the consequences very far ahead—that life presents problems; and one result is that the entrepreneurial function in economics exists and comes to be in all degrees specialized in a limited number of individuals.

The principles involved are not changed if some of the "co-operators" furnish property services instead of personal ones to the enterprise—or furnish both types of "productive capacity." The entrepreneur himself, as so designated, inevitably furnishes at least a small amount of both types, even though he may be actually bankrupt and his services really of no value or of negative value. In current business life, the relationships are further obscured and complicated, without affecting the basic principles, by two or three facts. One is the explicit *delegation* of the managerial function to an agent, paid a salary. The real, ultimate entrepreneurship cannot be delegated. In these cases the actual entrepreneur function is that of appointing the agent, fixing his powers and duties and his remuneration, and assuming responsibility for the results of his acts (or, as just noted, the function may be foisted off on unsuspecting laborers and property owners who take the risk of loss without intending to do so and who also make the responsible decisions in committing their resources to the use and the control in question). The appointment of agents obscures the relation between the entrepreneurial and "labor" functions. The hired and salaried manager is a "laborer," whatever the level at which he formally makes decisions.

A second source of confusion is in the entrepreneur-property owner relation. It is common practice for an enterprise to secure property services by borrowing "money," liquid capital, and constructing whatever equipment it wishes, instead of leasing equipment from owners. These latter might construct it *ad hoc* and lease it, as individuals and families produce and hire out capital in the form of more or less specialized labor power. As we have already intimated, there are two forms or levels of the entrepreneurial function: (1) "commitment" of productive capacity to a particular form; (2) direction of the use of equipment in a particular way. The role of the "capitalist" in relation to that of the property owner is not simple. It is not unusual for one person, or a group (partnership, company, corporation), to "own" property which is "mortgaged" to any part of its full value. Who, then, is the "real owner"? Only a complex legal analysis can give the answer, and it might require a trial before a court to decide various issues.

Further complications arise when the entrepreneur is an organized group, a company, or a corporation. In the first place, a group of substantial size inevitably acts through agents, who may or may not be "members," and the principal-agent relation never makes a clear division of power and responsibility. Moreover, the modern corporation may issue a bewildering variety of "securities" and may make contracts and incur debts on all sort of terms, involving a sharing of both assets and control, as well as earnings. With respect to a typical large corporation, it is often hard to say where "membership" ends and outside contractual relations and claims begin. Much actual power to control the operations and to appropriate the income may reside in a labor organization, i.e., in its officials, who may in any degree really "represent" the actual employees.

It is a common misconception that property employs labor; the entrepreneur is the employer (in the mediative sense, representing the ultimate consumer) of both property (or "capital") and labor. He "owns" the enterprise; but it may have no net worth. Property and labor work together, operatively, nominally for him, really more for the consumer who not only gets the product but exercises the final control; and finally, each works for himself. As everyone knows, business enterprises, so often condemned as exploiters of consumers and laborers, incur losses as well as make gains. It is indeed a question whether on the whole and on the average, or as a class, they secure any income at all. Whether losses are greater or less than gains cannot be certainly determined from statistical evidence. Inference from the gambling motive (where people regularly buy "tickets" at far above known actuarial value), and from such other empirical evidence as there is, suggests that over-all net gains cannot be substantial and may well be negative. Even including monopoly revenue, more or less distinguishable from "legitimate" profit, no statistical study is accurate enough to find any "profit" share in the national income. Entrepreneurs in the same and in different industries compete in one set of markets for the purchase of productive services and in another set for the sale of products. Effective competition "tends" to raise the former set of prices (entrepreneurs' costs) and to lower consumer goods prices. It seems that the "spirit of enterprise," akin to the spirit of gambling but including both emulation and the creative urge, has been strong enough to bring costs up and prices down at least to equality, on the average. Of course, either gains or losses may be large in individual ventures, though over time these tend rather rapidly toward "mediocrity," the ordinary return on investment, which contains no "pure" profit, and to fluctuate between gain and loss. Since entrepreneurs usually have other sources of income than "pure profit," there is no paradox in this share being zero or negative.

Theoretical analysis must start from the conception of a "perfectly competitive" economy organized through a system of theoretically ideal markets. Here all profit (and loss, negative profit) is excluded. Such ideal or "frictionless" conditions would make all costs equal to selling prices, the whole value-product being distributed among those who supply the various productive services. The prerequisite is errorless foresight of future conditions in all business decisions. Omniscient direction becomes identical with automatic adjustment to conditions. If a particular entrepreneur had perfect foresight he would clearly never incur a loss; and if his competitors had it he could never make a gain. This condition is a necessary hypothesis, though absurd if taken as realistic. Since productive commitments must precede consumption changes by an indeterminate and various but usually long interval, "responsible" decisions are required, subject to a wide range of error in numerous factors. In a society of self-sufficient individuals or families each would make these for himself and take the consequences. Tremendous gains in efficiency are to be had through specialization and co-operation, and there are other reasons for organized action. Concentration on particular products gives place to concentration on particular operations, dozens or even thousands of which may contribute to a completed product. Things have worked out most to the satisfaction of all parties concerned when implemented through individual initiative under control of exchange in the market at prices fixed by "demand and supply." Organization of a large labor force and distribution of product through explicit negotiation or quasi-political process on the pattern of representative government, called "producers' co-operation," is often advocated on ethical grounds but in practice has never succeeded so as to reach any considerable development.

In any free-market economy, insofar as "competitive" conditions prevail, each participant unit is in effect, like a Crusoe, working for himself, using his own resources to satisfy his own wants. Production for exchange is indirect production of the product received; it is intelligently done only because it is more efficient than direct or self-sufficient production, yielding to both parties a larger or a better product from the same resources. The effect of organization through free exchange is merely to increase efficiency, and it does this to the maximum extent consistent with the human limitations of the parties and the amount of freedom they have. ("Of course" freedom in association means freedom on both sides, not freedom of one to coerce or defraud another.) The theoretically ideal free-market organization enables everyone to use whatever resources (personal or external) he has in the way which yields the maximum value (given the known techniques) to the most willing and able consumer, and hence to their owner, and it gives the owner this yield as compensation.

With the world as it is, and men as they are, infinitely

varying in knowledge, wisdom, and managerial capacity, a gain in efficiency comparable to that due to specialization in occupations is to be had through specialization of management, particularly with modern technology calling for production in large, integrated organizations, in contrast with individual or "family" units. Under these conditions, analysis requires a "proximate ideal": that of "effective competition" between entrepreneurs (in the markets for products and for productive services) under the condition that the entrepreneurs and others have such ordinary human qualities as they do have, not omniscience. But it is assumed that there are numerous competitors, on both sides, with offers ranging widely (no collusion). In this situation, the same conclusion as above would hold. Each works for himself at maximum effectiveness, except that in consequence of uncertainty and error, some enterprises will make a gain and others incur a loss. Which predominates will depend on the "eagerness" of the entrepreneurs; if optimism predominates they will on the whole incur losses—and this latter statement seems to accord with the facts, specifically in the United States.

This is the *meaning* of a *free* economy. No one has any arbitrary *power* over another, since every buyer and seller has a choice of equally good opportunities. And, by the same argument, every member is made secure—secure of being able to sell, at their full value, whatever productive services he is in a position to render. Or, he can use his productive capacity himself to gratify his own wants directly. He can also pledge future income to realize present goods, either by borrowing or outright sale of productive capacity—to the extent that the legal system of society actually allows. In fact, this opportunity is normally available to property owners, but to a more limited extent to those who only possess productive capacity in the form of their own personal abilities. In the freest economy, needless to say, anyone's ability to consume depends either on his having productive capacity for direct use or sale to others (or for sale of its product), or on a one-sided transfer. Those who cannot produce can consume only at the expense of someone who can and does produce (except for eating up capital); this is axiomatic, regardless of the system of organization or absence of organization. The main ethical problem centers in the "right" to consume on the part of those who for some reason do not produce—or to consume beyond what they produce, as measured by free choice of other consumers.

5

Finally, we may offer a brief critique and a few observations on policy. The most important general observations which the economic theorist has to offer, bearing on social policy, are the truisms that "business is business," and that "charity is charity." The two truisms involve different conceptions of "justice," or "rights." (And "law is law" and involves still other norms of justice and right.) But such truisms are repugnant to large numbers of people and are accordingly repudiated. The cry for "Justice, not charity!" may be valid or nonsensical, depending on the definition of justice. In general, the definition of justice is what men dispute and fight about; not many demand more than they have a "right" to—i.e., think they have.

There is a kind of "natural justice" in the principle of the exchange (open or competitive market) economy, i.e., that each shall consume what he produces, i.e., adds, to total social production, as production is organized. (The family is the unit and voluntary charity or help is always allowed.) This norm would apply "ruthlessly" to an isolated individual (Crusoe) and must axiomatically apply to any community considered as a unit (allowing for some consumption of capital for a time, at the expense of the future). On the other hand, rigorous application of this norm to individuals in a society would be not only immoral but impossible and absurd; it is meaningless or grotesque or hideous in relation to babies, for example.

The next proposition is akin to the first and, like it, self-evident. Any unsatisfactory condition in an economic society may be due either to the fact that the "competitive system" does not work effectively in accord with the theory as stated, or to the antithetical fact that it does. Low wages, for example, or wages "too" low. The worker in question may be getting less than his "productive contribution," or may be unemployed because of imperfections in the organization machinery (or interferences with its working); or he may be getting all he is worth (to any ultimate consumer) but this may be inadequate for "decent" support, or less than a socially tolerable minimum, apart from humanitarian considerations. For the baby, and many others, it is zero, and for others it is or "ought" to be zero or small, while their consumption ought nonetheless to be high according to the standards of need and of justice which prevail in our society. However, we cannot say that anyone "ought" to have more than his own contribution without saying that somebody else has an *obligation* to *sacrifice* consumption of some part of his productive contribution, to make up the difference. The main problem is to locate, appraise, and apportion this obligation, determined in relation to needs and possibilities, and to find a way to effect the redistribution without such cost or loss of productiveness (destruction of incentive) as would nullify the gain.

Perhaps the first task of economics teaching is to counteract the tendency of the general public to say that "competition does not work" or has ceased to work, or is a myth, because many people do not get the incomes they "need" or are thought to need. Competition merely tends to give everyone his productive contribution, which is limited by his resources; and these latter bear little or no relation to his needs or those of his dependents. There are, indeed, serious "mechanical" weaknesses in the organization. Competition is "imperfect," for many reasons (not only monopoly of various kinds and related conditions). Much technical monopoly is accidental, or inevitable, or even functional (cf. patents and copyrights; most monopolies are similar in stimulating innovation and are also limited and temporary). The importance of this evil is vastly exaggerated in popular thinking. Moreover, labor unions and farmers, supported by public opinion and often by the law, are now the monopolies that do the most damage. Another and most important phenomenon is the "business cycle" of boom (partly pseudoprosperity) and depression (real), with unemployment, loss, and suffering by all classes, not merely wage-workers. In the first place, much if not most of the real imperfection of the market organization is due to ignorance and prejudice on the part of the individuals acting in every functional role—as consumers, workers, owners, and entrepreneurs in every branch of production, including trade. And much more is due to stupid governmental action and other well-intended interference. Unquestionably, selfishness, greed, and power-lust play a large role. They always will, particularly in any large organization. And the individual wage earner is at a disadvantage here since he is not often in a position to get away with much. But he is not the only victim, and it is far from easy to gauge these things, to separate and define legitimate rights or remediable evils, before discussing remedies. It is especially hard to identify evils remediable democratically by law and administration based on general free approval. The government is the largest organization of all, and "politics" is certainly not less liable to error, and prejudice, and skulduggery of every kind, than is "business." It is discouraging to see how much that is really wrong is due to ill-advised governmental action—action largely demanded by public opinion or at least by the majority; some of it is, of course, "put over" politically by selfish—or indeed by honest and well-meaning—"special interests." The fallacies of "protectionism" in foreign trade and "inflationism" internally are grievances of the economists as old as the science of economics itself, and little if any price-fixing is ever defensible; at the moment, the rent freeze on residential housing is doubtless both the most stupid and the most popular example.

The more serious problems of the free economy lie in the very meaning of economic freedom; but these can be dealt with here only by summary and rather haphazard mention. In fact, while they can be discussed endlessly, what can be said with confidence and in general terms can be put in relatively few words. The essential fact is that, fundamentally, society is not made up of individuals, but rather of institutional groups, beginning with the family as the minimum real unit: that is, considering society as an ongoing complex and looking either backward in history or forward in policy. Again, the heart of the matter, the veritable foundation of society, is the rights of babies—and the locus of the corresponding obligations to give them their rights. Here, obviously, the "individuals" directly in question can have no obligations themselves, and "freedom" for them has no meaning. Otherwise stated, the problem centers in the relations of right and duty between the family and, in the first instance, "the state." But the state—a free state—has nothing to give anyone except what it takes from someone else (if not from himself!)— and only part of that, since the transfer itself necessarily involves costs. The state, in free or individualistic society, serves as a sort of legalized Robin Hood, an intermediary for enforcing the "right" of the weak or unfortunate to be supported at a "decent" level at the cost of the stronger or luckier.

Now it is indisputable (as we have noted before) that within some bounds this right and the corresponding obligations exist. They are not merely dictated by humane sentiments; their acceptance—up to a point—is an absolute requisite to the existence of any society whatever, both sentimentally and practically. What point? is the first question. And the question impinges on every individual as either more or less "weak or unfortunate" or "strong or lucky" as the case may be. We cannot measure either of these variables—cannot even (as already noted) define economic inequality at all sharply. Obviously "individuals" cannot be allowed to be the judges of their own rights and the obligations of others to them or to their children and other dependents. And there is no impartial judge, and little hope of approach to agreement. Further, it is necessary, in the world as it is, to distinguish between inability and unwillingness on the part of those living below approved standards to provide for themselves and their own, and necessary to apply different treatment; and here there is an almost complete absence of objective norms. Yet the incompetent (morally blameless), and the unwilling too, have children, whom society must (both ethically and in self-defense) safeguard and provide for. Reasonable freedom to reproduce is perhaps the most sacred freedom and right, and it carries the heaviest responsibility.

The notion of freedom is meaningful only in relation to "given" individuals, given as to their ends and means, their tastes and their wants, their capacities internal and external. But in fact individuals are not "given." Both the wants and the capacities with which they enter responsible adult life are determined principally by the institutional complex which is society on the basis of innate physical, mental, and moral qualities and what must be classed as "accident." It should be stressed, because it is so generally ignored, that this cultural determination is just as important in connection with wants or tastes as in connection with "means," and that it is true and important in practically the same sense for the internal qualities that make a human being economically productive (his labor power) as for his endowment with external "property." The moral contrast between property rights and "human" rights will not stand examination.

The first requisite for intelligent discussion of wage policy—action to raise wages where they ought to be raised, or to supplement them by relief where they are inadequate—is a genuine interest on the part of the public in intelligent discussion itself, and in truth and understanding, in contrast with action by snap judgment, aimed at symptoms of maladies. Problems must be approached without prejudice in judging facts and the consequences of acts, as well as with high moral ideals. Science must be separated from wishful thinking, and co-operation for mutual advantage through business separated from charity, either voluntary or politically enforced. This has little appeal to the romantic-sentimental nature of man; but it will only confuse council and do more harm than good to define "wages" as what anyone thinks he or someone else ought to have, regardless of the person's contribution to production. And what one ought to have cannot be asserted without considering who is to contribute to his income, fixed by the value of his service to some willing buyer.

Short of slavery, neither the government nor coercive organizations of workers can force anybody to employ labor on any terms; they can only prohibit employment on specified terms. The result ordinarily to be expected from any coercive action to raise wages will be unemployment, i.e., no wage at all, or else the displacement of some workers into a stiil lower-paid occupation. There is no sense in minimum wage laws apart from provision for supplying the prescribed income in some other way, and this would make any prohibitive measure superfluous. And the only discoverable reason for existence of large national unions is to coerce the public, rather than the employers. According to the first principles of economics, employers as a group, in an entrepreneurial economy, have nothing to give or to be taken away. Some make gains, which are offset by losses on the part of others. Forcible expropriation of profits where and when positive profits arise must reduce the general inducement to risk resources in employing labor at all. It is simply impossible for all labor to benefit significantly at the expense of all employers. But the public statements of top labor leaders and other advocates of wage legislation express indifference as to where a demanded wage increase is to come from, whether from others better off than the beneficiaries or worse off. The "just" objective, of course, defined in terms of relative capacity in comparison with need, is to assist those badly off at the cost of others enough better off to justify the violation of freedom, as well as all the political and social costs and losses. It will be self-defeating to take away gains where there are gains and not reimburse for losses, destroying the incentive to strive to be better off. Men will not carry on business on terms of "heads you win, tails I lose." That policy must soon lead to a general stoppage or to dictation of all economic life by some authority, with loss of personal freedom and political responsibility.

It is impossible to say, even in theory, who will finally pay any particular wage increase forced from an operating firm. The first impact will be on the proprietors, but they may or may not have anything to lose; and anyhow, it may be passed on to creditors, consumers, or salaried employees, depending on circumstances that will hardly be ascertainable even by careful investigation of the particular case. The firm will in general employ fewer workers and turn out less product. We know that any increased consumption for some must come either from increased production, or from the consumption of others, or from saving. Workers might save a little out of an increase, and there are conditions in which higher wages may stimulate greater productivity, but both cases are unusual. The main effect of an enforced wage payment, beyond the competitive rate (the value of the service to the final consumer), will be to reduce the incentive to entrepreneurs and property owners, actual or potential, to save and to make investments and expand production. If people whose incomes are "inadequate" are to get more, apart from voluntary charity, the means should be secured by taxation levied in a morally and prudentially defensible way and amount, so as not to have too much negative effect on production. Wage earners are by no means the only persons receiving inadequate incomes; they are not as a class identical with propertyless persons, and many of them receive incomes which make them fit subjects for levies to support others.

Whether persons owning a little wealth but not enough to support them at a tolerable level should be forced to consume all of this before receiving any aid at the cost of others is one of the difficult questions of social policy.

In any attempt at redistribution of income, many considerations have to be taken into account. Presumably the question of "desert" should be given some weight, on the side both of the provider and the receiver of aid. But this is a factor where even a crude working definition is hard enough, and anything like measurement is hardly possible at all. In what are commonly thought of as economic terms, the first main consideration rendering an income a proper subject of taxation is its size, relative to the socially recognized claims against it. The latter include the number of persons it must support, their health and various special needs, the extremely difficult matter of separating real net income from expenditure properly required by one's business or profession, and the like. Society sometimes requires its functionaries to keep up appearances, to maintain the dignity of a calling, by living even more expensively than they themselves prefer. A second consideration is the security of the income, its steadiness in time and its prospective permanence. The major fallacy in popular thinking is the notion that size and security of income correspond simply to property versus personal services as the source. (This is apart from confusing property owning with entrepreneurship, which affords the most precarious and doubtful income of all.) There is probably a considerable correlation; but it is certainly not enough to justify treating "owning versus earning" (property rights versus human rights) as a principle in the determination of policy. These matters must be decided by discussion on their merits and in accord with facts, in specific cases, by collaboration of specialists in ethics with students of taxation who are up against the detailed facts and practical difficulties. General analysis tells us chiefly that most concrete measures of reform are crude substitutes for taxation and subsidy, and are hard to defend either in ethical terms or in terms of their economic or social-political effects—if their actual effects are brought out into the open.

Before and above all, the problem of social justice must *not* be discussed, as it so commonly is, on the assumption that a given social dividend is to be divided up among the individuals of a given population. The dividend is a current product, with the possibility of drawing a little upon the future by consuming capital—surely to be treated as a recourse of near desperation. But it is only too easy to sacrifice the future to the present by measures which undermine the incentive to activities contributing to growth. An intelligent social policy must strike some balance with respect to action that redistributes income more equitably, but at the cost of reducing the total below what it would otherwise be. And, on the other side, the sharers are not at all "given," either in numbers or in any of their important and relevant characteristics. A drastic redistribution, conforming to some abstract ideal of justice, may both decrease the amount to be distributed and increase the number of claimants; and the moral effects of "indiscriminate charity" constitute another problem about which little is known except that pauperization and disintegration of personality often result. Our moral sentiments seem to be as much out of accord with the possibilities of the world in which our lot is cast as they are in conflict with the basic natural propensities that make up immediate self-interest. He that would love his fellow man, and express his love in a way that will do more good than harm, must indeed learn to be (in scriptural language) as wise as a serpent and harmless as a dove. Freedom, justice, order, efficiency, and progress are value imperatives all essential within wide limits, but there is conflict among them—conflict practically between each one and all the rest; more of one can be had only by giving up more or less of the others. And there is no formula to tell the policy maker where or how to strike the best attainable balance.

The conclusion, which it is not pleasant to reach, but which must be drawn, is that the most needed lesson for public opinion at this historical juncture is not to expect too much. We must "live in the world" as it is until (and if) we can change it. Neither accepting it nor changing it is easy, and, if our powers are limited, attempting much or rapid change is certain to be to make things worse instead of improving them. The forces of nature show no detectable preference for the human virtues of gentleness or justice, or for any "good intentions"; and the basic drives of human nature are those required for survival in a world of the kind this one is. Freedom of the individual in particular is a historically anomalous product of conditions peculiar to the Western world in the past few centuries. It seems to be natural to human beings to turn to a "savior" when they are in trouble of any kind. As a great Founding Father of the American Republic well said, "Eternal vigilance is the price of liberty"; but he should have said "intelligent" vigilance. If we care for freedom we must respect it, and not hasten to pass laws and set up authorities for enforcing them unless there is very sound reason to expect the result to be an improvement over that "natural liberty" which is anything but natural in view of history as a whole.

This means that laws must be chiefly in the negative form, like the Decalogue, made up of thou-shalt-not's, but summed up in the proposition that none shall infringe the liberty of others; that is, relations shall be by mutual assent. Intelligent positive policy has as its first requisite a clear understanding of how the free economy works, and of whether the evils we see are due to freedom or to its absence or—which is largely the case—to some unalterable condition of life. With respect to wages, the only proper meaning of the term is the price the most willing and able buyer will pay for the most valuable product the individual is able and willing to turn out (or contribute toward); and this is the wage which "tends" to be established in the free market. In no wise does it imply ethically ideal results; for, in the demand for labor, "able" counts as much as willing and might does not make right. Ability and even will (tastes and interests), is in large part the creation of brute facts and forces along with ethical factors. Society is not made up of given individuals; as we have seen, both productive capacity and wants are socially created at least as much as they reflect activities of the individual for which credit or blame can be imputed; and "luck" is perhaps the largest factor of all. Social policy must aim first at giving the worker his wage, in the proper meaning. Beyond that, interference must be directed to supplementing the wage where needful and feasible. But, more especially, social policy must strive to enable the individual to earn as much as he is potentially able to earn through property and personal services, and to achieve security, through reducing the vicissitudes of economic life and through an honest application of the insurance principle.

Finally, social action must not simply be sweepingly identified with state action, as there is such a tendency to do. That can easily lead to submergence of all freedom in a totalitarian regime and to the destruction of civilization, if not of humanity, in international strife. There is no formula, no easy or satisfactory answer to the problem of the distribution of responsibility between the individual, the family, the local community, the nation-state; and the world order, which is slow in coming, must imperatively be somehow built up. And there are innumerable other important groupings, political or nonpolitical in various ways and degrees. There are grave dangers in the tendency of reform to transfer functions from individual, family, and voluntary associations to the state. The family is particularly threatened, and the problems of rich and poor nations, of inequality and alleged exploitation between regions and peoples, are coming to be as serious as the same differences and conflicts within a particular state. Nations no more than individuals can live to themselves alone, in the world of modern technology and humanitarian feeling.

Any serious effort to discuss the social problem, of which

the wage problem is merely an inseparable aspect, and to consider all the factors which patently have to be considered and give them their due weight must tend to emphasize caution and conservatism. The time has passed when the world needed simply to be aroused to action, on the assumption that what to do was no serious problem, evils being due to people not doing what they know it was good to do. There is of course plenty of "sin" in the world, and "vested interests" resist change; but it is not to be assumed that "reformers" are either more disinterested or wise than opponents of particular measures, and it is an infinitely harder problem to change things for the better than to preserve law and order in roughly their wonted course. The modern social order is an infinitely complicated and sensitive mechanism, and there is vastly more chance of injuring than of improving it by tampering with it at random, or without the clearest understanding of what one is doing, however well-meant the action may be. At this time, ill-considered measures of interference are a greater danger than indifference to evils. One of the first conclusions from any candid investigation of our problems, from the standpoint of inadequate wages as from any other standpoint, must be the inevitability of gradualness, or of disaster as its alternative.

CHAPTER V

Selections from the Discussion
of Knight's Paper

[*Editor's note:* After Professor Knight's paper there was a discussion of the extent to which even the "purely" competitive solution can be said to be "optimal"—especially from the point of view of the individual. This led into a general discussion of "welfare" economics as follows:]

WRIGHT. I don't believe the welfare economists have yet established any proof that redistribution would increase happiness.

SAMUELSON. It seems to me a proposition incapable of proof. Under certain specified ethical assumptions the greater the inequality of income the better. The economist can't deduce ethical norms.

WRIGHT. Why then talk of it as a scientific proposition? I don't see there is anything in economics or mathematics to show redistribution would raise the happiness of the world.

SAMUELSON. That's, by the way, quite irrelevant in this.

WRIGHT. No, it's not irrelevant if you're going to talk in terms of ethics, or political organization.

SAMUELSON. The only question I am raising here is whether somebody's client will say that is a better situation.

WRIGHT. I know, but you're beginning to talk about utility functions and redistribution and so on, and that elaborate mathematical calculus doesn't amount to a hill of beans, because it's all based on assumption of comparability of wants, and we don't know they are comparable. . . .

SAMUELSON. It isn't the business of the economist to say what is better or not; what the economist can do is to interpret to different people with different welfare functions, whether in terms of their particular welfare functions they will consider one distribution better than another, and it's up to the noneconomist to specify to us the full range of variables that he wants included in the welfare function in terms of which we are to make such an appraisal.

WRIGHT. Don't you think you might start with the assumption that not all the welfare functions could possibly be satisfied?

SAMUELSON. That's obvious.

WRIGHT. And work out to see what is the best method of settling this pull of interest?

SAMUELSON. You mean a superwelfare function which defines a compromise?

WRIGHT. No, we might say: Here we are. We all want different things. What is the best way of finding out who shall get what—of deciding?

I might know that under one method I might get more, and yet I might prefer the method of settlement because I believe that to be ethically better even if it doesn't happen to yield a result that suits me, and it might yield a result that might not give the maximum return to any particular person. But the belief in a method of settling the dispute might override our personal interest in the actual award, so to speak.

SAMUELSON. I might even define that as the problem of politics—the way, in fact, compromise welfare functions are worked out—since generally speaking people agree that they both want more of a limited total of economic goods.

WRIGHT. Well, a distribution of wealth achieved under certain generally accepted systems of rights and sanctions might therefore have some ideal content in the sense that you believe in that particular set of rights and sanctions.

SAMUELSON. And to the extent that people acquiesce, as say Burke would have done, in the inherited institutions, it's at the low political level a very good solution, but to the extent that they don't, and we all recognize that there is a revolt against the competitive imputation of income even after it has been changed by progressive taxation, the solution doesn't always work. The particular warring parties have not been able to reach general belief and hence they resist the results the market actually yields. . . .

One last point, if you have a large group and if it is selfish and if the rest of the community will play the part of passive competitors, it is always to the advantage of the large group to exercise monopoly power, as it puts it, in a Robin Hood fashion. This is what you might call the Launhardt-Bickerdike theory— that if all but one large group will play the part of competitors, the last group will maximize its own welfare by deviating from competition.

FRIEDMAN. Sure, given a generally competitive society, a person who can get a monopolistic position is in a position to exact tribute from others.

SAMUELSON. You can't tell your client that labor unions are incapable of improving themselves by non–income tax policies. You can warn them that other people will do the same and they can't necessarily get unilateral monopoly. But if you have only their selfish interests at heart, and if the other people are competitive, then you must tell them, "Depart from the rules of the game of perfect competition in your own interests."

This isn't ignorance. This is interfering with the competitive order not through ignorance but avarice and power.

BOULDING. The real question is why is the power of the state always being used to destroy the market? Why is the political power inimical to the market, as it has been for the last hundred years? I mean it always has been except for the brief interval between Adam Smith and Cobden.

FRIEDMAN. It's partly ignorance. It's partly because two people think they can benefit by the intervention of the state without benefiting at the expense of one another.

SAMUELSON. It's more. It is that the market hasn't left them in any "uniformly" complete defensible position.

WRIGHT. Could you say that it has left them that way by and large? I never get very much excited when somebody says the market is entirely perfect or not entirely perfect—

SAMUELSON. This is a perfect market.

WRIGHT. I think that you can see that if as a matter of practical belief—it may not be so, but if people on balance feel that by and large on the whole they get a greater degree of fairness in the general method of distribution if there is a considerable amount of competition and a workable market, that that might be the basis of having the market—that they feel that there is less coercion and compulsion and, on the whole, on balance, a fairer result.

What you are trying to do is to run an economy without ethics, and you say that your client is going to prey on the market. Society as a whole, as long as it believes in some approach to a market, is then quite justified in turning on your client and saying, "No, we are not going to allow people to prey on the market. You have got to subordinate your welfare to general considerations of justice, and one of our general considerations of justice is that the distribution emerging from a tolerably competitive market is on the whole the best." Since personal welfare functions cannot all be satisfied they must be reconciled in some way. May it not be best to reconcile them in a manner involving the minimum of coercion?

SAMUELSON. You see, I am trying to examine this result in terms of each and every possible prescribed ethical scheme. . . .

BOULDING. It seems to me this discussion largely misses the point of the problem. As far as the subject which is supposed to be on the table is concerned [Ed.: the price mechanism], the real problem of the price mechanism isn't the question as to what you get when you have solved your simultaneous equations. It's the process of solving them, and what happens in the process of solving them. That is the main subject of ethical or policy judgments.

SAMUELSON. May I second that?

BOULDING. Yes. That is, in economics we have a strong prejudice in favor of price flexibility; if there is an excess demand or excess supply, then we say the price ought to adjust itself. We do this because of our prejudice as economists, because that is the way our system works out. Actually, there isn't much justification for it. If we look at the thing in dynamic terms as a sort of ecological succession—that is, how Monday turns into Tuesday—then it is obvious that the strains in society which result from price disequilibriums can have other consequences than movement of prices, and these other consequences may be more desirable. If your price is not at the intersection of all your demand and supply curves, or what lies behind the demand and supply curves, there is disequilibrium. We admit that. But the disequilibrium does not have to operate on the price alone. It may operate on variables such as technologies, tastes, or other things, and these operations have to be taken into consideration. But you can't just assume that determinants of the price system are given and that they determine the price system and that's wonderful.

You have to look at the way disequilibrium prices change these other things. If you look at Sidney and Beatrice Webb's masterly discussion of price competition versus nonprice competition in the labor market and their defense of nonprice competition in the labor market, which is extremely cogent, in *Industrial Democracy*,[1] you see that price adjustments aren't always desirable. Sometimes they are; sometimes they aren't. But there isn't anything which says they are always desirable.

And, of course, that is precisely why there is a revolt against

[1] (Longmans, Green, 1926.)

the market. The history of the last hundred years is a flight from the market everywhere—in protection, labor policy, cartels, agricultural policies, socialism. That's what the whole thing is. And there are good reasons for it.

SAMUELSON. Let me illustrate your very important point. Let's suppose that the mathematician figured out the competitive imputation and gave it to you and gave you a choice between that situation and what you would get in a situation where the government foolishly all over the map, but in a neutral manner, put on not lump sum taxes but unit taxes in a haphazard manner. People would still have all the freedom to buy and sell in perfectly organized markets. It would come about that the final system of equilibrium prices would be not the configuration that would give people the most if they valued economic goods and services as sole ends, and yet they might prefer a regime where they had full freedom to truck in the market place, even though it meant less efficient imputation than would be the case under a perfectly planned mock competitive solution doled out to them.

BOULDING. It is extremely instructive to draw up a model of an economy in which all prices are absolutely fixed, in which there is no price flexibility whatever, and in which all prices are arbitrary. What happens is that if the price, the arbitrary price system, of course, is not the same as your equilibrium price system, you will get shortages and surpluses, and then these shortages and surpluses will produce operations on the determinants of the price system that change these determinants until they determine the price system they have.

For instance, if you have a shortage, you get rationing of the commodity. You have a perfect market. There isn't any emphasis on selling. Then technological change will go into that commodity rather than into the surplus commodities, and you will have adjustments in the determinants of the system. And who is to say whether this is better than the other? You can't say, and there is a lot to be said for nonprice competition or nonprice adjustments in many fields. . . .

It isn't only revolt against imputation of income. It's revolt against the market. That is also the result of its general instability I think to some extent. How much that and how much the other I don't know.

FRIEDMAN. Most important of all in all of this—this goes back to one of Professor Knight's points—a large part of the so-called revolt against the market is the result of ignorance. I think in case after case you have people differing concerning social policy because they have different ideas as to what the effect of the policy will be, so you have A in favor of minimum wages because he thinks it will reduce poverty and B against minimum wages because he thinks that minimum wages will increase poverty. There isn't any difference in standards. One analysis is right and one wrong. That is the situation Knight was referring to in the case of an obvious thing like rent control. Thus differences in programs often reflect differences in analysis of the consequences of economic action rather than differences in objectives.

BOULDING. Why did we ever have a market? It's rather baffling, because all the forces are arrayed against it. Everybody's individual interest is to be a monopolist.

KNIGHT. Always has been.

BOULDING. Who is actively interested, as purchasers, in the institution of the market? It's the trader.

CLARK. Weren't the townspeople interested in market institutions for the people who came into the town to sell things the townspeople would buy?

BOULDING. Yes, but that's the difference between, say, a workingman and a trader? The workingman hits the market once a week at the pay desk, whereas the trader hits it all the time. He's always buying and selling. I mean that's the difference between the middleman and the people at the end. The people at the end only hit the market occasionally—the farmer and the worker. Even the manufacturer for that matter.

SAMUELSON. No, under conditions of anarchy and with the right psychological and technological conditions, it seems to me a market is inevitable, because the small man cannot exercise monopoly power if there is really free entry due to perfectly flat cost conditions; though nobody planned it, the market would then form itself. This is the only teleology you might find.

FRIEDMAN. The market is almost inevitable in some form or another because of the technical problems to be solved. . . .

KNIGHT. One more thing about the general principle here. You approach a game from two propositions. What is fair according to the rules of the game? I suppose we agree people shouldn't cheat. They should play the game according to the rules. But the rules may be the problem, and they are the problem for our discussion here. Now, when you go to change the rules you confront the question of costs. You suspend the game as long as you discuss the rules. You can't discuss the rules and play the game at the same time. That is one of the serious limitations of political action.

SAMUELSON. Can we not, as a theoretical matter, discuss the problem at this table without suspending the rules outside?

KNIGHT. It's our game. But society, which is playing the game, can't discuss the rules and play the game simultaneously—

WRIGHT. —can't run trains and argue over firemen at the same time. Every society has to have certain general beliefs which make the thing click. . . .

BOULDING. The only thing wrong with capitalism is that nobody loves it. You take the Canadian wheat farmer. That is a wonderful example. He hated the Winnipeg wheat exchange. He still hates it. I mean he is willing to suffer, I think, a considerable economic sacrifice in order to satisfy his hate of it; but this is something you have to take into the picture if this is going to be social science and not just economics. I mean all this ignorance. Why are people ignorant? Well, because as you say, we haven't succeeded in putting truth into a myth.

FRIEDMAN. But the reason he hates is because he thinks there is an alternative which will eliminate the real problems that are what bother him. That is, he thinks he can have his cake and eat it too.

CHAMBERLIN. Among the species ignorant, what is there ignorant about a monopolist, for instance, who thinks that by pursuing a monopolistic policy he can improve his own position?

FRIEDMAN. Nothing. He's absolutely right.

CHAMBERLIN. A great deal of the interference is of that sort, isn't it? It doesn't involve ignorance at all. We like to say that the labor unions are bad economists; that they ought to take a course in economics. I think they are very good economists myself.

FRIEDMAN. I don't doubt that for a moment, and I didn't intend to imply that the action by the labor unions was necessarily ignorant in terms of their members. But the actions by society in identifying the welfare of the union members with the welfare of society, in providing them with weapons, in the mistaken idea that this will benefit society at large, is the ignorance.

CHAMBERLIN. It's the tolerance of it by society.

FRIEDMAN. That's right.

CLARK. The action of the politicians in society on the assumption that they will get votes and stay in office by a certain course of action may not be ignorant.

BOULDING. The way scarcity hits the individual is through the market. He can't afford to buy all these things on sale because he doesn't have enough money. Then we wonder why people don't like it.

SAMUELSON. In rationing it's "those" people that get dramatized—the officials who limit ration tickets in the austere countries. They're the ones who have created the scarcity. And there is an element of truth in it. You find if you travel there much the same discontents as with us, only it's not the ticker tape of the auction market that is making people poor, it's the edicts of the planners. "Mr. Brofföss is keeping Norway down to a low level of consumption," and so on.

CHAMBERLIN. I think it's very important to recognize that it is quite natural for the state not to act in this case in a way in accord with the social maximum because it acts for political motives. It permits labor unions to do certain things because laborers have votes and it's quite important to get their votes. And there's nothing ignorant about it. The same is true with agricultural policy and any number of other policies. And if we recognize that, we avoid the prime error so common in the theory of socialism of identifying state action *per se* with state action in accord with a social ideal.

SAMUELSON. Multilateral monopoly is self-defeating. And in that sense there is an element of irrationality in it. Isn't that true?

CHAMBERLIN. Well, there may be irrationality in it from the point of view of a defensible social objective, yes. That's what you are saying. But I am saying there is no reason to expect the political state to act in accord with the defensible social objective.

FRIEDMAN. That may be quite right, and I didn't mean to imply ignorance in that way. And yet it seems to me there is a real point here. How can those people who are deliberately, let's say, seeking to get farm programs in order to benefit farmers, in order to get votes—how can they sell it to the rest of the country? The reason they sell it to the rest of the country is because they can persuade the rest of the country of something you and I think to be fallacious, namely, that not only farmers but everybody will benefit from this. And the protective tariff is the extreme case.

I quite agree with you that this ignorance of some is deliberately manipulated by others.

CHAMBERLIN. They sell it to the rest of the country mainly because the rest of the country isn't interested. The ones mainly interested in the agricultural handouts are the farmers. The ones mainly interested in policies favoring some particular industry are those in that industry. And, for the most part, other people simply would prefer to think about other things and live independently of those problems. Isn't that the reason why?

FRIEDMAN. Sure, that's right.

CHAMBERLIN. If people were actually alert and interested in the further implications of all policy questions, they wouldn't have time to do anything else.

WRIGHT. I think the main reason people hate the market is because they attribute the restraints of social life to the market. What I have been trying to do in my "Capitalism" book that I am just finishing is to show how much of what we don't like is quite irrelevant to capitalism.[2] Capitalism happens to be the vehicle by which these constraints are imposed upon us. And if we invent another vehicle, many of the same constraints, the same barriers, will turn up.

And another aspect of it is that as long as one person doesn't play the game, as Professor Samuelson says, he always makes a profit. So you have two things: (1) restraints supposedly only imposed by the pricing system but which would be imposed in other ways in other systems; and (2), "If *I* don't play ball *I* can do very well." Therefore we jump to the idea that if *everybody* doesn't play ball *everybody* can do very well.

CLARK. "In Philadelphia almost everybody reads the *Bulletin*." And it's fine for the one who doesn't.

SAMUELSON. Under conditions ideally suited for *laissez faire* that isn't quite true. One man is always too small. If he can't get together with the state, and cost conditions are right, he has no potential monopoly power, and he can't exercise it.

---

[2] D. McC. Wright, *Capitalism* (McGraw-Hill, 1951).

WRIGHT. Did the classical economists really think that they really had such a situation? Don't you suppose they allowed for a good deal of monopoly and special privilege?

I think in terms of the "reasonable, prudent man" all the time because I studied law. But they probably thought in terms of a "reasonable, prudent" approach to competition. And they admitted some people could get antisocial action, but, on the whole, they thought they kept it pretty well down.

KNIGHT. I want to say one thing. Man is romantic. People hate trade. They hate profit. As somebody just said, they'd hate the planner under planned economy. They don't realize that the planned economy would just shift the object of the hatred. They hate truth. They hate the incommensurability of the circumference of the circle with its diameter. And it's the smartest, best-educated ones that keep on trying to beat it and square the circle. And they hate the law of the conservation of energy. And a very large proportion of the brightest young men in the world spend a certain number of years of their lives inventing perpetual motion machines.

You can't get that out of the picture and talk about reality. I won't take any more time.

CHAMBERLIN. May I make one comment? Don't you think another thing they hate is measuring things? Part of their revolt against the market is due to its reduction of everything to quantitative measure.

SAMUELSON. They even hate analyzing the market mathematically.

KNIGHT. Some great author said the ability to do algebra is a form of low cunning. I have a great deal of sympathy with that. [Laughter.]

CHAPTER VI

Wages as a Share
in the National Income

BY KENNETH E. BOULDING[1]

THE problem of the distributional shares—that is, of
the determinants of the proportions in which the national income is divided among the various "ranks of the people"—has
interested economists at least from the days of the physiocrats.
In classical economics the problem is conceived as a threefold
division of the total product between wages, rent, and profit. In
this paper we shall consider only the twofold division into
wages (labor income) and "gross profits" or nonlabor income.
Nonlabor income is the same as Marx's "surplus value."

·In the classical system the problem of the distributional
shares is recognized both as what we should now call a "macroeconomic" problem, involving the main aggregates of the system,
and also as a dynamic problem, involving what happens in the
progress of society and the course of economic growth or decline. Total labor income, or aggregate wages, is regarded as a
constant at any given short period of time, determined by the
wage fund, which in its turn is determined in some way by the
decisions of capitalists as to the distribution of the use of their
capital. Exactly how the wage fund is determined is never made
quite clear, and this, of course, is the weak link in the whole
chain of argument. Given the wage fund, however, nonlabor

---

[1] *Editor's note:* No annotations are given in this chapter. For comments
see the discussion, chap. vii.

income is a residual—the difference between the aggregate total income and labor income.

Even with this crude apparatus the classical economists managed to develop at least the beginnings of a dynamic theory—i.e., a theory of economic development, and of what happens in the "progress of society." The subsistence theory postulated a perfectly elastic supply of labor at the subsistence level, wherever that might be. It assumed, that is to say, that there was some *average* wage above which the population would grow indefinitely, and below which the population would decline indefinitely. This average wage is the subsistence level, and it does not, of course, have to be determined by the level of physical subsistence. The average wage is equal to the wage fund, or total labor income, divided by the working population. If, therefore, the wage fund is constant, and the average wage is above the subsistence level, the population will grow, and therefore the average wage will decline until the subsistence level is reached and further growth of population ceases. In fact, however, the wage fund is not constant, but grows itself with the increase in capital. Hence we get the concept of the historical course of the average wage as the result of a race between population growth and capital accumulation, ending in the stationary state, where neither population nor capital grows. As population growth outstrips the growth of capital, the average wage falls; as capital outstrips population, the average wage rises; but eventually the race must be won by population—creation being no match for procreation—and the wage will settle down at the subsistence level.

It is instructive to examine a version of the classical system by means of graphical analysis. We suppose first of all that the aggregate income (Y) is a function of population (P) and capital (C). This function is shown by means of contour lines (Y-isomers) in Figure 1, where population is measured vertically, capital horizontally, and the solid lines marked 100, 200,

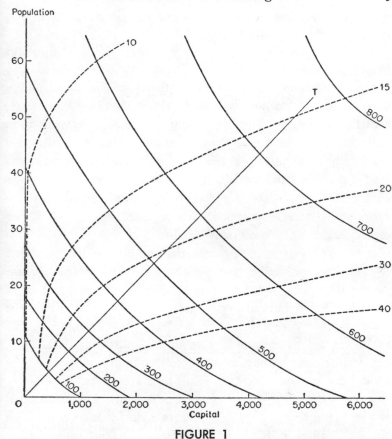

FIGURE 1

etc., are contours of equal aggregate income. These are drawn so as to exhibit a law of diminishing returns: An increase in both capital and population increases income at a decreasing rate, so that at high levels of population and capital a greater increase in population or capital is necessary to give a given increase in income than at low levels. This is reflected in the figure by the fact that the contours become further apart as we proceed upward or to the right. It is not necessary to assume any particular curvature in the contours, though a diminishing marginal rate of substitution between population and capital, as in the figure, is not unlikely.

By dividing the aggregate income at each point of the field by the population the per capita income can be calculated, and per capita income contours drawn (these are the dotted lines, marked 10, 15, etc.). It will be observed that the diminishing returns assumption—which is, of course, based on the assumption that there is some factor (land) which cannot be increased—results in a curvature in the per capita income contours, so that if per capita income is to be constant, capital must increase continually faster than population. If capital and population, historically, increase proportionally as along the line OT, per capita income will continually decline.

The classical system assumes that aggregate labor income is a function of capital, not population. In the extreme form of the wage fund doctrine it is assumed that aggregate labor income is some constant proportion of total capital. There is no need, however, to limit the model by this assumption, and in Figure 2 I have drawn, again on a population-capital field, aggregate labor income or wage bill contours, which are the solid lines marked 100, 200, etc. These are vertical, indicating that the wage bill is independent of population. I have assumed in the figure that the wage bill bears a diminishing proportion to total capital as total capital increases—a not unreasonable but by no means necessary assumption. From these wage bill contours average-wage contours can be constructed, the average wage at each point in the field being the wage bill divided by the population. It is assumed here that the population and the working population are identical—a rather general assumption in classical economics. The average-wage contours are the dotted lines marked 5, 10, etc.[2] Now suppose that the average wage

[2] The geometrical construction of the average-wage and per capita income contours is as follows: to construct the average-wage contour x in Figure 2 we take the points on the wage bill contours w_1, w_2, etc., at

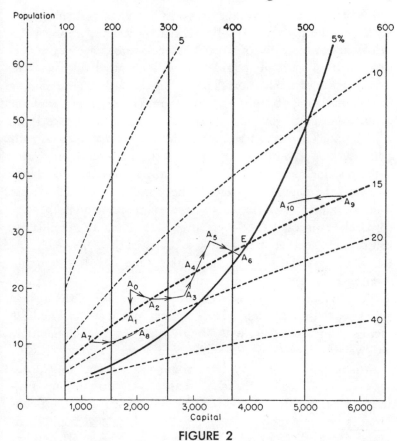

FIGURE 2

represented by one of these contours—say the wage of 15 units—
is the subsistence level. The corresponding average wage contour
is drawn heavily in Figure 2. At any point above and to the

which they are intersected by the lines $P = w_1/x$, $P = w_2/x$, and so on.
Thus the average-wage contour marked 10 in Figure 2 is constructed by
taking the point on the 100 wage bill contour where $P = 10$, the point
on the 200 wage bill contour where $P = 20$, on the 300 wage bill contour
where $P = 30$, and so on. The line joining these points is the average-
wage contour. A similar construction gives the per capita income contours in
Figure 1.

left of this line the average wage is less than the subsistence level and the population will eventually decline; at any point below and to the right of it the average wage is above the subsistence level and the population will eventually grow. The actual course of population depends on the factors determining the accumulation of capital and on the speed of response of the population to a wage which diverges from the subsistence level.

The actual course of population and capital may be shown by a line such as $A_0A_2A_3A_4$ . . . in Figure 2. A_0 represents some initial position of population and capital. If there was no change in capital the population would simply move to the subsistence level contour at A_1. Actually however there may be growth (or decline) in capital: if there is growth in capital, population and capital together may follow a course such as $A_1A_2A_3$ . . . etc. Population falls from A_0, as the wage is below the subsistence level contour. Capital continues to grow, however, and if the population is not immediately responsive to the rise in wages above the subsistence level we may move to A_3. The high average wage, however, will stimulate a growth of population, and we move back to the subsistence level contour A_4. The growth in population may have some momentum, which will carry us to A_5, below the subsistence level, this in turn producing a further decline to A_6. The more responsive the population is to the level of wages, the closer the actual population-capital path will approximate to the subsistence level contour; population will always just keep pace with the growth or decline of capital. When population is increasing faster, per unit increase of capital, than the slope of the subsistence level contour we see a decline in the average wage; when it is increasing more slowly the average wage rises. This is the "race between capital and population."

The foundation of Adam Smith's dictum that wages are likely to be high in an advancing society and low in a declining society can also be seen from this diagram. The basic assumption involved is that the reaction of population to a divergence of the

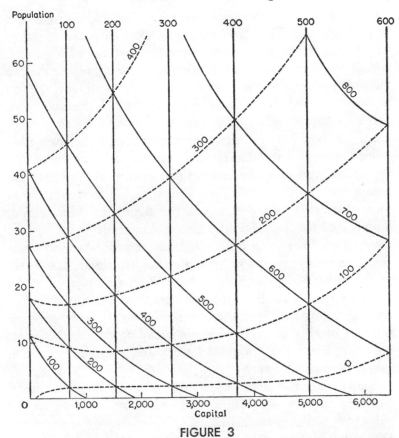

FIGURE 3

actual wage from the subsistence level is slow—slower, that is, than the rate of adjustment which would compensate for the change in capital. Thus in a society in which capital is increasing, even starting from the subsistence level, say at A_7, the population-capital course is likely to be like A_7A_8: the rise in population is not sufficient to bring the society back to the subsistence level contour. When capital is decreasing, however, as from A_9 to A_{10}, the population does not fall enough to keep pace, and the wage is continually below the subsistence level.

From the aggregate income and wage bill contours of Figures

1 and 2, contours showing the aggregate nonwage income can be derived as in Figure 3. Here the solid lines are identical with the aggregate income and wage bill contours of Figures 1 and 2. As the nonwage income is equal to the aggregate income minus the wage bill, the nonwage income contour, say, of 100 is drawn through the points of intersection of the 200, 300, 400 . . . aggregate income contours with the 100, 200, 300 . . . wage bill contours. The dotted lines are nonwage income contours. The "diminishing returns" assumption of the aggregate income function draws them upward to the right; the assumption of a diminishing ratio of wage bill to capital draws them downward to the right; in the figure the "diminishing income returns" assumption is clearly dominant.

The most interesting ratio in the case of nonlabor income is not the ratio to population [3] but the ratio to capital; this latter gives us a sort of gross "rate of return" on all capital. Thus in Figure 4 the dotted lines represent contours of equal "rate of return," constructed in a manner similar to the average wage contours of Figure 2. They slope sharply upward to the right, indicating that a rise in capital lowers, and a rise in population raises, the rate of return.

Suppose now that there is some rate of return at which capital will neither grow nor decline, and that above this rate capital will grow, while below this rate it will decline. We then have a long-run "subsistence" theory of the rate of return, or "profit." The "subsistence" rate of return need not be zero, as Ricardo seems at times to imply; indeed, in a society which is naturally averse to risk it is likely to be positive. In a highly risk-loving society it might even be negative. Suppose in Figure 4 that the subsistence rate is 5 per cent: the 5 per cent contour is then the subsistence rate contour. Putting this into Figure 2 as the heavy

---

[3] The per capita nonwage income is not a particularly significant figure, unless distribution of capital is practically equal. It is interesting to note in passing, however, that the per capita nonwage income function is quite likely to exhibit a maximum in the population-capital field.

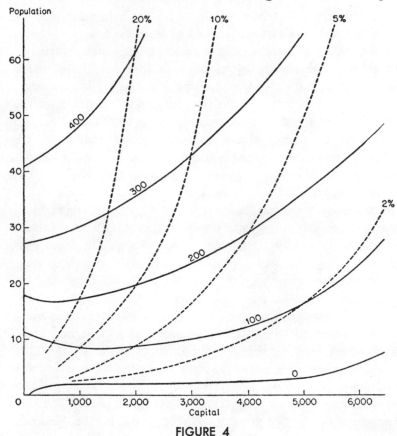

FIGURE 4

solid line, the "stationary state" is then found at *E*, where the subsistence wage contour and the subsistence rate contour intersect. This equilibrium is stable if the subsistence rate contour cuts the subsistence wage contour from below.

The model which I have outlined is substantially the same as that of classical economics. I have expounded it in some detail because I believe that it is much more relevant to present-day problems than is usually conceded. In modern economic thought the marginal productivity theory—or more generally, the refined marginal analysis—is supposed to have superseded the crude models of the classical school. In fact it has not done so. The marginal analysis has proved to be a very useful tool in dealing with problems of microeconomics. It is most instructive in dealing with the theory of the firm and with the demand, supply, and pricing of particular products and particular factors of production. It is not particularly helpful in dealing with the aggregates of the system, because its use is constantly likely to involve us in fallacies of composition. The functions which are deduced from the marginal analysis—e.g., demand functions for labor—are not aggregable, as they are derived on the assumption that other elements in the system remain stable. Consequently I can hardly help regarding the development of marginalism as a retrograde step as far as the theory of over-all distribution—i.e., of the macroeconomics of distribution—is concerned. The marginal analysis tells us a good deal about what determines the demand for plasterers in Podunk; it tells us very little about total wages. The famous "adding-up" problem relating to the homogeneity of the production function is quite unreal as applied to the whole economy, though it may have some significance in discussing the distribution of the revenues of a particular firm. Instead of superseding the classical analysis of distribution, marginalism has simply created a vacuum in this field. This vacuum has not been filled by the Keynesian analysis. In spite of one or two pregnant suggestions (e.g., the "widow's cruse" theory of profits in the *Treatise on Money* and the modified "wages fund" of the *General Theory*) Keynes never succeeded in developing a theory of distribution in macroeconomic terms, and this gap remains one of the prime weaknesses in his theoretical structure.

It is worth while, therefore, to re-examine the classical model to see how much of it actually remains valid in the light of present-day knowledge. We may examine first some misconceptions regarding the part played in the classical system by the wage fund doctrine. It must be confessed, of course, that the wage fund doctrine exhibits strong marks of that confusion between stocks and flows which is so characteristic of classical economics (and even more of Marxian economics!). In the form in which it is stated by Adam Smith and Ricardo it remains a somewhat inappropriate extension and generalization of a phenomenon which was clear enough in the agriculture of Adam Smith's Scotland, where wages were paid in oatmeal out of the barn, and the more oatmeal in the barn at the end of the harvest the higher wages would be in the forthcoming winter! [4] It is important to observe, however, that in the model outlined above no assumption is necessary that wages are paid "out of capital"; the only assumption necessary is that the total wage bill is an increasing *function* of total capital. This is a much less restricted assumption than is made in the usual exposition, and while it may not be particularly true, at least it is not ridiculous. The model could easily be extended, of course, by making the total wage bill a function both of population and capital, though we are in real danger here of postulating purely formal functions which have no basis in individual behavior. The really critical questions here are: (1) What are the *decisions* which actually determine the distributional pattern? (2) Can these decisions be expressed in terms of fairly simple aggregate parameters?

I cannot do much more here than sketch the outlines of the type of theory that will be necessary.[5] The basis of it may be

---

[4] In the course of the discussion Professor Knight raised the question as to why more oatmeal in the barn should mean higher wages. The answer is, of course, that the powers of consumption of oatmeal on the part of the capitalist are strictly limited, and once he has eaten his fill of porridge there is nothing he can do with his oatmeal but feed the "laboring poor and laboring cattle" with it. He will try to attract labor away from his competitors if he is particularly flush with oatmeal (perhaps to get gardeners!), and so will push up the oatmeal wage. The case is exactly analogous to the effects of increased money stocks of entrepreneurs on the money wage. Of course, if the laboring poor are so full of oatmeal that they cannot stand any more we will run into a "backward-sloping supply curve" for labor, but that is another story altogether.

[5] A more detailed exposition will be found in my book, *A Reconstruction of Economics* (Wiley, 1950), chapter 14.

called the balance-sheet view of the profit-making process. We suppose the accounts of the economy to be divided into two groups: households and businesses. Profits all accrue in business accounts, though they are of course distributed to household accounts as dividends, interest, and rent. Some practical difficulties of definition may arise here because of the confusion of household and business accounts in farming and other household-centered enterprises, but normally the distinction is clear enough in practice to make it valuable in theory. The accrual of profits is the same thing as the accrual of *net worths* in business accounts. If no profits were distributed the profit in a given period in any one account would be equal to the increase in net worth. If profits are distributed then the total gross profit accruing to the account is equal to the rise in the net worth plus the amount distributed in dividends, rent, and interest.

We thus see the profit-making process, in the case of an individual firm, as a process of manipulating assets by transformations through exchange and production in order to increase their total value in terms of the unit of account (usually money). This increase may be accomplished in two ways: (1) by increasing the physical quantities of assets in the account, or (2) by valuing existing physical quantities at higher "prices" or valuation coefficients. This means in effect that when one set of asset quantities is transformed into another set the value of the assets given up (cost) must be greater than the value of the assets which appear in the balance sheet as a result of the transformation. Profit, indeed, is the difference between the value of the assets produced by the transformation and the value of the assets given up—in more familiar terms, revenue minus cost. It is important to understand, however, that revenue and costs are not money flows: indeed, they need not be defined as flow at all, although a series of successive transformations can be so regarded. In the broadest sense cost consists of the assets which are consumed or destroyed or given up to another account;

revenue consists of assets created or received from another account.

For an individual business we can classify assets (positive and negative) into several groups. For purposes of a two-part model consisting only of households and business we need only seven classifications, including net worth, and can write the balance sheet as follows:

ASSETS		LIABILITIES	
Money	m_b	Debts to businesses	k'_{bb}
Value of goods (real capital)	q_b	Debts to households	k'_{bh}
Debts from businesses	k_{bb}	Net Worth	g_b
Debts from households	k_{hb}		

Treating contractual liabilities as negative assets, the balance sheet identity can be written in the form of a net worth identity thus:

$$g_b \equiv m_b + q_b + (k_{bb} - k'_{bb}) + (k_{hb} - k'_{bh}) \qquad (1)$$

This identity can be differentiated as follows:

$$dg_b \equiv dm_b + dq_b + d(k_{bb} - k'_{bb}) + d(k_{hb} - k'_{bh}) \qquad (2)$$

Here the prefix d before each symbol signifies the *change* (say increase) in the corresponding variable in a unit period of time. Each of the terms of this identity has economic significance: dg_b is the increase in net worth during the period, which may properly be called "business savings"; dm_b is the increase in the firm's money stock; $d(k_{bb} - k'_{bb})$ is the increase in the net debts owed to the firm by other firms; $d(k_{hb} - k'_{bh})$ is the increase in net debts owed to the firm by households. We are not considering here how these increases (or, if negative, decreases) arise from the particular transformations in which the firm engages; we are considering merely the end result.

Identity (2) can be summed (consolidated) for all businesses, and when this is done the term $d(k_{bb} - k'_{bb})$ reduces to zero, as the debts of all firms to all firms must be equal to the debts of all firms from all firms, being the same quantity. Every inter-firm debt, in other words, appears in two balance sheets, once as a liability and again as an asset. When all balance sheets of firms are consolidated, then, these terms cancel out. If we represent by capital letters the sums of the corresponding quantities for all firms, we have then

$$dG_b \equiv dM_b + dQ_b + dK_{hb} - dK'_{bh} \qquad (3)$$

This is a very important identity which may be called the *business-savings identity*. From it can be derived immediately an identity for gross profits (V), which must be equal to business savings plus business distribution (D):

$$V \equiv dG_b + D \equiv dQ_b + (dM_b + D + dK_{hb} - dK'_{bh}) \equiv$$
$$dQ_b + T \qquad (4)$$

The total product (Y) can be divided into two parts in two ways: into the distributional shares, gross profits (V) and wages (W); and into its absorptional composition, the increase in business real capital ("investment"), dQ_b, and household purchases ("consumption"), C_h, for if we suppose that the product originally is produced in business accounts, then that part which is not taken off the hands of businesses by households must still remain in the possession of businesses. We have therefore:

$$Y \equiv V + W \equiv dQ_b + C_h \qquad (5)$$

Comparing equations (4) and (5) we obtain an identity for wages:

$$W \equiv C_h - (dM_b + D_b + dK_{hb} - dK_{bh}) \equiv C_h - T \qquad (6)$$

This identity can also be derived directly from the summation of household balance sheets. The item T

$$T \equiv dM_b + D + dK_{hb} - dK'_{bh} \qquad (7)$$

I call the "transfer factor": added to business accumulation it gives us total profits; subtracted from household purchases it gives us the total wage bill.

The significance of these identities is that each item in them, apart from W and V, represents in some degree a parameter of behavior, and is affected fairly directly by the decisions of broad classes of individuals. The item dM_b is essentially a balance-of-payments item as between businesses and households. In the simple identities above I assume no creation or destruction of money; however, they can be modified to include such changes. If, however, the money stock is constant, the positive (or negative) balance of payments of businesses must equal the negative (or positive) balance of payments of households; the money stock may be regarded as a shifting cargo, sometimes shifting out of household into business balances, sometimes out of business into household balances. Such a shift—other things being equal—clearly affects the distributional pattern. A shift into business balances shifts distribution into profits and away from wages, as the additional money in business balances increases the total net worths of businesses. A shift away from business into household balances diminishes profits and increases wages—assuming, of course, that national income remains constant. We may regard this internal balance of payments as determined primarily by the relative changes in liquidity preference (or velocities of circulation) of businesses and households. If both businesses and households change their velocities (Expenditure ÷ money stock) in the same degree (either absolutely or relatively), the total of payments will change but neither will succeed in forcing money stocks onto the other: if both businesses and households start spending more freely, in the same degree, both will find that their receipts expand in an equal degree; for the receipts of businesses are the expenditures of households and the receipts of households are the expenditures of business, interbusiness and interhousehold payments being neglected as they cancel out in the total. If, however, businesses increase their expenditures toward households more than households increase their expenditures toward businesses, then the money stock will shift out of business into household balances.

There may be, of course, important other results of a disequilibrium in the internal balance of payments. If the reactions to positive and negative balances are not symmetrical, as may well be the case, the appearance of positive and negative balances of payments in general—i.e., a shift in the ownership of the money stock—may produce marked effects on the *total* of payments. If we suppose, for instance, that a positive balance of payments (i.e., an increase in money stock) on the part of an individual produces a slower reaction than a negative balance of payments (a negative balance produces a rather immediate curtailment of expenditures, while a positive balance is allowed to accumulate for a while without producing a corresponding increase in expenditures), then a disturbance in the *balance* of payments is likely to produce a net decline in the total *volume* of payments, and this in turn may react upon prices, income, and output, depending on the varying flexibilities of prices and outputs.

In general it may be said that the longer the period we take, the smaller will be the balance of payments item dM_b in relation to the other items: i.e., in the long run the balance of payments of one sector of the economy cannot persist for very long, since otherwise all the money of the system would be concentrated into one part of it. We should normally expect positive and negative balances to succeed each other for any given part of the system as the money cargo surges first into one part and then into another part. Unfortunately we have very little data on these internal balances of payments, especially in regard to their movement through time. Over periods of a year or perhaps two years they may be quite a significant factor in the distributional proportions, though the fact that profits are so generally reckoned annually means that fluctuations of smaller period are not likely to be reflected in the accounts. With a total money stock of the order of magnitude of 100 billion units, however, a "surge" into or out of business balances of the size of, say, five billion in the course of a year is by no means out of the question, and some of the short-period fluctuations in the distributional pattern may well be due to this factor.

The "business distributions" factor D is fairly directly connected with business decisions as to "business savings." We run into a paradox here: If the other elements in the identity can be assumed constant, decisions of businesses to save (i.e., to add to their net worths) do not determine the total of business savings but the total of profits. In other words we have a "widow's cruse" effect: the more businesses distribute out of their profits, the more profits they will have to distribute! This proposition, of course, does not hold for individual businesses— it is the distributions of one business that help to create profits for all. Even for all businesses, of course, the "other things" may not be constant. Increased distributions may simply remain in the pockets of the households to which the distributions are made: in that case the increase in D will be offset by a decline in dM_b and there will be no shift in the distributional structure. Even in short periods, however, it is most unlikely that increased distributions would be completely offset in this way. There is also a possibility that increased distributions may be offset by a decline in consumer credit, which would render dK_{hb} negative, or by an increase in household holdings of business securities, which would create a positive dK'_{bh}. These changes, however, are not likely to be directly related to dividend policy. There may also be a relationship between business decisions to distribute profits and business decisions to accumulate (invest) which may be offsetting. With all these offsets, however, the longer the period of time that we take the smaller they are likely to be, relative to the total volume of business distributions. Subject to the above-mentioned qualifications, therefore, we can say that an increased "propensity to distribute" profits on the part of businesses is likely to lead to a shift in the distributional structure toward profits and away from wages.

The other items in the transfer factor, dK_{hb} and dK'_{bh}, may be dismissed briefly. The first represents mainly changes in consumer credit, and is clearly capable of spontaneous and decision-determined changes: an increased "propensity" to extend or to accept consumer credit is likely to have a direct effect in increasing profits at the expense of wages. Here also certain offsets are possible. An extension of consumer credit may cause a shift in the money stock away from households toward businesses, if households regard a "line of credit" as a substitute for holding money. This is a "negative offset," actually intensifying the shift toward profits. More consumer credit may also mean a depletion of the inventories of businesses, and hence a decline in dQ_b; changes in relative liquidity preference may do likewise. If, however, there is any elasticity in output, a decline in business inventories is likely to be made up from production, so that this offset is also smaller as the period taken is longer.

The second debt item, dK'_{bh}, represents mainly the increase in business securities held by households. This acts to shift the distributional structure *away* from profits toward wages—a somewhat paradoxical result, as it is usually in the hope of profits that securities are issued! Here again there may be the usual offsets: money may flow into business balances, thus raising profits; the sale of securities may permit businesses to expand their consumer credit; and so on. In this case, however, there is one offset which will not generally diminish in importance with longer periods; an expansion in business indebtedness to the public is very likely to be associated with an expansion in the real assets of business (i.e., an increase in dK'_{bh} is likely to be associated with an increase in dQ_b). If, indeed, business investment is financed entirely by the sale of securities to households these two items will be equal and will cancel, and the distribution pattern will be determined by the other items in our identities, or rather by the behavior patterns to which they correspond. Insofar, however, as business investment is financed out of profits (i.e., without the corresponding issuance of securities to households), this investment will itself create the profits out of which it is financed—another delightful "widow's cruse."

It is impossible to proceed much further in this argument without considering the impact of these various variables on total output and employment; and to discuss this in detail would carry us far beyond the scope of this paper. Two kinds of models can be constructed based on the above identities: (1) By postulating various functional relationships among the aggregates of the identities equilibrium models can be derived, on the lines of the Keynesian or the Walrasian systems, with equal numbers of equations and unknowns. The equilibrium models can then be used to discuss the effect of changes in the underlying determinants of the system by the method of comparative statics. (2) The other type of model is "period" analysis along the lines of the Swedish school, in which the identities are used to show how the decisions of one period determine the *data* of the next. I have developed some equilibrium-type models in my *Reconstruction of Economics* (Wiley, 1950). An interesting model is the one which expresses household absorption (C_h) as a function of total income (Y) and wages (W) (cf. the Keynesian consumption function), and in which business accumulations (dQ_b, or I) are written as a function of income and profits. As income is equal to wages plus profits, C_h and I can also be written as functions of wages and profits. We have, then, five equations to give us the five unknowns, C_h, I, W, V, and Y:

$$Y \equiv V + W \equiv C_h + I$$
$$T \equiv V - I \,(\equiv C - W)$$
$$C_h = F_c(V, W)$$
$$I = F_i(V, W)$$

In the above system T is supposed to be given by the complex of decisions determining its components. We can easily extend the system, however, to suppose that T also is a function of V and W, in which case we add another equation, $T = F_t(V, W)$, and another unknown, T, to the system.

This model is shown graphically in Figures 5, 6, and 7. In all three figures we measure V (gross profits) along the horizontal axis, and total wages (W) along the vertical axis. In Figure 5, the solid lines are lines of equal household absorption, or C_h-isomers: they are the contours of the "consumption function": $C_h = F_c(W, V)$. This consumption function is assumed to have two significant properties. A movement toward wages with constant income (i.e., an increase in the proportion of income going to wages), as represented, for instance, by a movement along the line Y_vY_w $(Y = 50)$ from Y_v to Y_w, *raises* C_h, indicated by a movement to higher C_h-isomers. It is also assumed that at least after a certain point C_h does not increase proportionally with income, W/V being constant: thus, as we move out along a line OP, successive C_h-isomers become farther and farther apart. The C_h-isomers are likely to have some curvature also. The dotted lines marked CW_0, CW_{10}, etc., are $(C_h - W)$-isomers. Thus, the CW_0-isomer is constructed by joining the points where C_{30} cuts $W = 30$, C_{40} cuts $W = 40$, C_{50} cuts $W = 50$, and so on. Similarly in Figure 6 we have I-isomers marked I_0, I_{10}, I_{20}, etc.: contours of the function $I = F_i(W, V)$. These have somewhat similar properties to the C_h-isomers, except that they are assumed in the figure to be much more curved, so that as we move along a line of constant income (Y_wY_v) from Y_v (100 per cent profits) we find that investment rises to a maximum but then falls. This is a plausible but of course not essential assumption. We also assume that investment does not increase in proportion to the increase in income. The dotted lines VI_0, VI_{10}, etc., are $(V - I)$-isomers, constructed in similar manner to the CW-isomers of Figure 5.

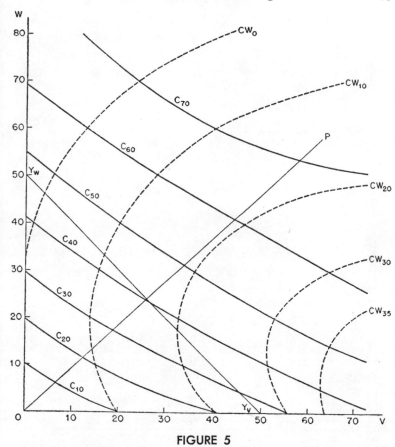

FIGURE 5

Thus VI_0 is drawn through points where I_0 cuts V_0, I_{10} cuts V_{10}, I_{20} cuts V_{20}, and so on.

In Figure 7 the dotted lines VI_0, VI_{10}, etc., and CW_0, CW_{10}, etc., are put together. The solid line *KLMN* is drawn through the points of intersection of VI_0 with CW_0, VI_{10} with CW_{10} . . . VI_n with CW_n. This is the line corresponding to the identity $V - I \equiv C - W$, or $V + W \equiv C + I$.

If now the transfer factor is assumed given—say, $T = 20$—the point of equilibrium of the system is given at Q where the

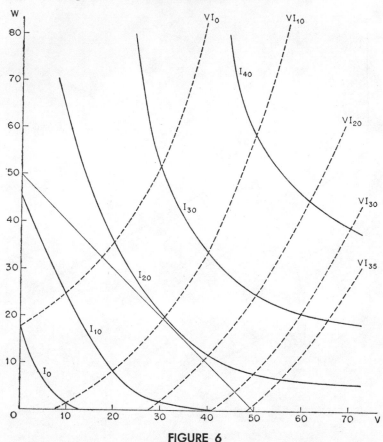

FIGURE 6

VI_{20}-isomer (or the CW_{20}-isomer) intersects with the line *KLMN*. It will be observed that there are apparent double solutions: that for instance VI_{20} and CW_{20} intersect twice, once at *Q* and again at *R*. Equilibrium, however, at points below *M* such as *N*, *R*, etc., is unstable, and the only stable equilibriums are above *M*.

Some interesting conclusions follow from this model. The maximum total income which can be obtained on the line *KLMN* is at the point *L*, where the line is touched by a 45°

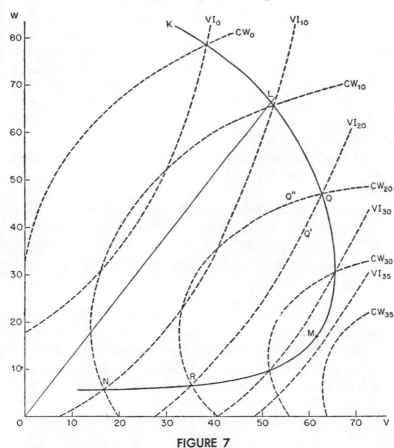

FIGURE 7

Y-isomer. We see also that a rise in T, moving the equilibrium point downward along the path KLQ, raises the proportion of profits and lowers the proportion of wages—proportionate distribution at a point, e.g., L, being given by the slope of the line OL. If T is below the value T_m which yields a maximum Y, then a rise in the profit proportion at the expense of wages through a rise in T will raise income: here "incentives" are more important than "markets." If T is above the value T_m than a rise in the wage and a decline in the profit proportion will raise income: here "markets" are more important than "incentives." It is not necessary, of course, for Y to exhibit a maximum such as L within the possible range of values of the various variables, but it is interesting to note that such a case is by no means impossible. The national income (Y_m) at L is not, of course, necessarily "ideal" income (i.e., the point L does not necessarily represent full employment); ideal income may be greater than Y_m, in which case no amount of distributional manipulation will achieve it. These models, like all Keynesian-type models, tend to break down as the capacity of the system is reached, as no specific provision is made in them for the mechanism of inflation; if the equilibrium output as given by these models is "above capacity" then there will be inflationary pressure of some sort which will shift the functions themselves to adjust to the capacity income.

A fall in the consumption function (i.e., a decrease in the C_h at each level of W and V) will push the C_h-isomers outward, which will bend the CW-isomers outward and to the right also. This will move the $KLMN$ curve of Figure 7 inward and to the left, lowering the national income. The point of equilibrium (with, say, $T = 20$) moves from Q to, say, Q'. In Figure 7 this represents a shift toward a higher proportion of profits, as OQ' has a smaller slope than OQ: such a result is plausible, but not absolutely necessary. Similarly, a fall in the investment function may move the equilibrium from, say, Q along the CW_{20}-curve to Q'', also with a fall in income and a rise in the proportion going to wages.

To return now to the focus of interest of classical distribution theory: What is the implication of these macroeconomic distributional models for the "progress of society"? If we examine the constituents of T (equation 7) we see that only the business distributions item D has any future in the stationary state. As we move toward the stationary state, investment $(dQ_b$ or $I)$ must decline to zero—unless of course there is perpetual inflation—the credit items likewise will decline toward zero, as debt cannot expand forever; the balance of payments component of the increase in business money holdings obviously approaches zero in the long run, or at best fluctuates between positive and negative values. A perpetual increase in the money stock will, of course, be reflected in a positive dM_b, but this is a poor way out of the difficulty. It is evident, therefore, that in the stationary state business savings, along with all other savings, must disappear: there can be no building up of net worths if assets cannot increase. Profits then are reduced to business distributions; but this fact alone shows that *profits* do not disappear in the stationary state, and that therefore there is no *necessary* contradiction in capitalism. Profits are the price that we pay for a polylithic, nontotalitarian economy. If it were inevitable that this price would become insufficient, we should have to capitulate to Marx eventually as we approached the stationary state. The analysis of this paper shows, however, that such is not the case, and that the stationary state is not necessarily inconsistent with the institutions of capitalism.

A striking feature of the macroeconomic theory of distribution outlined above is that it shows quite clearly that the principal determinants of the distributional shares are human decisions rather than physical relationships. The success of the marginal productivity theory has given rise to a certain feeling that distributional shares are determined by the physical production function. Such a view is not of course implied in the marginal productivity theory when correctly stated, but the absence of any macroeconomic theory of distribution places a certain premium on the improper extension of the marginal theory to some over-all physical production function involving "Labor" and "Capital." The theory outlined above makes quite clear what the classical economists knew very well—that though production might be the result of the immutable laws of physics and chemistry, distribution was the result of human decision, and that consequently distribution could be changed within a wide range of values. The macroeconomic theory, however, also makes clear another point with which the classical economists were familiar—that distribution was not directly determined by what happened in the market for factors of production, e.g., in the labor market, but that it was determined directly by quite a different set of decisions. That is not to say, of course, that wage bargains cannot affect distribution very sharply. In regard to the over-all distribution between capital and labor, however, the wage bargain and the labor market only affect distribution indirectly, as they affect the direct determinants of investment, financial, loan, and monetary behavior. A rise in money wages will only raise real wages, and will only shift proportionate distribution toward labor, if it produces appropriate secondary effects on household absorption, business accumulation, dividend and financial policy, etc.

What we have done, therefore, is to effect a partial rehabilitation of the wage fund doctrine by defining more carefully the types of decisions regarding investment and finance which determine the total wage bill. The wage fund is perhaps more flexible than Ricardo thought (though certainly no more flexible than Mill thought). Nevertheless the general *conclusions* which follow from the wage fund doctrine, with the exception of the conclusion that the total wage bill is independent of income, are of the right order of magnitude—that distribution depends on decisions, and mainly on the decisions of capitalists about the use of their capital and their methods of finance; and that distribution, hence, is largely independent of what happens in the labor market. The history of trade unionism, and the evident impotence of trade unions in increasing the share of labor in the national income, are telling tributes to the accuracy of this insight.

CHAPTER VII

Selections from the Discussion
of Boulding's Paper

KNIGHT. Referring to Dr. Boulding's oatmeal example, why were wages high? Why did the farmer pay more wages because the farmer happened to have more oatmeal in the barn?

BOULDING. Because his demand for labor was higher, and because of the competition among farmers, you see, for laborers—I don't know the answer to that question really. I don't think there is a very good answer to it.[1]

CLARK. It was one of the questions raised in the controversy that finally put the wages fund under the table. . . .

WRIGHT. Would you state once more the assumptions necessary to meet your widow's cruse theory?

BOULDING. Yes. The assumption is that there are certain parameters of behavior, that is, quantities in the system which are related in some way to aggregates of individual behavior. Suppose we have an increase in business distributions. This can take place without any change in investment policies, without

[1] *Comment by Wright:* Professor Boulding's reply to Professor Knight in footnote 4 of his paper seems to me to run too much in terms of one commodity. "The powers of consumption of *oatmeal* on the part of the capitalist" may be "strictly limited" though even this is debatable. But not their "powers of consumption."

Comment by Boulding: The "classical" wage fund theory arose precisely because of an extension of an argument which was valid in the one-commodity case to the many-commodity case, where it was more dubious.

any change in consumer credit policies or financial policies, you see.

WRIGHT. I don't get it. Shall we argue about this now?

SAMUELSON. Suppose that down at the office I decide that instead of holding a thousand dollars in cash my wife will hold a thousand dollars at home. I declare a dividend. I would call it a capital transaction, not a current transaction. It would appear in the Department of Commerce as a dividend. I see no "cruse."

BOULDING. That's because your wife hangs on to it. That increase in distributions is offset by the diminution in the balance of payments item. But I'm assuming that these offsets are going to be small, which I think they are as in—

SAMUELSON. Wait a minute. Does this assume an increased marginal propensity to spend?

BOULDING. We are not assuming anything about the consumption field.

SAMUELSON. She spends none of it.

BOULDING. That has nothing to do with consumption. I can't make any sense of the marginal propensity to spend. She doesn't hold on to it.

SAMUELSON. She doesn't hold on to it?

BOULDING. No. She spends it.

SAMUELSON. Why?

BOULDING. Are you going to suppose that every time business pays out money to anybody this only results in a shift in the money stock?

SAMUELSON. No, but I'm simply supposing that some unknown part of what's called dividends is a capital transaction in which people move their security holdings from one domicile to a different domicile.

BOULDING. All transactions are capital transactions, aren't they? All transactions are an exchange of assets. All transactions are capital transactions. There is no such thing as an income transaction.

WRIGHT. The decision to disburse more of profits, and by inference I gather a decision to spend more on the part of the community, if investment plans are left unchanged, must imply a rise in total national income, doesn't it?

BOULDING. No.

WRIGHT. How can you leave investment unchanged and have everybody spending more unless they are eating out of inventory?

SAMUELSON. But then investment isn't constant.

BOULDING. Well, I think this effect may depend on the existence of a certain amount of slack in the economy. Of course, one of the things that worries me about some of these Keynesian models, as somebody mentioned this morning—and he was right—is that we have never succeeded in putting the price system explicitly into these models. Until we do that they have to be treated with kid gloves. They have been very dangerous.

But suppose that we have situations of less than full employment. Well, then, the distribution of dividends on the part of an *individual firm*, of course, simply diminishes its cash on the assets side and diminishes its net worth on the other side, doesn't it?

Nevertheless from the point of view of firms as a whole you see that the cash will not stay out in households. It will, of course, come back to firms. Now, how does it come back? If it comes by the purchase of inventories, then I would say that if firms have a constant inventory policy they will replace these inventories.

SAMUELSON. But why "of course"? I would think there would be dm_b, in your paper, matched often in depression times by a dm_h. An outgoing from firms might well be an addition to the cash balance of households.

BOULDING. Oh yes, I am saying that you can have offsets here all along, you see. And in some cases the offset may be complete or even adverse. That's absolutely true.

CLARK. Did you call a bank a household? I have forgotten.

BOULDING. I wasn't quite sure whether I put banks in this system. They're rather troublesome.

SAMUELSON. A bank's a business.

BOULDING. It can be a business. I think you have to put banks almost in a category of their own to get a really satisfactory system out of this, and I haven't done that yet.

But the general assumption here—especially, as I say, the longer the period of time that you take, you see, the more significant this factor is in relation to this factor [indicating on blackboard]—as the first approximation, the assumption of the distribution of the money stock as constant is not ridiculous. The longer the period of time you take the more likely it is to be true.

FRIEDMAN. For this purpose money stock is not what we regard as money ordinarily. It's really net obligations of the Federal Government. So your banks are in there as businesses, and that part of bank deposits which correspond to loans outstanding is not money in your context? Is that right?

BOULDING. If we regard banks as part of government, it is.

SAMUELSON. There is no fiduciary element in a government-owned bank which has assets to match the liabilities.

BOULDING. That's true, but you get the fiduciary elements in the issue of reserves.

FRIEDMAN. It's only net obligations of the banking system and the government combined.

BOULDING. That's about it.

WRIGHT. The widow's cruse must depend, not only on the existence of unemployment or slack in the production system, but also on change in MV, because if you merely transfer existing balances without a change in velocity, then you can't maintain investment constant. The stimulus will come from an increased consumption. And if MV is fixed and you have more money being spent on consumption, less money has got to be spent on investment.

BOULDING. Yes. Well, of course, it's absolutely true an autonomous increase in dividend distribution without any changes anywhere else in the system constitutes an increase in velocity. That is perfectly true.

WRIGHT. But that has got to assume that prior to this occurrence the businesses have been sitting on some idle money all this time.

BOULDING. All money is always idle, isn't it? I don't see any way of distinguishing between idle money and not-idle money.

WRIGHT. It sounds rather like D. H. Robertson's essay on Foster and Catchings where he has the profit streams speeded up to pay twice quickly. But I don't see why an increased disbursement of dividends by corporations necessarily would raise velocity.

FRIEDMAN. In the long run also if you have this kind of change it is going to manifest itself mostly in prices. The argument that it will manifest itself in the portion going to wages versus the portion going to nonwages is far less obvious. If people decide to spend money more rapidly, the stock of money will support a higher price level.

BOULDING. If there is a rise in prices, you will have a rise in this thing [indicating dQ_b on the blackboard] which has as part of its components the rise in the price of existing assets. Of course that's why an inflation creates profits.

FRIEDMAN. That's in the transition.

BOULDING. If we look at the great depression and we ask why did profits disappear in 1932 and 1933, the main answer is that investment disappeared.[2] It was a shift in the composition of the national income which was responsible for the shift in its distribution. And the simplest assumption is to say that this thing altogether (T) is zero; that all these things always offset one another, you see; and that in that case the distribution of the na-

---

[2] *Comment by Wright:* This statement is true as description. But *why* did investment disappear? See, in this regard, the comments of Professor Samuelson (pp. 160-61).

tional income and its composition are identical and irvestment always creates profits equal to the amount of investment. This may be also a thing you don't like. I don't know.

WRIGHT. Before we get off on this, it seems to me this demonstration, stated in the form you have used—I think it can be phrased to be correct under special circumstances—but, as you phrased it, this demonstration seems to me to show some of the most questionable characteristics of simplified Keynesian analysis. You have taken a statement which requires a condition of less than full employment, not explained, and which applies to changes in velocity, not explained, or else an increase in the money supply, not explained, and a condition of constant prices, not explained, and then you jump from that to the statement that generally the more profits are paid out the more profits will be made, which doesn't follow at all.

SAMUELSON. May I illustrate with an example? Take a perfect capital market where money left in the company is regarded by the consumer as the same thing as money in pocket. Now, there, to pay out more dividends is simply to create more flotations in which they get it back in that way.

BOULDING. Offsets here, yes. Then you get offsets in other parts of the financial system. That's all right. But, of course, it isn't and you don't.

SAMUELSON. I don't want to prejudge it, but it seems neither fish nor fowl. It is neither grounded in the physical facts of life nor in at all plausible money expenditure propensities.

WRIGHT. I looked up the quotation and Keynes doesn't say that the increased disbursement of profits makes for *more* profits.[3] He only says that if entrepreneurs spend more of their profits they will still get them, and the only profits which increase, in his example, are profits in the consumption goods in-

---

[3] Cf. J. M. Keynes, *A Treatise on Money* (Macmillan, 1930), p. 139: "Thus however much of their profits entrepreneurs spend on consumption, the increment of wealth belonging to entrepreneurs remains *the same* [italics added] as before."

dustries, which could just as well be offset by losses in the investment goods industries. Of course, however, you're holding investment constant, which implies a rise in income.

BOULDING. I don't think Keynes ever followed this out, you see. The "widow's cruse" was one of his brilliant asides actually, and he never really thought it out. And it does seem to me this identity provides a set of aggregates the relationships among which are interesting to discuss. . . .

[*Editor's note:* The discussion from this point on cannot be given consecutive abridgment. Professor Samuelson questioned Professor Boulding's asset and accounting theory of profits as follows:]

SAMUELSON. In the situation I am thinking of, which is highly competitive, profits are a very definite thing subject to commercial law; that has almost nothing to do with the names given by accountants to the process.

BOULDING. If you don't think profits are produced by the accounting system, what are they produced by?

SAMUELSON. By competitive imputation.

KNIGHT. I say when I live in a house that what I am consuming is services, and it's consumed continuously. If I pay the rent on the house once a month or once a year it doesn't affect the fact.

BOULDING. Consumption has nothing to do with that. It's when the wind blows the shingles off.

SAMUELSON. Let's adopt your view of assets which is just integrated flows. The question is whether this profit is simply a superficial bookkeeping thing which happens to depend upon the particular corporate structure and rules of thumb, or whether this represents more basically two kinds of decisions: basic physical, technological decisions; and, in a world where aggregate demand is important, sticky wages, or perhaps inflexible prices, and basic spending propensities.

I don't think that, taking those into account, profits are arbitrary at all.

FRIEDMAN. I think what Professor Samuelson is saying in an altogether different way can be expressed in terms of a conflict between your system of equations and the Walrasian system of general equilibrium equations. We have a society. It has some resources. It has some tastes. The Walrasian system of general equilibrium will generate prices. There will be a set of prices that are consistent with the given resources, tastes, etc. Correct?

BOULDING. That's right.

FRIEDMAN. That set of prices—

BOULDING. A set of relative prices.

FRIEDMAN. —precisely—will generate a relative distribution of income. The system generates it. It's a relative phenomenon, not absolute.

All right. Now, this is one theory of relative distribution that you and I both agree with. Yet, you seem to have said here that we will throw it out and start all over again, and get something else that also determines the relative phenomenon. If you were arguing that your system of equations determined the height of the *numeraire* it would be something else, but you're saying that it determines relative distribution in terms of the *numeraire*. How can that be?

SAMUELSON. Is it even a good theory to explain deviations from the Walrasian system in, let's say, even a world of frictions and price inflexibilities? It seems to me that what people write down in ledgers isn't the essence of the problem—such things as the particular rules of thumb they use, or what part of business enterprise is incorporated, and the extent to which a farmer separates his kitchen from his barn—

BOULDING. I mean that isn't important in this system at all. The thing I am discussing here is the profit-making process. That is the process by which the possession of assets enables you to increase them.

WRIGHT. I think you are confusing profit-making with accumulation.

BOULDING. No, I'm not at all. Income is gross addition to assets. It always is. It's always what it is.

SAMUELSON. No, it isn't always.

BOULDING. The gross. You start off with this kind of picture. You have the total of assets here. Production, which is income—do you agree to that?

SAMUELSON. Yes.

BOULDING. —is the process of adding to them. The consumption is the process of subtracting.

SAMUELSON. No. it's the process of an opera singer singing and I'm listening.

BOULDING. The opera singer is singing. She is creating a capital good which is—

SAMUELSON. That is—

BOULDING. —that capital good depreciates.

FRIEDMAN. Suppose we grant you all that. What do we do with our systems of equilibrium equations? I don't understand. If we are even going to start taking your theory seriously, you have to convince us of some reason for throwing overboard the existing theory.

BOULDING. Profits are not a reward of a factor of production. That's the answer.

KNIGHT. Under a proper definition I would agree with that.

SAMUELSON. Under stable conditions where there are no entrepreneur profits in Boulding's sense, it seems to me the nonlabor income is a reward to factors of production.

BOULDING. It isn't. That is, you cannot derive it from any production function because it's something which is thrown up in the process of valuation.

KNIGHT. Why can't you have a production function in a barber shop or a symphony orchestra just as well as anywhere else?

BOULDING. You can.

FRIEDMAN. Your system ought to apply to a completely stationary state.

BOULDING. That's right.

FRIEDMAN. In a Walrasian stationary state, in stationary equilibrium, we don't have any of the risk-taking functions. We don't have any profits in any sense. We have wage and nonwage income in your sense.

BOULDING. I don't think you have anything but wage income in a stationary Walrasian state.

SAMUELSON. Why?

CHAMBERLIN. What about land income?

BOULDING. I don't think there is any land in the sense of an original factor of production. . . .

[*Editor's note:* The discussion passed on to the problem of the stationary state as follows:]

BOULDING. As I have been trying to make some remarks about business savings here, suppose we take this question of what happens in the progress of society. It seems to me quite clear that business savings along with all other savings have to disappear. Isn't that right? That in the stationary state business savings are zero? Does anybody disagree with that? [4]

SAMUELSON. Nobody is approaching a stationary state in the societies we know.

BOULDING. That's what I was interested in. That seems to me one of the objectives—to tell people what happens in the progress of society. This is a neoclassical model, you see. And in the stationary state savings disappear, business savings.

All right. How do you get any profits in a stationary state? And do profits disappear? . . .

(Simultaneous discussion.)

BOULDING. Profits are equal to business distribution. They have to be. Now, is there any reason why business distribution should not be arbitrary?

SAMUELSON. Yes.

FRIEDMAN. Yes, there certainly is.

---

[4] *Comment by Wright:* This is of course true as logic. But as a practical matter unless we first know *why* we are in a stationary state, or *why* society is tending toward one, it does not have much practical significance.

SAMUELSON. You can't keep zero net savings of business unless they distribute full earnings, and earnings are determined by competitive—

FRIEDMAN. Business concerns won't get the use of the resources they have unless they bribe people in order to let them use them, and in order to do that they have to pay them the equivalent of their marginal product.

BOULDING. There are limits there.

FRIEDMAN. Exactly. By the same token, in your system wages are arbitrary. Wages are arbitrary down to the subsistence level.

SAMUELSON. I would deny that. That isn't so in a competitive full-employment world.

BOULDING. I was not saying you can't deduce out of this what you might call Marxian models, in which there would be no equilibrium short of the subsistence level. I say we have societies that may be like that.

WRIGHT. I can see that if a business makes profits and disburses all of them there would be no net saving and therefore your equilibrium would be one without growth. But I still don't understand why the business is making profits in the stationary state, because I agree with Professor Samuelson if you have pure competition they will all be bidding against each other. They will compete away those profits.

SAMUELSON. They are paying rents though.

FRIEDMAN. Yes, they will be paying rent. Let's try to talk in terms of nonwage incomes instead of profits.

WRIGHT. There would be rents but no profits.

FRIEDMAN. It seems to me you're doing yourself an injustice by taking the position you did just now because you're putting yourself squarely up against the Walrasian dilemma. It seems to me if you want to try to keep away from that you ought to argue that this model may be useful in explaining short-run shifts, or what happens in the process of going from one equilibrium position to another. But the point, it seems to me, at which your model can have the least possible relevance is in the stationary state.

BOULDING. I don't really agree. I am absolutely willing to confess that there is a dilemma here that I haven't resolved, and I don't think anybody else has either. This is one of the real gaps.

[*Editor's note:* Professor Samuelson next queried the usefulness of Professor Boulding's profit theory as follows:]

SAMUELSON. There has been for about the last fifteen years a kind of aggregative theory of how corporate finance affects the total of aggregate demand. And let's waive this deeper Walrasian question, whether if we had wage-price flexibility it would be unnecessary to analyze such things, but let's assume what you might call pre-1937 Keynesian assumptions, *freezing* of all wages, *freezing*, relatively speaking, of the wage structure. It certainly is easy to imagine unemployment in such a system.

Let's further assume that consumption depends upon disposable income and that people don't think of money held for them by the corporation as the same thing as money in the pocket. It's very difficult to learn about this. But assume that the capitalization in the stock market is imperfect and that to a first approximation it's disposable income of people that's important. Let's assume the rich and poor—that is, those who receive dividends and wages respectively—have about the same propensity to consume, marginally speaking.

Let's assume investment—this is a very simple Keynesian assumption—is an exogenous thing because the interest rate is as low as it is going to get for whatever reason—

FRIEDMAN. Or lower.

SAMUELSON. Or lower. Now, this conventional theory I think posits that there is assumed to be for each corporate level of corporate earnings a propensity to disburse dividends. At high earnings, dividends are disbursed higher.

Now, actually, there are certain shifts in this schedule. We know when a company has reduced its debt it changes its dividend habit, but let's work in oversimple terms in that way and let's assume, which I think is a very dangerous assumption, that this dividend propensity is not something closely geared to the investment opportunity. Now, for firms which have liquidity problems that's just nonsense, of course.

BOULDING. Quite.

SAMUELSON. But, nevertheless, it's a deep depression model. Now, in such a system I know exactly how a change in autonomous investment will affect total employment, total production, total consumption. I even know, if you assume certain fixed committments on the part of business, or if break-even curves are specified, how the division of income into labor income and residual income will behave. And it explains all the facts which you mentioned occurred in the depression—why profits were negative. I think because it caught business with old commitments and their volume went down.

What I would like to know is how it squares with this five-equation system here which seems to me doesn't have the simple merits of that very simple conventional fifteen-year-old theory that we have all been using all these years. . . .

[*Editor's note:* After considerable further discussion, Professor Chamberlin shifted the discussion to the question of marginal productivity.]

CHAMBERLIN. I would like to say a word or two about marginal productivity theory. I am mystified by the position taken earlier which identifies it with microeconomics. I think that idea is true if we talk of marginal *revenue* product in the sense that marginal revenue product is a concept belonging to the *firm* and you can't add the marginal revenue products of firms without getting into fallacies of composition. Thus the marginal productivity theory when interpreted as marginal revenue product theory has difficulty going beyond the firm. All that is in agreement with what you have said earlier.

What I wanted to say is something else. I think we might

discuss marginal revenue productivity later. But marginal productivity has been during most of its history a theory of what happens under purely competitive conditions identifying incomes, not with marginal revenue product, but with the value of the marginal product. Thus Hicks in his *Theory of Wages* [5] clearly defines the theory in terms of the *value of the marginal product* and asserts that this is the theory generally held, which I think is a true statement for the middle of the thirties. Certainly this was the general theory of marginal productivity.

Let's simplify by taking a static state and conditions of pure competition.

FRIEDMAN. It isn't in Marshall. Marshall explicitly distinguishes.

CHAMBERLIN. He does just the reverse. Marshall clearly defines marginal revenue product, distinguishes it and says that for the usual case we may dismiss it. [6] Marshall's theory is essentially a purely competitive theory.

SAMUELSON. The Walrasian theory is, in its usual exposition, a theory of pure and perfect competition.

CHAMBERLIN. What I want to say is: under purely competitive assumptions, what's the matter with the marginal productivity theory as an explanation of aggregates as well as of rates of pay?

It's a perfectly respectable theory which held sway for a good many years as a theory under purely competitive conditions. I for one see no objection to the theory under those conditions.

(Simultaneous discussion.)

FRIEDMAN. It's all right as a theory under noncompetitive conditions too. That's what we are all saying.

CHAMBERLIN. As a theory of marginal revenue product it is, which is quite a different thing.

[5] (Macmillan, 1932, pp. 8, 9.)
[6] *Principles*, Mathematical Appendix, note XIV, pp. 849-50.

FRIEDMAN. For the purpose of this argument—

BOULDING. All right, except it doesn't tell us anything.

SAMUELSON. But there isn't anything to tell.

BOULDING. There is something to tell. The marginal productivity theory does not really give you any illumination as to what are the decision-making factors which affect the distribution.

CHAMBERLIN. It gives you a theory of what each of the various factors—which may be either four or maybe twenty-five if we want to make them more finely divided—it gives you a theory of what each one gets in a total social complex of factors in which they are allocated in purely competitive markets.

HABERLER. On page 133—at the top you say that there is a real danger here of postulating purely formal functions which have no basis in individual behavior. I think that for that reason you need something like the marginal productivity theory qualified with marginal revenue.

SAMUELSON. Take this general equilibrium theory. Let's take it under pure competition for a moment. Prices are what they will be as determined by the structure of all the Walrasian markets. How do they change over time? They change over time the way they will change as determined by the structure of the markets. Now, you don't get out of that a grand Kalecki's theory—exactly .666 goes to certain kinds of labor. All I am saying is that there isn't any quantitative theory other than a competitive market that will impute what a competitive market will impute.

CHAMBERLIN. But according to the principles of diminishing marginal productivity for the total social aggregate of factors—

SAMUELSON. There need be nothing social about it.

CHAMBERLIN. As new units of factors are added, of course, they are added to firms. But they have a net result upon the total amount going to these factors according to the principles of diminishing marginal productivity applied to the social aggregate of factors. What's wrong with it?

SAMUELSON. You can say something like this: If you add a certain number of seventeen-year-old youngsters of some special skill group to what you already have—the society before that had a very complicated menu of all goods, services, and alternatives open to it—I think one should be able to say something about how this complicated menu shifts, namely, that the first seventeen-year-old youngster shifts it in one way and the second one cannot give the whole menu a bigger uniform shift than the first one did. Depending upon how classical your assumptions are concerning constant returns to scale and varying proportions, there are some very complex—

CHAMBERLIN. Defining seventeen-year-old youngsters as a factor of production, if they are distinguished from the others and they are simply added at various places throughout the system where they will add most to the product and where entrepreneurs will therefore employ them for the highest wages, and they add a certain amount to the total and they get paid a certain amount—

KNIGHT. I would like to make every individual agent a separate factor. Continuous gradation between every factor and every other factor. There is a lot to be said here. And the productivity theory means in the real sense that every productive agent gets what it adds to the social dividend.

CHAMBERLIN. I'm amazed at the way it has been dismissed as what might be called microeconomics.

(Simultaneous discussion.)

WRIGHT. I have always been troubled by the notion of taking all the capital in the world and adding all the labor in the world and then calculating the general share of labor. It seems to me that you have a lot of calculations back and forth in particular markets which, added up, give you a result but I don't think you can add it.

CHAMBERLIN. If your objection is to lumping all of labor together and treating labor like one enormous homogeneous factor, I quite agree with you on the objection. But you can solve that by simply having more factors and getting factors which are reasonably homogeneous and measuring them by efficiency. Professor Knight wants to make every person a factor. I wouldn't go that far, but certainly it is possible to classify factors into meaningful groups which are, let's say, reasonably homogeneous. I'm always talking about pure competition.

SAMUELSON. Is not such a vocabulary rather unsatisfactory in a scientific discipline?

KNIGHT. The fundamental analysis would be the same as in the Crusoe economy.

SAMUELSON. Crusoe doesn't have any problem except production, the problem of allocation. He has no problem of imputation. He never needs to impute how much is due to labor.

KNIGHT. He absolutely must. I simply take issue. To make any rational decision he has to do that.

SAMUELSON. I believe I can state the same conditions of equilibrium that your analysis would end up with, without giving them that interpretation.

FRIEDMAN. I don't have to decide in the market, either, what part of my return is appropriately regarded as return to original indestructible capital, so in the sense that what you say about the Crusoe economy is true, it is also true about the non-Crusoe economy.

SAMUELSON. That's my point. Why add this completely un-illuminating and unnecessary color language that this is what labor really gets, what he deserves, or even what he "produces"?

FRIEDMAN. What's colored is the statement, that he ought to get what he produces, and this statement you need not add.

SAMUELSON. All you can say is that he gets that which in a rational world—the accounting, bookkeeping point prices which we use must have at the margin the same conditions of equilibrium as would exist in a competitive market where you do impute to people the incomes according to supply and demand.

CHAMBERLIN. You seem to object, for J. B. Clark's theory,

even to calling it the product of labor, quite apart from the further issues of whether there is anything ethical about it.

SAMUELSON. I can identify the wage rate in the market with a certain partial derivative.

CHAMBERLIN. That's the marginal productivity theory, isn't it?

SAMUELSON. All I'm saying is why add the provocative language that this is really what labor produces?

CHAMBERLIN. That seems to me to be a very minor point that this is "really what labor produces." What it is, is the partial derivative.

SAMUELSON. That's only my point.

CLARK. I wouldn't want to admit that that is the only content. But we have passed the time that was suggested as a deadline for this session.

[*Editor's note:* Professor Boulding began the second morning's session with the following statement:]

BOULDING. There are one or two things that I had not quite gotten formulated yesterday so that I thought I perhaps might clarify my position a little now. First of all, on the widow's cruse and how you get widow's cruses. All these widow's cruses around economics arise because the system as a whole can't get rid of money by spending it. The fundamental widow's cruse is the quantity of money. The widow's cruse theory of profits that I was talking about yesterday is fundamentally, I think, an aspect of that.

Now, in regard to the relations of my system with the Walrasian system, I have had some thoughts about that. The Walrasian system, fundamentally, is a system of exchange relationships. Do we agree with that? It is a system of prices and price determination. Now, what I am really arguing is that certainly dividends stand in a different category from purchases. You see that if you look at it again from the point of view of the balance sheet. Purchase of labor or of raw materials or of any kind of capital item or of land or of the use of things for a period, anything of that kind, represents an exchange. It is an asset transformation in the balance sheet. It represents a diminution in money and an increase in the thing purchased. Now, dividends are very different. Dividends do not represent an asset transformation. They represent an asset destruction; that is, dividends are very much like transfer payments; and it is because the Walrasian system does not have any transfer payments in it that results don't correspond with mine and that my system has this element of indeterminacy in distribution which the Walrasian system would not seem to permit. That is, if you did not have any transfer payment in the structure, then I think it is true that the solution would be quite determinate; but the presence of these transfer payments is the thing that introduces the indeterminacy. Now there is, of course, a real question as to the extent to which things are transfer payments and the extent to which they are really purchases of something, that is, factors of production. This is really the question of surplus value, I suppose, in one aspect of it.

[*Editor's note:* Professor Clark commented upon the "widow's cruse" theory as follows:

> In case financial status totters
> And you have little left to lose
> Just cast your bread upon the waters
> And thus acquire the widow's cruse.]

CHAPTER VIII

The Monopoly Power of Labor

BY EDWARD H. CHAMBERLIN

ORGANIZED labor in the United States at the present time numbers about 15 million in round figures. This is a far cry from the three million of 1933 and the still smaller number over a long earlier period during which the ideas and attitudes of both ordinary citizens and economists toward collective action by laborers were being formed. Organized labor can no longer realistically be described as the "underdog," or as an "underprivileged" element of the population. Among labor unions are to be found some of the largest and most powerful organizations in the country, both politically and economically. Professor Slichter has coined the phrase "a laboristic economy" to bring home to those with a time lag in their thinking the tremendous shift in relative power between labor and "capital" which has taken place in recent years.

Allowing for families, organized labor as an element in the population is roughly one-fifth of the total. There are in addition millions of unorganized laborers, including agricultural workers, white-collar workers, government and institutional employees, farmers and small businessmen, members of the professions, students, old people, insurance beneficiaries, and receivers of pensions and of interest and dividends. Among these latter are many of small incomes, as well as endowed institutions, educational and other, endeavoring to carry out various types of disinterested activity. All of these have their real incomes reduced when the prices of commodities produced by organized labor are increased by a rise in labor costs. It may seem strange that such banalities should have to be said. But it is even stranger that anyone saying them should risk being labeled as a person of no social sympathies. Verily, Henry Simons was right in his much-quoted observation that to criticize unionism is like attacking motherhood or the home. Large segments of the American public seem to accept uncritically that what is good for organized labor is good for everyone, and that no one can claim to possess any feeling for his fellow man who does not ally himself completely with the cause of unionism. One wonders in what degree this general attitude may contribute to explaining the fact that the typical university course in "Labor Problems" is a course in trade unionism, with little, if any, attention paid to the unorganized sector and to the possible means of alleviating the lot of the *really* underprivileged by means other than collective action.

Labor in a broader sense, including unorganized labor and all those who receive "wages" as the term is ordinarily defined in economics, is clearly a majority of the population (again allowing for families), and it is this fact which no doubt serves most often as a rationalization for the proposition that labor's interest and that of society are one and the same, via the specious identification of the majority with the whole. It is again strange that in these days when we are generally so sensitive to the political and economic oppression of minority racial and other groups, it should need to be asserted that no group, whether a majority or not, has unlimited rights over other elements in society, and that therefore it becomes the duty of every good citizen (including every good economist), in the interest of promoting the *general* welfare, to seek to define reasonable limits for particular elements and to become "anti" whoever attempts to go beyond them.[1]

[1] The standard of "reasonable limits" in the present paper is not the familiar competitive one; for, in accord with the general theory of

This latter appears to me to be such a reasonable position that it is of interest to contrast it with that of Henry Simons, whose famous indictment of "labor monopoly" is preceded by solemn affirmations of concern only for this segment of society. "My central interest," he says, "and the criterion in terms of which I wish to argue, is a maximizing of aggregate labor income and a minimizing of inequality. If unionism were good for labor as a whole, that would be the end of the issue for me, since the community whose welfare concerns us is composed overwhelmingly of laborers." [2] Professing less partisanship than Simons, I shall nevertheless emerge with conclusions less sweepingly hostile to collective bargaining than his.

Similarly, Machlup, in an article which is lavish in its praise of Simons, says: "If monopolistic wage policies 'exploited' only the business man and stockholder, but *no one else*, these wage policies would have my blessing. Since there are not even a million business men and stockholders in this country earning $5,000 or more per year, we should recognize that what is good for the sixty million jobholders and job seekers (and their families) constitutes the interest in the nation." [3]

It is such a professed lack of concern for anyone *but* laborers—

monopolistic competition, it involves a recognition of ubiquitous monopoly elements in product markets and of possible monopoly elements in the labor market. It should be said, however, that the chief purpose of this paper is analytical—to examine the extent to which collective bargaining is correctly described as monopolistic. Where policy implications emerge, they involve mainly a prejudice in favor of allowing labor as much monopoly as anyone else, but not any more.

The general position that the "welfare ideal" must contain a substantial element of monopoly is developed more at length (with particular reference to product markets) in my article, "Product Heterogeneity and Public Policy," *Amer. Econ. Rev.*, XL, No. 2 (May, 1950), p. 85.

[2] "Some Reflections on Syndicalism," *Journal of Political Economy*, LII, p. 1.

[3] "Monopolistic Wage Determination as a Part of the General Problem of Monopoly," in *Wage Determination and the Economics of Liberalism* (Chamber of Commerce of the U. S., 1947), p. 61.

and on the ground that nonlaborers are a mere minority—that seems profoundly shocking to me; and I believe I may claim a more fundamental concern for labor than either Simons or Machlup: if there were less than a million laborers, and sixty million businessmen, I should still hold that the laborers deserved protection from overreaching policies on the part of the businessmen. In brief, I see no more reason to identify the interest of labor with that of society because labor is a majority, than to show a special concern for the population of the United States east of the Mississippi River, or for the population under the age of thirty-five or over the age of twenty-five, these in each case being also majorities.

Obvious as such propositions may be, there can nevertheless be no doubt that what I am proposing constitutes a major departure from a strong "prolabor" bias in traditional liberalism. This being the case, it is of interest to inquire how the liberal tradition, so strongly against monopoly in general, could at the same time have so warmly espoused the cause of collective bargaining. Indeed, this is only one of the many avenues by which one may approach the issue of whether and to what extent collective bargaining *is* monopolistic. It seems to me very clear that traditional liberalism did not regard it as monopolistic and that we must find out the reason why.

On this issue, as on many others, F. W. Taussig may be taken as the embodiment of the best of the liberal tradition. His textbook [4] was widely used and the views it expresses have been of tremendous influence. It was characterized by great sympathy for "reform" in general, a consistently "public" point of view, and at the same time an especial concern about the problems of labor and the improvement of the lot of the laboring class. Collective bargaining was in general approved because of the belief that it could not obtain for labor more than a "competitive" wage, meaning by this the wage at which

[4] *Principles of Economics* (Macmillan, 1912). Last edition 1939.

the existing body of laborers could be absorbed into the system
according to the familiar principles of marginal productivity
The overwhelming consideration, here, was undoubtedly the
number of laborers, and the fact that their *numbers*, either in
the aggregate or in any particular trade, would not be changed
merely by collective action. Wherever union policies *did* take
the form of restricting numbers, as directly in the closed union
or indirectly by high initiation fees, etc., such actions were
condemned as roundly as were the corresponding restrictive
actions on the part of business monopolies. Restrictive union
policies were labeled for what they are—actions designed to
benefit a particular group at the expense of society in general
and in particular at the expense of other laborers. But col
lective action as such appeared to be something different from
restriction. The distinctive feature of this view, and what gave it
an appearance of consistency, was its identification of monopoly
with the *literal* restriction of output. The error is a simple one
as we now know, but since it is still highly prevalent it had
better be made explicit.

A monopolist in any field may seek to increase his total profit
by adjusting either the quantity he sells or the price at which
he sells it. If he had perfect knowledge of his demand curve
the two types of adjustment would blend into one, for he would
be able to announce both his higher price and his smaller sales
with precision. Since he does not in any case have such perfect
knowledge, he must either restrict his output and look to the
market to discover at what price it will be taken, or raise his
price and look to the market to discover how much he can sell
The two actions are equally monopolistic. The second is the
one almost universally followed. The monopolist is able to raise
his price because he *controls* the supply, but not because he
literally restricts it: within the area of his monopoly there is
no one who can undercut his price for the reason that there is
no one else who has any supply to offer at a lower price. His
sales are less at the higher than at the lower price but, far from

restricting his supply in any *literal* sense, he is always eager to sell more than he does, and in the typical case even spends money on advertising in order to do so (*vide* those indisputable monopolies, the public utilities). With these considerations in mind it is easy to see how far astray one may go if one identifies monopoly with "restriction of supply" in any literal sense. In the labor field, as elsewhere, it is the market which does the "restricting" in response to the higher price (wage), and the unsold supply (labor services) either joins the unemployed, or drifts away to some other area, or may be absorbed by the reduction of hours or working days, by institutionalized work stoppages as in coal mining, or by other work-sharing devices.

Returning to the liberal position, it seems clear that, monopoly being generally condemned, it was a colossal error to suppose it to be present in the labor field only to the extent that the common varieties of restrictive practices could be observed. A union which achieves a higher wage rate and lets the market do the restricting for it is on equal terms with one which engages in restriction of the direct and observable variety. The time is past when the economist who wishes to be friendly to organized labor and critical of monopoly at the same time does not at least have something to explain. He can no longer retreat into the comfortable position which I have identified with traditional liberalism.

One ground on which collective bargaining has always been defended is the allegedly weak "bargaining power" of the laborer when acting as an individual. Again it is interesting to note that in traditional liberalism (1) this defense is standard, and (2) it was never imagined that "increasing bargaining power" could do more than assure the laborer of the "competitive wage," defined, as will be recalled, with reference to his numbers. The term "bargaining power" has, as we know, an extremely ambiguous meaning, and has been subject to a variety of interpretations. One of its primary meanings has reference to an indeterminate range of prices, any one of which will equate supply and demand so that competition within this range is inoperative as a determining force. Such a range may appear with discontinuous demand and supply schedules as in the typical analysis of the Austrian school; the range is automatically compressed to a point where the schedules are continuous, as, for instance, in Marshall, where *"natura non facit saltum."* The limits to such a range, if it exists, are set by competition, and beyond them no bargaining takes place. Conversely, within them there is bargaining but no competition. *Any* wages within such limits would be "competitive" wages, and in theory they would be nearer the upper limit as labor's bargaining power was stronger, and nearer the lower limit as it was weaker. Is it not highly probable that such a frame of reference, an integral part of the then prevailing theory of value, contributed consciously or unconsciously to the view, still highly prevalent, that bargaining power has nothing to do with monopoly power? And is it not equally obvious that such an analysis has virtually no relevance to a modern wage negotiation where each side is acting as a unit and where the problem is therefore one of bilateral monopoly with the bargaining strength on each side being inseparable from its *monopoly* position?

Who is the weaker in bargaining power under these circumstances? There is certainly no simple answer to this question, but several aspects of it may be laid open for examination. It has frequently been urged that the individual employee is only one of, say, a thousand in a plant, and that therefore his threat to quit work is as nothing beside his employer's threat to discharge him. In the one case the employer is left with 99.9 per cent of his labor force; in the other the employee is left with zero per cent of his job. By such logic, for all workers to walk out together merely re-establishes the balance, and leaves the two sides precisely equal in this type of bargaining power. This appears to me to be both valid and important. The objection may be made that *mere* disparity of numbers does not *necessarily* put the more numerous group at a disadvantage; and this is true. A retail grocer, for instance, has many customers, and there would hardly seem to be a case for the customers to organize and to deal with him collectively in order to equalize bargaining power. Yet in fact there is. It is only under the artificial assumption of pure competition—a homogeneous product and a very large number of grocers at the identical location—that it would be a matter of no consequence to consumers that their numbers were, say, a thousand times greater, so that the conclusion would be warranted that there was no case for their organizing into groups of a thousand equal in number to the grocers. (Even here one would have to conclude also that there was no case *against* their organizing into such groups; for, since the number of groups would still be large, no one of them would have any monopoly power.) But when we drop pure competition and recognize that, in spite of a great deal of competition, generally speaking, between retail grocers, there remain substantial elements of monopoly which attach customers in some degree to one grocer rather than to another, there *is* a case for customers' organizing, in the sense that they could in this way offset some of the monopoly power in the hands of the individual grocer and drive a better bargain. To be sure, the case is evidently not strong enough, considering also the difficulties, to be exploited by an organizer. But in the labor case, where a particular job is a means of livelihood (in contrast to a source of obtaining a retail good), and where a worker "takes roots," not only with reference to the job itself, but to the community in which he lives, the element of "immobility" is typically much greater, and the power in the hands of the employer may be great indeed if he deals with each laborer individually. There is, I believe, a genuine and compelling case on this score for collective bargaining within the firm, and it is not to be put off by demonstrating that it puts monopoly power in the hands of the union. So far there is no reason to suppose that this power would be any greater than it already and necessarily is on the side of the employer.

But this argument deals only with the situation within a single firm; no case has been made as yet for collective bargaining on an industry- or trade-wide basis.

Let us pass over with only brief comment such considerations as the alleged perishability of labor and the alleged lack of reserves which put the laborer under pressure to find work or to go back to work with a minimum of delay. As to the first, labor *services* which are unsold today produce no *goods* for the employer to sell, so that these latter "perish" equally with the services; and it should be added that the loss of good will may extend into the indefinite future, far beyond the period of actual work stoppage. To the extent that goods already produced may be sold, the depleted stocks must be replaced later, which replacement requires labor, so that the labor is no more nor less perishable than the goods. Where a concern produces services, as in the case of public utilities, there is again equal perishability on both sides. As to lack of reserves, the argument first appeared at an earlier period, when wages and the level of living for laborers were much lower than they are now, and when the "reserves" on the other side were more often the bank account of an individual capitalist employer. In any event, although it remains true today that the average representative of management has more money in the bank than the average laborer, it is not *his* reserves that are relevant, but those of the firm. Firms range from those that could hold out for a very long time if they were willing to swallow the losses to those on the verge of bankruptcy, and evidently no generalization can be made. On the other hand, workers who are already receiving good wages may be able to cut back their expenditures severely, postpone all purchases but food, run up bills, borrow, get help from friends, from the union, and from relief, and take terrific punishment before they give in. It does not appear to me that any safe generalization can be made as to which side is at the greater disadvantage for want of ability to hold out. In some cases it will be the firm; in others the striking laborers.

In fact it is this very ability to hold out on both sides that is so alarming, for it opens up the possibility of the long-drawn-out strikes which we now seem to take as a matter of course. Occasionally a strike is won or lost by one side exhausting the staying powers of the other. But more often it is settled long before such exhaustion, and the appropriate measure of relative bargaining power seems to be, not relative ability to last, but the relative ability of each side to inflict damage upon the other. Certainly this is a major factor, in the first place, in deciding whether there shall be any strike at all; and it must be in the forefront through the duration of any actual conflict. Again, ability to inflict damage is bound to vary with circumstances, and I see no possibility of generalizing as to which side is the more powerful in this type of warfare. It seems much more relevant to say that nowadays the power on both sides is so great that there is not much point in comparing them. It has become a commonplace that in warfare nobody wins. And it seems clear that in warfare, whether international or industrial, "bargaining power" is no longer an appropriate term to apply once war has actually broken out.

The fact that strikes are a form of warfare needs to be stressed, because to many they seem to be regarded as a natural and inevitable concomitant of collective bargaining; and since this latter is taken to be a *sine qua non* of "democracy," they take their place, in the minds of such people, as a necessary feature of the democratic way of life. Yet the Bureau of Labor Standards has estimated that before the last war nine out of ten union agreements were renegotiated each year without interruption of work and without arbitration. The goal is ten out of ten. It is no more desirable to settle industrial relations by putting the ultimate strength of the two sides to a test than it is to settle international relations in this way. In either case there is confession of failure in the peaceful means of negotiation and compromise. It can be said flatly that a strike, being a test of strength, implies victory by the stronger, and hence could hardly be expected to yield results bearing any relation to standards either of justice or of desirable economic policy (except, of course, that the conflict is finally terminated). Yet strikes take place within a larger framework of law and social restraint, which might as reasonably be expected to prevent them as it is expected to prevent people from burning down each other's houses, or from fighting any other kind of private war which involves the infliction of material damage on one another and on innocent third parties.

It might be held, however, that in this particular type of economic issue the most "workable" social policy would be to permit the two parties to settle a disagreement by inflicting as much damage as possible on each other until one of them gave in, *provided* no one else were involved. But surely there is no need to expand on the familiar complexity and interdependence of the economic system, and to point out that third parties are *always* involved in some degree and often in overwhelming degree. It is easy to understand why unions should try to persuade both themselves and the general public that to deny or in any way to qualify the so-called "right" to strike is to establish "involuntary servitude." Since no one favors involuntary servitude, there can be only gain for the labor cause by such a confusion of issues. But where is the "servitude"? Workers are always free to leave any occupation individually. And what is at issue is not even the freedom of any *group* of workers to leave their occupations collectively, for no one expects to leave them at all. If anyone did he would find work elsewhere, and would offer no obstacles to someone else moving in and taking his job. Whatever may be said against the legal injunction in a case of emergency—and I hold no brief for it if a better method of protecting the public interest can be found—economically considered, it merely aims to compel a collective body of men for a limited period of time *actually* to work at the jobs they have freely chosen, jobs which they claim the right to prevent others from taking, and jobs to which they expect soon to return. The essential problem is one of protecting the public interest against an aggregate of private power which puts it in jeopardy. It is hard to believe that the public will in the end be persuaded that the restrictions on *collective action* necessary to achieve this end constitute in any sense a re-establishment of that "involuntary servitude" to which the Thirteenth Amendment to the Constitution sought to put an end.

Most of the traditional arguments as to the weak bargaining power of labor seem to apply, if at all, within the firm, and the disparity they indicate would be corrected if the laborers within each single firm bargained as a group with their employer. As has already been indicated, I see no case against collective bargaining per se within the firm' as monopolistic. The employer is already a single unit, and for employees to become one through collective action only restores the balance, whether we think in terms of the hardship caused to the other by either side terminating the work contract, or whether we think in terms of monopoly power in the labor market, possibly already enjoyed by the employer, and now offset by a similar monopoly power on the employee side. In this latter case we now have a bilateral monopoly in the labor market, one more or less restricted by competitive elements on both sides: alternative employers for the employees; alternative employees for the employers. In short, whatever the power gained by labor within the firm, it can at best no more than offset similar powers already in the hands of management.

If the firm is making monopoly profits in the sale of its product, the question of labor sharing in these gains arising from the product market must also be raised. I have argued elsewhere that such monopoly profits exist very generally throughout the economy; and it is quite possible, of course, that members of a particular union may be able in some degree to share in the monopoly profits, if any, of the enterprise by which they are employed. One may well ask why the laborers in one firm should be paid more than those in another, and the "orthodox" answer to this question is that they should not. But it appears to me that the case for labor sharing in the extra profits in question is no better or worse than that for the entrepreneur himself making off with them; *as long as the monopoly profits are tolerated,* it seems not to be an objection to labor's getting a part of them to point out that this is possible only because labor too has some monopoly power in the situation. When and if the monopoly profits are disallowed by appropriate social action, the case for labor having any share in them will no longer arise. It should be mentioned that all of the above is reasoned on the assumption that labor is not accorded any special weapons in bargaining, such as the right of intimidation or of preventing others from taking over jobs left vacant. This is obviously a major qualification, and will be discussed further, below. But so far it would appear that for laborers within a firm to bargain collectively with their employer is quite defensible so long as there is no collusive action among laborers beyond the firm. Evidently this would mean no industrial or trade unions, but it is a substantial departure from the sweeping condemnation of all collective bargaining as monopolistic.

Beyond the firm it would appear that the considerations by which collective action by labor over a wider range such as an "industry" or a trade are to be judged are strikingly similar to those whereby collective action by businessmen over such an area are judged. There are no problems of weak bargaining power, except in the sense that, generally speaking, *anyone* can strengthen his economic position by acting in concert with those who otherwise would appear in the market as his competitors. Of course, to the extent that businessmen may enter into agreements, actual or tacit, to keep wages down, there is a similar case for the laborers in more than one enterprise acting together as trade- or industry-wide unions against their collective employers. But in this area the organizations of labor which extend beyond the firm appear to be far ahead of those of employers, so that the actual power is on the side of labor, whose industry-wide organizations can play one employer against another by tying up either the entire industry at once, or particular units of it in succession, all in accord with the most advantageous strategy as it appears in the larger perspective.

In this wider struggle the odds appear to me to be heavily with the labor unions. The first and chief reason is that public sympathy is fundamentally with the unions. For this there is a variety of explanations: (1) A majority of the public consists of laborers, in the broad sense, who regard particular unions as representing the interests of labor in general and hence their own interests. (2) Labor is regarded as the "underdog," and though the public may be very angry with John L. Lewis it will never be angry with coal miners, even when they earn $15 a day, at which rate there appear to be only about two hundred days a year of employment for the existing body of workers in the industry. (3) The public is unaware of any connection between unduly high wages and unemployment, because such a connection involves long-run considerations to which the public almost never pays any attention. This natural human propensity, against which economists have fought for generations, has now been fortified by the depression economics of J. M. Keynes, presented in the garb of a "general theory" in which the long run doesn't matter. (4) The public does not (usually) deal directly with labor, and, being unfamiliar with the theory of value, readily believes that high wages come out of profits instead of out of its own pockets through the influence of higher costs upon prices. For all these reasons and others public sympathy is with labor. And public sympathy is of vital importance in this type of warfare, since the public determines the rules under which it takes place, and since in the last analysis it could not take place at all without public sanction.

A second and related reason why the odds are with labor is the political one. In any major conflict, government participation as an umpire of some sort is inevitable, and the attitude and policies of the government may be of primary importance. A prominent labor economist said to me of the recent coal strike, "Don't forget there's lots of votes in those coal-mining districts." The point does not require elaboration.

A third reason arises from the principle that the prices of commodities tend to express their cost of production, including an appropriate allowance for profit. This is a principle which operates with many refinements and qualifications, of course, but by and large it means that the more fundamental clash of interests in any particular labor dispute is between labor and the consumer of the product involved, and not between labor and the businessman or corporation who employs it. The laborer is bargaining about his own income, whereas the businessman can usually in some measure, and perhaps entirely, protect his own income by a price adjustment. To the extent that he *can* protect it by a price adjustment he will be more ready to give in; this gives us another important reason why the pressure to increase wages may not be matched by an equal opposing pressure. To understand the importance of this factor we have only to ask if the businessman's position in a wage dispute would not be transformed in a regime of price fixing where he was forbidden by law to increase his prices. Who can deny that it would be?

This last consideration has its application chiefly to warfare conducted over a broad front, and including a number of firms in substantial competition with each other in the product market. To the individual firm, although higher costs mean a recomputation of its maximum profit position, the possibilities of a price adjustment are severely limited if its rivals, not subject to the same pressures, hold their prices at the same level. The extreme of this situation would, of course, be pure competition, where the individual firm could not change its price at all, merely because its own costs had changed. In any event, wherever a *general* upward adjustment of costs has taken place among firms in substantial competition with each other a *general* price adjustment will be a natural result, since no individual firm will have reason to fear any substantial loss of business to competitors. This contrast points up again the difference between the case which may legitimately be made for collective bargaining within the firm and the illegitimacy of extending it uncritically to areas beyond the firm.

A final reason why the greater power is on the side of labor in struggles beyond the firm arises from the fact that, although the laborer retains his freedom to seek other employment, the employer does not effectively retain his freedom to hire other laborers. Indeed he usually does not even retain the freedom to continue operations with that portion of his working force which, if not intimidated, would prefer to work. The techniques by which this result is accomplished are several, including the key one of picketing, which the American public for some curious reason continues to associate with "free speech." (It is heartening to record that the American Civil Liberties Union, one of whose primary objectives is the preservation of free speech, has issued strong protests against mass picketing.) But the fundamental fact appears to be that the public sanctions the proposition that when persons stop work collectively they may legitimately prevent from working, not only a minority of their own numbers who would prefer to continue, but also others working for the same enterprise whom they may successfully intimidate, and, more to the point, still others who might be glad to take their jobs either temporarily or permanently. It is certainly by public sanction that violations of the most essential freedoms of other citizens are tolerated in order that a group of organized laborers may press its case more effectively. We have here only one more instance of the importance of public sympathy and support.

The significance of this peculiarity of "bargaining" in the

labor area seems to me hardly to have been noticed. In earlier discussions of "bargaining power," collective actions used to be defended by making a contrast between the position of a single worker in a large plant and, for example, an individual housemaid who bargains supposedly on equal terms with the individual householder. If the mistress discharges the maid, the maid is put to the trouble of finding another job; if the maid quits work, the mistress is similarly put to the trouble of finding another maid. Here "bargaining power" appears truly to be equalized. But suppose now that the maid were to be given the power to quit and at the same time to prevent the householder from employing anyone else. Even the individual worker in a large factory might have great "bargaining" power indeed if he could similarly threaten to quit and prevent the company from having anyone else do his work as long as he chose to stay out. The corresponding power in the hands of an employer would seem to be not only to deprive a worker of his job, but also to prevent him from taking any other until he comes to terms. The "right" to strike is certainly not to be discussed in terms of the right of workers collectively to quit their jobs. There is no question of quitting their jobs at all. It is a question of *keeping* them absolutely, but of not working at them, and of preventing anyone else from working at them either. As has been brought out above, such a power greatly unbalances in favor of labor the relative position even within a firm. But it becomes vastly more significant in industrial warfare conducted over the wider area at present under discussion. This is partly because what is involved is mass coercion or, possibly, mass violence; and the magnitude of the forces which array themselves against the police power of the State is a matter of primary consequence. It is evidently easier to quell a riot of ten people than of ten thousand; and similarly it is easier to protect ten people from intimidation than ten thousand. But, on the economic side, the wider the area of conflict the smaller become the possibilities in realistic terms of replacing workers, either temporarily or permanently. Herein must lie a substantial part of the explanation of why such replacement is no longer a realistic possibility in an industrial conflict of any magnitude. "Something new has been added" to the idea of bargaining—the power in the hands of one party to prevent the other from considering any alternative offers from others who might like to make a contract with him. And such a power in the hands of labor seems to be commonly regarded as not merely compatible with, but by many as even essential to, a "free" society!

A number of special circumstances have now been mentioned which strengthen the hands of unionized workers in exerting pressure for wages higher than those they would be able to obtain if organized only within each firm to offset the unit opposition of their entrepreneur-employer. I suggest that the wages obtainable by merely intrafirm organization, with a strict prohibition of any collusive action by labor beyond the firm and of any action of intimidation to prevent the firm from making an alternative contract with nonstriking laborers, might be described, by a variation of Professor Clark's terminology (chap. i), as "workably competitive wages." Such wages would still involve substantial elements of monopoly, but, as pointed out above, no more substantial than those that the owners of individual firms already have, either in the labor market or in the product market. And to the extent that monopoly profits in monopolistically competitive product markets were found socially undesirable and subjected to regulation, a corresponding check would be put upon any participation in these profits by labor.

It is of interest to recognize that the possibilities for monopoly income through collusive action beyond the individual firm, although usually associated with the profits share of income, are equally open to labor. In fact they may be open *only* to labor if competition in the product market is effective in keeping down profits. For example, an industry-wide union may first obtain higher wages for any or all of the various reasons already given. With higher costs, prices are adjusted upward to cover them, but competition in this case keeps *profits* at the "competitive level" in the industry. At the higher price what has happened is that a portion of the area of possible monopoly profit for the industry has been taken over by labor. The process may be repeated, and by a series of such adjustments the monopoly income forbidden to enterprise by the antitrust laws may be enjoyed by labor as the sole factor and with the privilege of selling its factor services under unified monopoly control on an industry basis.[5]

A similar argument is equally valid for labor organized on a trade basis, the upward pressure on prices here being merely exerted in several industries at the same time. There is no reason to think that such is not the general situation—in fact there is every reason to think that it is. Economists as well as the public are fooled by the fact that the adjective "monopoly" is always attached to the noun "profit" and never to the noun "cost." But economists at least should not be fooled in a matter as straightforward technically as this appears to be.

One final observation. It has been an objection to analyzing labor unions as monopolies that they do not aim at maximizing total income, or that there is at least a good deal of uncertainty as to what it is they are maximizing—whether it is the income of *all* members, of those actually employed, of older members with seniority rights, who will be the last to be laid off, or of those in some other preferred position (politically within the union, etc.). Also it has been pointed out that the problem of labor monopoly varies in important detail from that of industrial monopoly: for instance, by the necessity of adding into the picture in this case the influence of political factors within the

---

[5] If neither competition nor the antitrust laws are effective in preventing unreasonably high profits over the area in question, I see no case against labor having a share in them. The argument is identical with that for monopoly profits within a firm (cf. above, p. 180).

union—the necessity of recurrent wage demands for internal political reasons, etc. But all these considerations merely indicate that the monopoly problem is not simple. If a monopolist, industrial or labor, moderates his policy for fear of an unfavorable public reaction, or if a union leader presses his advantages more vigorously because he must maintain his prestige as an officer, he is nevertheless in each case a monopolist. The economist will have to learn that there is more to the theory of monopoly than the simple maximizing of profits. Indeed, the behavior of monopolists in different circumstances is certainly one of the most fruitful fields for economic investigation.

The reaction of many to the above, or any similar, analysis will be that it is "unrealistic," and that "labor unions are here to stay" because it is "politically impossible to abolish them." I think the first reply to such a position is that made by D. H. Robertson in discussing a similar problem: "[Before we talk about politics], let us get the analysis right." [6] To this I may add a second observation: If the above analysis turns out to be reasonably "right," it seems to follow that the problem of labor monopoly is not one of a simple "yes" or "no" to collective bargaining. Rather, it appears possible to limit and restrict labor monopolies in a variety of ways and degrees, and to find workable solutions in appropriately adjusting their powers. Perhaps it is not too much to hope that, even in a democracy where pressure groups are disconcertingly powerful, such an objective may be achieved.

[6] "A Revolutionist's Handbook," *Quarterly Journal of Economics*, LXIV (February, 1950), p. 13.

CHAPTER IX

Selections from the Discussion

of Chamberlin's Paper [1]

KNIGHT. In harmony with the rest of your paper, would not "labor-unionistic economy" be more accurate than a "laboristic economy"?

FRIEDMAN. Of course, he is using labor as synonymous with trade unions. The longer phrase would lose some of its catch quality.

KNIGHT. Some of the propaganda prestige. . . . Is it true that the majority of American society are working for wages?

CHAMBERLIN. Including families—and I am including all labor.

HABERLER. Farmers included?

CHAMBERLIN. Yes, including farm labor. Here I am using labor—

HABERLER. It is awfully vague where you draw the line.

KNIGHT. It must be pretty close, if you mean people who work for wages, whether it is a majority or not.

CHAMBERLIN. There are about 60 million jobs right now, I believe?

[1] *Editor's note:* The discussion of Dr. Chamberlin's paper, unlike the preceding sessions, was not reserved to the end but took the form of a running commentary on the paper as it was being read. Accordingly it is even more difficult than in the other sessions to give a consecutive abridgment.

FRIEDMAN. But that includes all the entrepreneurs, or about 10 million independently employed.

CHAMBERLIN. Take 50 million and add their families, and, as a proportion of the population, it would be more than half.

FRIEDMAN. If you take just the manual workers as you want to do it would probably be a minority.

BOULDING. And I suspect a decreasing minority.

CHAMBERLIN. Of course, the point here is *not* to take just the manual workers. . . .

[*Editor's note:* Professor Samuelson here recurred to "welfare economics" (cf. chap. v).]

SAMUELSON. I think we ought to discuss the delicate question of why monopoly is generally to be condemned.

CHAMBERLIN. Yes, but please note that I say, "*If* monopoly is generally to be condemned," and not that it *is* generally to be condemned.

SAMUELSON. I say that is the implicit element that runs through the paper.

CHAMBERLIN. Yes, it is implicit that joint action between units, beyond certain limits, is to be condemned rather than that monopoly is generally to be condemned. As someone has observed, I would be a strange person to say monopoly was universally to be condemned since I hold that the welfare ideal must have a lot of monopoly in it.

SAMUELSON. The most ardent laborphile would say the labor movement should not indulge in abuses, should not carry its actions beyond what is in the general welfare.

WRIGHT. If he gives you that much, you could start in from there and begin to argue about what is the general welfare.

CLARK. I wonder if this is not affected by the same kind of attitude that my father used to express sometimes, that he was willing to discuss the issue of socialism on a basis of benefit for labor as a whole because he thought he could get the answer he was satisfied with on that basis and, a fortiori, if he got the answer on that basis it would be valid if you took in the other elements.

SAMUELSON. I am interested in Professor Chamberlin's preconceptions, and I am interested in them only to understand them, not to criticize them. I get the impression here, nowhere stated but everywhere implied, that wherever there is a competitively determined income, whatever its size, that that is the proper check and balance between the rights of a minority and the rights of a majority; and if that is your view, I think you should state it; and if it is not, I think you should state that, because a reasonable man will infer that.

CHAMBERLIN. I use the word "overreaching" here instead of exploitation so as to carry the meaning that there is need for considering the claims or rights of all elements in society. That is all. I don't see that I need to make explicit at this point any particular criteria for the different elements in society. Certainly it is not needed as a logical element in the argument. The case I want to make is simply (1) that every element in society deserves some consideration, and that the problem is to define what degree of consideration there should be, and (2) that beyond that point one should restrain the person who has gone too far. Both of these are general propositions.

SAMUELSON. Suppose "John Doe" says John L. Lewis is "Robin Hood" and, despite the monopoly exploitation of Lewis, Doe approves of him because he behaves like Robin Hood. Lewis may not do it as well as some other Robin Hood does it. In that case one might harp on the damage done by that. But what is wrong with monopoly power which in terms of this particular ("John Doe") ethical frame of reference improves the total situation? If I may coin a phrase, the "general welfare."

CHAMBERLIN. I don't think there is any inconsistency. All I have said so far would be related to what you say by the proposition that you have to set a limit to the activities of Robin Hoods, wouldn't it?

SAMUELSON. If we condemn monopoly in other fields, we must condemn monopoly in the labor field?

This may be a bad way to discuss your paper by taking sentences before you come to them, but I am giving you the whole Gestalt of the conclusion one derives from your paper.

FRIEDMAN. The John L. Lewis case is a poor case for the present purpose. The most famous reference to a discrepancy between private and social cost is certainly the smoke nuisance case. The conclusion is that the price of coal ought to be higher than the competitive price, and John L. Lewis is making it higher.[2]

SAMUELSON. John L. Lewis is a terrible Robin Hood. That is absolutely true. He is not even a Robin Hood who is doing what Robin Hood is supposed to do. That isn't the question. The question is whether a price—

WRIGHT. A community of Robin Hoods, however well motivated, would stymie the working of the whole system. In other words, you might have a gain for some by taking from the rich and giving to the poor (what I call the Jesse James theory of taxation), and it is true that there is an immediate benefit to that particular group of poor who are benefited; but when all social life is organized among, let us say, fifteen or twenty Robin Hoods, then in this process of giving slight benefit to a few poor, or even to many, the Robin Hoods may cut off the possibilities of an expansion which would make their small benefit from extortion look like nothing at all.

SAMUELSON. Absolutely true; and if that is what you mean, say it.

WRIGHT. That is what I got out of Professor Chamberlin's paper.

CHAMBERLIN. I think the answer to what you say about Robin Hoods is simply that if you are going to permit Robin

---

[2] *Comment by Wright:* Should this be "the" conclusion or only one conclusion?

Hood activity in a society, there will have to be some criterion as to where it should stop.

SAMUELSON. And the good economist can investigate and spell out where the limit is?

CHAMBERLIN. I don't think that follows.

SAMUELSON. I thought that is what the earlier paragraph says. Was that your purpose?

CHAMBERLIN. The "good citizen," including every good economist.

SAMUELSON. And every reasonable man will come to the same opinion? . . . I suggest what you are giving us is an implicit, voting system of the market place; and all of our feelings of opprobrium about monopoly you are quite properly, from the mechanical viewpoint, in my view, putting onto labor; and just as it is bad in one field, it is bad in the other.

BOULDING. Just as good in one field as in the other. We cannot accept the proposition that all monopoly is bad, really.

FRIEDMAN. Why can't we?

BOULDING. Because some of it is good.

FRIEDMAN. Some may be inevitable. That is a far cry from saying it is good.

WRIGHT. I will side with him and say that sometimes "monopoly" is good.

SAMUELSON. Against some ideal alternative? [3]

FRIEDMAN. It is a difficult question whether it is meaningless to say something is a necessary evil. That may be a contradiction in terms. It means you are contrasting what exists with something you think cannot exist. Yet I really think that that is the sense in which we mean all monopoly is bad and that yet we might tolerate some.

CHAMBERLIN. The main objective here is to show that monopoly in the case of labor is not different from other

---

[3] *Comment by Wright:* I should say that if growth is the standard then even the ideal must contain "monopoly" elements—better described as a minimum of "essential friction."

monopoly, for instance, from monopoly on the part of business-men. It would still be possible to say that there is no inconsistency in permitting laborers to exercise monopoly powers and not permitting businessmen, if that were a conclusion drawn from a premise that one *likes* laborers better than businessmen.

SAMUELSON. Or John Doe likes poor people better than rich people; or the Lord's chosen people better than the Lord's non-chosen people. There are a lot of clients in this game.

CHAMBERLIN. I don't see that it is necessary here to adopt any definite standard as to what the limits should be for any particular social group. I agree that the general line of the argument implies a great deal of competition in the standard, although certainly not pure competition.

SAMUELSON. Within narrow professional discussion nothing but good could come, in my opinion, if for a number of years we would wage an unending campaign to make all welfare economic assumptions as explicit as possible. Now, it is obvious that I have been riding that horse here. Such an approach is not for the purpose of the public press or the platform. Obviously, there are subtleties that are not appropriate there, but in professional discussion it seems to be long overdue. Let's go on. . . .

[*Editor's note:* The question next came up of what the earlier economists thought union action could do.]

SAMUELSON. Did Taussig [4] actually think that collective bargaining could not obtain more than a competitive wage in one particular industry?

HABERLER. Does he specifically say that?

CHAMBERLIN. I am paraphrasing Taussig. That is certainly the tenor of what he said—for an "open" union of course.

CLARK. Of course, that view was formulated in a period long before the techniques of restriction, picketing, and so on were worked out to the extent they are now.

[4] See Professor Chamberlin's comments, pp. 171 ff.

CHAMBERLIN. Yes, I think it was certainly an analysis of what was possible by collective bargaining as such, and did not include some modern techniques used by unions. I certainly don't want to misrepresent Taussig in any way, and it should be made clear that this was at a period when certain techniques had not yet developed.

HABERLER. The same kind of collective bargaining which you propose later on—or to which you do not object—without picketing, and without everything which I think is characteristic of collective bargaining.

SAMUELSON. I am surprised that by 1911 when the first edition of the book came out that a man as sage as Taussig should have been of the opinion that collective bargaining couldn't raise wages, even at the plant level. I would have thought it was something of a commonplace by that time.

CHAMBERLIN. I am sure I can supply quotations from Taussig to support my paraphrase of his position: that mere collective bargaining does not change numbers and that the general level of wages is influenced predominantly by the number of laborers. And that is the logic whereby the conclusion was reached that collective bargaining could not affect the general level of wages—because it would not affect the number of laborers. With the exception of those restrictive activities that I speak of, that certainly was the tenor of what he held—but the important thing is that it was held more widely than by Taussig alone.

CLARK. In my father's view, unions could not raise wages in general above their "natural level"; but without unions they might be substantially below it. . . .

[*Editor's note:* Another topic discussed concerned that raised earlier pp. 63 ff.) in connection with Dr. Clark's paper: Could wages "push up" prices without monopoly?]

FRIEDMAN. I don't see that there is any difference between the laborer and the businessman. If the businessman can protect his income by a price adjustment, that means he had the wrong price before—that is, a price that did not maximize his profit.

CHAMBERLIN. No. In the case of a competitive industry, when all laborers in the industry receive higher wages, he may protect his income by raising his prices.

FRIEDMAN. But every employer in the industry can't do that.

CHAMBERLIN. If they all pay higher wages, they can.

SAMUELSON. A perfectly elastic supply of enterprise?

FRIEDMAN. Even then, it would only be those who remain who had protected their incomes entirely—still not all of the employers originally in that industry.

CHAMBERLIN. At the higher price there will be some reduction in output.

FRIEDMAN. It can't be that the laborers can get more than they did before and the employers as much as they got before.

CHAMBERLIN. What would you say to what is coming here? Let me go on: "To the extent that he *can* protect it by a price adjustment he will be more ready to give in; this gives us another important reason why the pressure to increase wages may not be matched by an equal opposing pressure. To understand the importance of this factor we have only to ask if the businessman's position in a wage dispute would not be transformed in a regime of price fixing where he was forbidden by law to increase his prices. Who can deny that it would be?"

You wouldn't deny that it would be?

FRIEDMAN. I think this final statement is very different from the earlier one. The objection I have to the earlier statement is that by implying the businessman could protect his income entirely you were in effect saying that the businessman had not chosen the optimum price. The present statement is all right, since you are restricting the businessman's freedom. Suppose the state forbids him to choose the optimum price? Wouldn't that change the situation?

CHAMBERLIN. That is not what I am saying, because in the case of the individual seller under pure competition, of course, he couldn't change his price at all. In the case, however, of a general wage adjustment in an industry the individual may change his price because the wage adjustment is general and competitors also have higher costs. So the reason he did not raise it before was that he did not have this higher cost which made it possible for him to raise his price. It is not an answer to say that if he can raise his price because of the cost adjustment, he could have raised it anyway, and therefore why didn't he?

FRIEDMAN. That isn't what I was saying. If he can protect his income *entirely* by raising the price, then it follows that the price was not the appropriate price before. So put the two parts together.

CHAMBERLIN. If at the higher price less is sold and some firms drop out of the industry, then the firms remaining may in the end have protected their incomes entirely.

FRIEDMAN. The firms *remaining* . . .

[*Editor's note:* We next encounter some semantic problems.]

SAMUELSON. Collective bargaining is itself a form of "warfare."

CHAMBERLIN. I don't see why it is. I quite disagree.

SAMUELSON. It is power against power.

CHAMBERLIN. There is no reason why collective bargaining within a firm should be warfare. Bargaining may be carried on collectively, and the results may be reached by negotiation and compromise and no warfare break out.

SAMUELSON. It is a power struggle, a welfare power struggle.

WRIGHT. Both are power struggles. In one you are throwing bombs and in the other you aren't, in the other you are merely talking to him. You can't draw a line philosophically between the collective bargaining session and a strike. One is just a point of view backed up by more violent sanctions than the other.

CHAMBERLIN. You may say that international politics is a power struggle. Yet it does not need to lead to warfare. So collective bargaining is not necessarily warfare. It simply means that there is bargaining and negotiation, and the bargaining is carried on from the labor side by a collective group of laborers, but it does not need to mean that warfare breaks out. The results may depend upon the relative power that can be exerted in the bargaining or upon relative skill and various aspects of power.

SAMUELSON. You think there is more damage to third parties when there is a strike than to the first and second parties?

CHAMBERLIN. There certainly is damage from the strike through stoppage of activity. There is the further damage, which is quite distinct from that covered directly by the strike, in the nature of the adjustment which comes out of the negotiation; in other words, even if there never were any strikes, there obviously would be damage to various people, depending on the nature of the bargain which was reached. . . .

[*Editor's note:* In the following section Professor Haberler raises a protest against indiscriminate use of the word "monopoly."]

HABERLER. I think we should distinguish between labor monopoly confronting labor monopsony on the one hand, and a monopoly in the product market on the other. In the first case, I think the validity of organization is pretty clear. There is much to say for labor monopsony being confronted with labor monopoly. In the other case, where you have a product monopoly, I think it is not at all clear that you correct it in any way if you confront it with labor monopoly. Such a labor monopoly will just try to cut in on the monopoly profits and leave output unchanged. You don't say that, but that seems to be the implication.

CHAMBERLIN. I agree that the cases are different, and the distinction between them is made later on.

KNIGHT. Employer monopsony presupposes labor immobility. Some laborers want to stay and some want to move anyhow, and such freedoms are one of the important issues in the case, the right to move or the right to avoid the inconvenience of moving. Other things being equal, what would be the labor turnover?

CHAMBERLIN. Labor is exceedingly immobile.

FRIEDMAN. I would argue the opposite, that the whole tenor of evidence is that labor must be extremely mobile. There is evidence of all kinds: the relation among incomes in different regions of the country, the actual degree of movement which takes place during times like wartime, etc., and other empirical studies.

CHAMBERLIN. But what of the differences in wages, geographical wage differences?

FRIEDMAN. There appear to be only small differences between family *incomes* in different regions of the country if you take into account size of community. In cities of the same size, incomes are roughly the same in different communities. Wage rates are not. If you take North versus South, a white family in a city of 100,000 will have roughly the same annual income in the North and South; but the wage for any specified occupation will be lower in the South than in the North. The reconciliation is, I believe, that you have a different occupational grouping in the South and North. The appearance of the Negroes in the South forces wage rates down in all occupations, but also pushes the whites into a higher upgraded occupation. So it is a very clouded picture.

SAMUELSON. The thing is very clouded. The Fitchburg and New Haven studies suggest there is quite a measure of mobility. Quite a lot of it seems to be unrelated to wages. Wage differentials exist even in the same market.

CHAMBERLIN. It is the wage differentials that I had in mind when I spoke of labor immobility. Very substantial wage differentials do exist.

FRIEDMAN. There is a real problem whether they are equalizing or immobilizing.

SAMUELSON. Unexplainable differentials.

FRIEDMAN. The fact that family incomes are equal strongly suggests equalizing differences.

SAMUELSON. In Fitchburg, the same area, same type of people, the studies are clouded on this point.

HABERLER. May I come back to the point that you have a product monopoly and labor monopoly? I think you cannot say now that the workers share in the monopoly profit, but under most circumstances it would be reduced further. I think that is not brought out here.

KNIGHT. Agreement between labor and employers, in establishing monopoly is terribly important, in sharing the fruits.

HABERLER. What do you mean by bargaining? That is what I would like to know. You admit collective bargaining "within the firm," but you say it is to be bargaining without restricting numbers, without the closed shop, without higher initiation fees, without intimidation, without strikes, and without threats of strikes. I don't know what kind of bargaining that is.

KNIGHT. I am bothered about that. The word bargaining, if you want to give it any definite meaning, just reduces to hypnotic power, because a monopolist does not bargain any more than the competitor. He fixes the price and says take it or leave it.

CHAMBERLIN. Yes, but in a bilateral monopoly, you certainly could not say that either side fixes the price, take it or leave it. If the prices they fixed were different, you would not have any bargain.

KNIGHT. It is kind of a mutual effort to hypnotize or browbeat, a psychological form of coercion. I think it is mysterious what you mean.

HABERLER. A question about relative power.

FRIEDMAN. The power appears to be heavily with labor unions chiefly because public opinion is with labor unions. True, a majority of the public does not consist of members of labor unions. The issue should be not whether the public are with "labor," but whether they are with labor *unions*.

CHAMBERLIN. Well, in the public mind there is substantial identification between the two, isn't there?

FRIEDMAN. You argued earlier that that is one of the problems, that people tend to make this identification, that they ought not to, and that it would be socially desirable if they didn't.

CHAMBERLIN. Well, public sympathy is heavily with labor and to that extent the odds are heavily with labor.

FRIEDMAN. I think that statement is correct chiefly because, fundamentally, the public, like economists, confuses the two.

[*Editor's note:* The discussion shifted to the standard problem of whether employers had greater "staying" power than labor. Professor Chamberlin doubted that they necessarily did.]

BOULDING. That is not really fair because the employer has the money.

FRIEDMAN. The goods aren't sold.

WRIGHT. What about good will? It seems to me that is a very perishable feature on the employer side of the thing. Take coal. One reason people have converted to oil is not because oil is less dirty, but because they feel they can get oil more reliably than they can get coal.

CHAMBERLIN. I think the case could be made stronger. Take the case of Chrysler automobiles. People may buy another automobile because they could not get a Chrysler during the strike. As a result, they may go on buying other automobiles. The loss may extend beyond the strike period.

WRIGHT. The highly perishable commodity there of good will. You may force the attached buyers to deal somewhere else, and there is a pecuniary loss to the producer.

FRIEDMAN. It is a loss to the employee too.

WRIGHT. I am only arguing concerning the proposition that the laborer has a perishable commodity and that the owner can sit down and not lose anything. It seems to me that it is false.

CHAMBERLIN. The people who couldn't buy Chrysler automobiles then buy General Motors; and Chrysler has to reduce the scale of its operations; and the laborer who was working for Chrysler may go and work for General Motors and produce other automobiles. In that case, the good will is even more perishable.

CLARK. That gets you into the tactical situation that I don't think you explicitly put into your analysis—the union bargaining with employers one at a time.

CHAMBERLIN. I think it is dealt with in one place, but it is not dealt with at length.

KNIGHT. Would the General Motors branch of UAW [United Auto Workers] freely admit members from the Chrysler branch automatically?

CHAMBERLIN. I don't think there would be any trouble to speak of.

SAMUELSON. This does not happen in strikes very often, but it does happen. In a two-year strike in New York everybody had a job in another city.

CHAMBERLIN. I meant over a longer period. Because people were prevented from buying Chryslers during this strike, there would be a major impact on operations. Certainly the workers who could not be employed by their employers would look for jobs elsewhere.

KNIGHT. Would the General Motors union chapter practice no monopoly exclusion whatever against the members of the Chrysler chapter?

CHAMBERLIN. I think they would not over the long period. Of course, to the extent that they practiced exclusion, they would be that much more monopolistic.

SAMUELSON. I agree with the point but would restate it. Workers on a fifty-day strike don't lose fifty days' income, in trades where workers don't work all year long. But a day's labor has perished, if you assume full employment, and the worker does not work that day. The fact that there are additions to stocks and depletions of stocks does not mean there is not a social waste due to the loss of one day of a man's life, since the days of our years are numbered.

KNIGHT. That is fantastically unreal. You are simply defining full employment in terms of intensity as well as hours.

SAMUELSON. State it that the workers would not have worked the full year anyway and you get a different time profile. In cases other than that there is something lost.

KNIGHT. The services may be more than completely perishable, deteriorate out of use.

SAMUELSON. The sentence can easily be fixed up.

CHAMBERLIN. That is what I mean to say, although in different language from what you have used. The stocks might be replaced even if you had a full employment situation by working overtime or by working Saturdays and Sundays. In that case you would have more than full employment for a period in order to replace them. The only point is that the stocks are perishable in the same way that the labor is. All I want to say is that there can be no generalization about it. In some cases the firm can hold out longer and in some cases the laborers can hold out longer.

WRIGHT. Particularly these quicky strikes, when you suddenly pull out in the middle of an order.

CHAMBERLIN. That is a matter of how much damage you can inflict, which is not the same thing.

BOULDING. Each side holds out the same length of time.

CHAMBERLIN. In fact, it is this very ability to hold out on both sides that is so alarming. Only a very rich country could afford the long-drawn-out strikes which we seem to take as a matter of course.

BOULDING. Even in the worst years strikes were never more than 1 per cent of the national income. Your statement seems to be a gross exaggeration.

CHAMBERLIN. You are agreeing with me, aren't you?

BOULDING. Not at all. I am saying that, quantitatively, strikes are not very important even in this country.

FRIEDMAN. I think two points are involved. I think you are right as far as the loss to the nation, but only a country of very rich people could afford separately and individually long-drawn-out strikes. That is really a different point—not because of the richness of the country, but because the laborers are relatively rich individually, for a strike does cost a lot to each.

BOULDING. I may have misunderstood. That is a different point.

CHAMBERLIN. That is what I meant.

BOULDING. I don't really think strikes are a serious problem; compared with the other problems, I would say they are quite secondary.

SAMUELSON. I think the strikes that could happen are very important.

BOULDING. They haven't yet.

SAMUELSON. But as far as influence at a collective bargaining table is concerned I think the situation is just like the loaded weapon that "never goes off." Some day it may.

CHAPTER X

Some Comments on the Significance of Labor Unions for Economic Policy [1]

BY MILTON FRIEDMAN [2]

LABOR unions are important political and economic institutions that significantly affect both public and private actions. This fact raises serious and difficult problems for economic policy. At the same time, laymen and economists alike tend, in my view, to exaggerate greatly the extent to which labor unions affect the structure and level of wage rates. This fact is one of the most serious obstacles to a balanced judgment about appropriate public policies toward unions.

We may distinguish at the outset three rather different ways in which unions affect the community:

(1) Unions are political as well as economic organizations. They use their political power to achieve their immediate economic objectives, as well as to promote legislation which they favor for any one of a wide variety of reasons. Currently, unions are generally regarded as exercising very considerable political power. It is clear that this could be so even if their direct economic power to alter particular wage rates were negligible, so that their political power is analytically distinguishable from at least certain types of economic power, though undoubtedly related to them as both cause and effect.

[1] I am deeply indebted to H. Gregg Lewis and Albert E. Rees for valuable criticism and constructive suggestions.

[2] *Editor's note:* No annotations are given in this chapter. For comments see the discussion, chap. xi.

(2) By choice or necessity, unions may follow tactics to gain their objectives that impose costs on the rest of the community. These "frictional effects" may be present whether or not unions succeed in attaining their objectives. For example, suppose unions seldom or never made wage rates different from what they would otherwise have been. This obviously would not mean that unions were of no economic importance. In the attempt—assumed unsuccessful—to influence wage rates, they might precipitate strikes and widespread industrial warfare, causing considerable harm to third parties. It is hard to pass any considered judgment on the importance of these frictional effects. The statistics on number of man-days lost through strikes uniformly show a negligible fraction of total labor time lost— generally well under 1 per cent. To some extent these figures overstate the loss, since time lost during strikes may be at the expense of subsequent or prior idleness rather than of work; to some extent they understate the loss, since they take no account of indirect idleness in complementary industries or of other indirect effects hinging on the strategic position of the struck activity. On the whole, however, I am inclined to believe that this frictional effect, while certainly significant, tends to be overrated for reasons that are much the same as those which will be adduced to explain why the effect of unions on wage rates is exaggerated.

(3) Unions may affect the structure and level of wage rates, and thereby the allocation of resources among alternative uses. A primary objective of unions is to affect wage rates, so what is in question here is the success of the unions in achieving one of their major objectives. This structural effect can be distinguished from the frictional effects just considered. Suppose unions always succeeded in gaining their demands without strikes or other interruptions of production. Then unions would have no frictional effects. They would have structural effects. Indeed, these two effects may to some extent be negatively correlated: the stronger the union, the less need it may have to

resort to strikes and the more successful it may be in gaining its objectives. In the first instance, unions operate on the wage rate for a particular craft or in a particular industry, and so tend to change relative wage rates. But it has been argued by some that this process may result in monetary reactions that change the general level of money and perhaps real wage rates, so changes in both the structure and level of wage rates should be included under this heading.

This paper is concerned almost entirely with the third way in which unions affect the community: the long-run effect of unions on the structure and level of wage rates and thereby on the allocation of resources. Of course, the other two aspects of union activity cannot be entirely neglected—if only because they are among the primary means for attaining the objective of altering wage rates—but they will not be considered in their own right.

From this strictly economic point of view, labor unions and enterprise monopolies are conceptually similar if not identical phenomena and have similar effects. In particular, the economic significance of both tends to be exaggerated for much the same reasons, and the fact of exaggeration tends to have much the same implications for policy. In my view, appropriate public policy calls for like treatment of both forms of monopoly—treatment designed to keep their extent and importance to a minimum.

Orthodox economic theory has significant implications for the circumstances under which unions can alter wage rates significantly. These implications are largely supported by experience. After summarizing them, I shall comment on the quantitative importance of the effects unions have had on wage rates, on why these effects tend to be exaggerated, and on the relation between unions and economic stability. None of these major problems will be examined exhaustively; my purpose is rather to emphasize a number of points that impress me as misunderstood or unduly neglected. Finally, I shall mention a number of conclusions for economic policy that follow from these comments.

Some Implications of Orthodox Economic Theory

The power of unions, as of any other monopoly, is ultimately limited by the elasticity of the demand curve for the monopolized services. Unions have significant potential power only if this demand curve is fairly inelastic at what would otherwise be the competitive price. Even then, of course, they must also be able to control either the supply of workers or the wage rate employers will offer workers.

DEMAND FOR LABOR

The theory of joint demand developed by Marshall is in some ways the most useful tool of orthodox economic theory for understanding the circumstances under which the demand curve will be inelastic. It will be recalled that Marshall emphasized that the demand for one of a number of jointly demanded items is the more inelastic, (1) the more essential the given item is in the production of the final product, (2) the more inelastic the demand for the final product, (3) the smaller the fraction of total cost accounted for by the item in question, and (4) the more inelastic the supply of co-operating factors.[3] The most significant of these items for the analysis of unions are the essentiality of the factor and the percentage of total costs accounted for by the factor. Now, a factor is likely to be far more essential in the short run than in the long run. Let a union be organized and let it suddenly raise the wage rate. Employment of the type of labor in question is likely to shrink far less at first than it will over the longer run, when it

[3] Alfred Marshall, *Principles of Economics* (8th ed.; Macmillan, 1920), pp. 385-386.

is possible to make fuller adjustment to the change in wage rate. This adjustment will take the form of substitution of other factors for this one, both directly in the production of each product, and indirectly in consumption as the increased price of the products of unionized labor leads consumers to resort to alternative means of satisfying their wants. This simple point is, at one and the same time, important in understanding how unions can have substantial power and how their power is sharply limited in the course of time.

The importance of the percentage of total cost accounted for by the factor leads one to predict that a union may be expected to be strongest and most potent when it is composed of a class of workers whose wages make up only a small part of the total cost of the product they produce—a condition satisfied, along with essentiality, by highly skilled workers. This is the reason why economic theorists have always been inclined to predict that craft unions would tend to be the most potent. This implication of the joint-demand analysis seems to have been confirmed by experience. While industrial unions have by no means been impotent, craft unions have in general been in a stronger economic position and have maintained it for longer periods.

Simple though they are, these implications of the joint-demand analysis have considerable value in interpreting experience, primarily because other economic changes frequently conceal from "casual" observation the action of the forces isolated in the theoretical analysis. This point can be exemplified by a brief examination of three major apparent exceptions to the generalization that industrial unions are likely to be less potent than craft unions. In each case, it will be found that other economic changes tended to make the strength of the unions appear greater than it actually was.

(1) The United Mine Workers' Union appeared highly successful from shortly before 1900 to about 1920. This period coincided with a long upward movement in general prices and wages, so at least part, and perhaps most, of the apparent success

of the union can be attributed to its receiving credit for wage increases that would have occurred anyway. Scanty evidence suggests that wages in soft coal may have risen somewhat more than wages in general during this period, so that all of the wage rise may not be attributable to general inflation. The difference may be evidence that the union had some effect on wage rates, or may reflect the operation of still other forces affecting the supply of and demand for labor in coal mining, such as changes in levels of education, in the composition of the stream of immigrants, etc. It would take a far more detailed examination of the evidence than we can afford here even to form an intelligent judgment about the relative importance of the various forces.

From 1920 to 1933, the general price level was stable or falling, coal was increasingly being replaced by oil, and the United Mine Workers' Union practically went to pieces. It was unable to prevent the underlying economic forces from working themselves out. Yet at least events of the earlier part of this period are a tribute to the short-run strength of the union: the union was clearly responsible for keeping coal wage rates from declining for some time in the face of the sharp drop in wages and prices generally after 1920. This illustrates the implication of the joint-demand analysis that the strategic position of unions will be stronger in the short than in the long run. It also illustrates a not atypical train of events. Attendant favorable circumstances enable a union to gain strength in the number and adhesion of its members by appearing to accomplish more than its basic economic power would permit; the attendant favorable circumstances without which the union might never have survived disappear, but the historical process is not completely reversible: the union for a time at least remains strong and capable of preventing the readjustment that would otherwise take place, though sooner or later it is likely to weaken and die if other favorable circumstances do not come along.

This train of events may be repeating itself in coal. Since 1933, prices and wages in general have again been rising fairly steadily, at a particularly rapid pace, of course, during and after the war, and the union has re-established itself. Once again, the union seems to be showing real strength less in the wage rises it has attained than in its prevention of a subsequent readjustment (see additional comments, pp. 226, 228).

(2) The garment workers' unions—the International Ladies Garment Workers' Union and the Amalgamated Clothing Workers—achieved their initial successes in the decade prior to 1920, reaching a peak along with the postwar inflation in 1920. Again, the unions may have made the wage rise somewhat greater than it would have been otherwise, but clearly a large and probably the major part of the wage rise for which the unions received credit would have come anyway. Though these unions declined in membership and importance during the 1920's and early 1930's, they fared better than the United Mine Workers' Union, in my view largely or wholly because of an attendant favorable circumstance. These unions were in an industry that had been largely supplied by immigrants from Eastern and Southern Europe. Union or no union, the stringent restrictions on immigration imposed after the First World War were bound to reduce the supply of workers and thus to strengthen their economic position. The next spurt in union strength came during the period of generally rising prices and wages following 1933. Thus these unions too have flourished only when underlying economic conditions were generally inflationary.

(3) The more recent large industrial unions—the auto and steel unions in particular—have been operating throughout their lives in a generally inflationary environment. The strength that this has permitted them to gain will be demonstrated in a somewhat paradoxical way: we shall argue later (pp. 217 ff.) that they were responsible for preventing the wages of their members from rising after the Second World War as much as they would have in the absence of the union. I doubt

that these unions had much effect on wages prior to 1945. The recent, much-publicized agreement between the United Automobile Workers and the General Motors Corporation seems to me almost a public announcement of union weakness.[4]

An interesting and instructive example of the tendency, suggested by joint-demand analysis, for the strategic position of unions to appear stronger in the short run than in the long run is provided by the medical profession. In economic essentials, the medical profession is analogous to a craft union. It consists of a highly skilled group of workers, closely organized, and in an especially strategic position to keep the supply of workers down through control over state licensure and, as a consequence, over admission to medical schools. True, the medical profession differs from the usual craft union in that the return to the worker (medical fees) accounts for a considerably larger fraction of the total cost of the final product. However, even this difference can easily be overstated; costs of hospitals, medications, and the like are by no means negligible. Moreover, this difference is typically supposed to be counterbalanced by inelasticity in the demand for medical care.

There is little doubt that the medical profession has exercised its powers on various occasions to limit entry to the profession fairly drastically: over a considerable period about one out of every three persons who are known to have tried to

---

[4] The agreement calls for a steady annual increase in the basic rate, plus cost-of-living adjustments. In considerable part, these changes are costless to the company, since, as experience in the automobile industry before unionization and in other industries amply documents, they are the kind of wage changes that come anyway, though they are perhaps larger in magnitude. They represent a clear case of a union seeking to gain credit for what would happen anyway. Assuring itself such credit in so public and dramatic a fashion may be extremely clever union tactics; the need for using such tactics is significant evidence of basic weakness. The length of the agreement is of major value to the company, which is assured thereby of uninterrupted control of its affairs. I doubt that a really strong union would have granted such terms.

enter American medical schools has been unable to gain admission, and it is clear that the number of persons seeking entry is considerably less than it would be if it were not for the known difficulty of entry; further, serious impediments have been placed in the path of potential entrants trained outside the country. Yet, restriction of entry has succeeded in raising average incomes in medicine only by something like 15 to 20 per cent.[5] Chiropractors, osteopaths, faith healers, and the like have turned out to be important substitutes, and the increase in their numbers has been one of the most important effects of the restriction of entry into medicine proper, an impressive example of the possibilities of substitution in the long run. The short-run effects of restriction are more noticeable than the means whereby the strength of the union is undermined in the long run, which, as noted below, is one of the chief factors that leads to an exaggeration of the effect of unions.

SUPPLY OF LABOR AND CONTROL OVER WAGE RATES

Another line along which orthodox economic analysis has some interesting implications is the role of so-called restrictive practices. It is clear that if a union can reduce the supply of persons available for jobs, it will thereby tend to raise the wage rate. Indeed, this will be the only way of raising the wage rate if the union cannot exercise any direct control over the wage rate itself. For example, in a field like medicine, there is no significant way of exercising direct control over fees charged, or over annual incomes of physicians. The only effective control is over the number of physicians. In consequence, medicine is a clear example of the kind of situation that is usually en-

[5] For evidence on the use of restrictive practices and on their effect on income see Milton Friedman and Simon Kuznets, *Income from Independent Professional Practice* (National Bureau of Economic Research, 1945), pp. 8-20, 118-137.

visaged in which the wage rate or its equivalent is raised by deliberate control over entry into the occupation.

This line of reasoning has led to the view that, in general, unions may be regarded as exercising control over the wage rate primarily by controlling the supply of workers and that, in consequence, the so-called restrictive practices—high union initiation fees, discriminatory provisions for entrance into unions, seniority rules, etc.—have the economic function of reducing the supply of entrants so as to raise wage rates. This is an erroneous conception of the function of these restrictive practices. They clearly cannot serve this function without a closed or preferential shop, which already implies control over employers derived from sources other than control over entrance into unions. To see the function of these practices and the associated closed shop, let us suppose that the wage rate can be fixed above its competitive level by direct means, for example, by legal enactment of a minimum wage rate. This will necessarily mean that fewer jobs will be available than otherwise and fewer jobs than persons seeking jobs. This excess supply of labor must be disposed of somehow—the jobs must be rationed among the seekers for jobs. And this is the important economic function the so-called restrictive practices play. They are a means of rationing the limited number of jobs among eager applicants. Since the opportunity to work at a wage rate above the competitive level has considerable economic value, it is understandable that the restrictive practices are important and the source of much dispute.

The question remains how the wage rate can be controlled directly by means other than legal enactment of a minimum wage rate. To do this, unions must be able to exercise control over employers—they must be able to prevent existing employers from undercutting the union wage rate, as well as the entry of new employers who would do so. They must somehow be able to force all employers to offer the union wage rate and no less. The devices whereby this is done are numerous and can hardly be fully enumerated here. However, one feature of the various devices whereby wage rates are directly enforced or entry into an occupation limited is essential for our purposes, namely, the extent to which they depend on political assistance. Perhaps the extreme example is again medicine, in which practice of the profession is restricted to those licensed by the state and licensure in turn is in general placed in the hands of the profession itself. State licensure applies in similar fashion to dentists, lawyers, plumbers, beauticians, barbers, morticians, and a host of other occupations too numerous to list. Wherever there is licensure, it is almost invariably in the hands of the existing members of the occupation, who almost as invariably seek to use it to limit entry. Of course, in many cases, these techniques are largely ineffective, either because it is not feasible to restrict drastically the number of licenses granted, or because it is possible to evade the licensure provisions. But they do exemplify how political power can be used to control entry directly. Only slightly removed from this kind of licensure provision and in many ways far more effective is local political support through building codes, health regulations, health ordinances, and the like, all of which serve numerous craft unions as a means of preventing nonunion workers from engaging in their fields through substitution or elimination of materials or techniques, and of preventing potential employers from undercutting the union wage rate. It is no accident that strong unions are found in railways, along with federal regulation. Again, union actions involving actual or potential physical violence or coercion, such as mass picketing and the like, could hardly take place were it not for the unspoken acquiescence of the authorities. Thus, whether directly in the form of specific laws giving power to union groups or indirectly in the form of the atmosphere and attitude of law enforcement, direct control over union wage rates is closely connected to the degree of political assistance unions can command.

Here again, there is a very close parallel between labor unions on the one hand and industrial monopolies on the other. In both cases, widespread monopolies are likely to be temporary and susceptible of dissolution unless they can call to their aid the political power of the state.

The Significance of Union-Produced Alterations in the Structure of Wage Rates

It would take a major research project—and, incidentally, one that is very much needed—to get a reasonably precise quantitative estimate of the extent to which unions have changed the structure of wage rates. Fortunately, no such precise estimate is required for our purposes. All that is needed is some indication of the order of magnitude of the effect, and this can be obtained fairly readily.

Total union membership is currently about 16 million, or something over one-quarter of the labor force. On the basis of our preceding analysis, however, it seems likely that many if not most members are in unions that have had only a negligible effect on wage rates. In the long view, it seems likely that unions have made wage rates significantly different from what they otherwise would have been, primarily in construction, railroads, printing trades, and in general the areas in which old-line craft unions are strong. Total membership in craft unions is probably not over 6 million, and by no means all these can be supposed to be in unions that have affected wage rates significantly. To this needs to be added persons in organizations like the American Medical Association that are the economic equivalents of unions though not counted formally as such, and members of those industrial unions that have had a significant effect on wage rates. Thus probably not over 10 per cent and certainly not over 20 per cent of the labor force can be supposed to have had their wages significantly affected by the existence of unions.[6]

[6] It is often asserted that nonunion members have had their wages raised because of the "pattern" set by the unions. This may have some validity for workers highly competitive with union workers, but in the

It is very much more difficult to say how much unions have affected wage rates. If the experience in medicine can be taken as representative, even quite strong unions have not in the long run raised relative wage rates by more than about 15 or 20 per cent above the levels that would have prevailed without unions; and this would certainly seem like a high estimate of the average effect.

Roughly, then, we might assess the order of magnitude of unions' effect on the structure of wages by saying that perhaps 10 per cent of the labor force has had its wages raised by some 15 per cent, implying that the remainder of the labor force has had its wage rates reduced by some 1 to 4 per cent, the exact amount depending on the relative wages of the two groups. Now this is by no means an unimportant effect; the danger of underrating it should be avoided as much as the danger of exaggerating it. Yet I suspect it will strike most readers as small, relative to their implicit expectations. Perhaps most readers, unpersuaded by what precedes, will regard it as a gross understatement, reflecting simply my own biases and inability to read plain fact. This may be correct, but I urge the reader to withhold final judgment until he has read the sections that follow, which seek to explain why supposedly plain fact may be exceedingly misleading.

Some indirect evidence on whether the magnitude of the unions' effect is vastly different from what I have supposed is

---

main, the assertions are supported by neither economic analysis nor empirical evidence. The observed general similarity of many wage movements in union and nonunion areas is better interpreted as the result of common influences from the side of demand. The presence of unions in some areas merely means that wage changes that would have taken place anyway are made through the medium of the unions. In general, one would expect that any rise in the wage rates of certain classes of workers secured by unions would tend to lower wage rates of other workers because of the increased competition of workers for jobs. But this should not be added to the effects considered in the text, which is concerned with changes in relative wage rates; it is simply the other side of the coin.

provided by a comparison of the behavior of prices and wages during the two important price revolutions in this country so far this century—those accompanying the two world wars. Union membership reached a maximum of something like one-eighth of the working population after the First World War (in 1920), and something over a quarter after the Second World War. In my view, most of this latter increase, and perhaps also of the First World War membership, was in largely ineffective unions, so, if I am right, the change in the apparent importance of unions should have had little effect on the relative behavior of wages and prices. On the other hand, if I am wrong, this change should have had a substantial effect, particularly in manufacturing, where union membership is relatively concentrated.

I have assembled a few relevant figures in Table 1, which also includes a few figures for yet another case: the Civil War, when unions were presumably even less important. The figures in the table are all ratios of the relevant series for a postwar year to the corresponding series for the year in which the war began (not the year in which we first participated), for the two world wars, and the year preceding the war, for the Civil War. So far as the data permit, the terminal year is the year in which wholesale prices reached their peak.

The rise in prices, as measured by the indexes used in Table 1, was strikingly similar in the three wars. Prices appear to have risen slightly more in the First World War than in either of the other wars; but this may simply reflect the use of annual averages or differences in the adequacy or coverage of the index numbers, all of which necessarily have a fairly large margin of error.[7]

[7] For the Civil War, Mitchell gives a quarterly index number of wholesale prices which reaches a peak of 2.16 times the 1860 average in January, 1865. For the First World War, the Bureau of Labor Standards' (BLS) monthly wholesale price index number reaches a peak of 2.46 times the 1914 average in May, 1920; and for the Second World War, a

TABLE 1. *Selected Price and Wage Rate Changes in the Civil War, First World War, and Second World War*

RATIO FOR INDICATED YEARS

Series	Civil War 1865/1860	First World War 1920/1914	First World War 1919/1914	Second World War 1948/1939
(1)	(2)	(3)	(4)	(5)

I. PRICE INDEX NUMBERS

A. Wholesale Prices

Series	(2)	(3)	(4)	(5)
1. BLS	2.17	2.27	2.04	2.14
2. Mitchell	1.85			

B. Cost of Living

Series	(2)	(3)	(4)	(5)
3. BLS		2.00	1.72	1.72
4. Mitchell	1.68			

II. WAGES

A. Manufacturing

Series	(2)	(3)	(4)	(5)
5. Mitchell (wages per day)	1.50			
6. Douglas (hourly earnings)		2.31		
7. BLS (hourly earnings, production workers)			2.14	2.13

B. Unskilled Labor

Series	(2)	(3)	(4)	(5)
8. Douglas (hourly rates)		2.29		
9. Employed in road-building (hourly rates)				2.43
10. Farm wage rates, composite index number		2.40		3.51

C. Building Trades

Series	(2)	(3)	(4)	(5)
11. Aldrich (wages per day)	1.61			
12. BLS (union hourly wage rates)		1.90		1.64
13. BLS, private building projects (hourly earnings)				2.01

D. Bituminous Coal

Series	(2)	(3)	(4)	(5)
14. As reported by BLS			2.11	2.14
15. Corrected for portal-to-portal and health and welfare payments				2.62

E. Printing

Series	(2)	(3)	(4)	(5)
16. Union hourly wage rates		1.63		1.70

The data on wages show somewhat less similarity, particularly between the Civil War and the two world wars. However, it is doubtful that the much smaller rise in wages shown for the

---

peak of 2.20 times the 1939 average in August, 1948. These figures suggest that annual averages understate the full extent of the price rise most for the Civil War and least for the Second World War. The fact that the peaks are successively farther removed from the end, or virtual end, of active fighting is, I feel sure, not an accident.

Parenthetically, there are few studies that seem more promising than a detailed examination of comparative price behavior in these three wars.

SOURCES FOR TABLE I:

LINE 1, cols. (2), (3), (4). U. S. Department of Commerce, *Historical Statistics of the United States,* 1789-1945, Series L-15; col. (5), *ibid.,* and U. S. Department of Commerce, *Statistical Abstract of the United States,* 1949, p. 1029, Series L-15.

LINE 2, col. (2). Wesley C. Mitchell, *Gold, Prices, and Wages under the Greenback Standard* (Berkeley: The University Press, 1908), p. 279.

LINE 3, cols. (3), (4). *Historical Statistics,* Series L-41; col. (5), *ibid.,* and *Statistical Abstract,* 1949, p. 1029.

LINE 4, col. (2); LINE 5, col. (2). Mitchell, *op. cit.,* p. 279.

LINE 6, col. (3). *Historical Statistics,* Series D-124.

LINE 7, col. (4). *Ibid.,* Series D-117; col. (5), *Monthly Labor Review,* May, 1950, p. 573.

LINE 8, col. (3). *Historical Statistics,* Series D-131.

LINE 9, col. (5). *Statistical Abstract,* 1949, p. 218. Series attributed to Federal Works Agency, Public Roads Administration, and described as "average rates per hour for unskilled labor employed in road-building on Federal-Aid Projects"; ratio given above based on figures for United States.

LINE 10, col. (3). *Historical Statistics,* Series D-176; col. (5), *ibid.,* and *Statistical Abstract,* 1949, p. 1001, Series D-176. Series compiled by Bureau of Agricultural Economics.

LINE 11, col. (2). *Historical Statistics,* Series 110, taken from Aldrich report.

LINE 12, col. (3). *Ibid.,* Series D-152; col. (5), *ibid.,* and *Statistical Abstract,* 1949, p. 1000, Series D-152.   ·

LINE 13, col. (5). *Statistical Abstract,* 1949, p. 220.

LINE 14, col. (4). *Historical Statistics,* Series D-147; col. (5), *ibid.,* and *Statistical Abstract,* 1949, p. 1000, Series D-147.

LINE 15, col. (5). Unpublished corrections by Albert Rees.

LINE 16, col. (3). *Historical Statistics,* Series D-158; col. (5), *ibid.,* and *Statistical Abstract,* 1949, p. 1001, Series D-158.

Civil War can be interpreted as a consequence of the lesser importance of unions. The wage data for the Civil War period are extremely unsatisfactory. They were collected some thirty years afterward from records of firms still in existence. The coverage is inadequate and probably biased, and examination of the individual records raises serious questions about their reliability.[8] On the whole, I would expect them to understate the magnitude of the rise in wages from 1860 to 1865.[9]

Further, if the lesser importance of unions explained the apparently smaller rise in wages for the Civil War than for the other wars, one would expect to find a similar discrepancy between the two world wars. Table 1 shows none. The statistically most satisfactory comparison is perhaps that based on the BLS series for hourly earnings of production workers in manufacturing, a comparable and broad series available for both wars. Unfortunately, this series is available only for 1919, not for 1920, which accounts for the inclusion of column (4) in Table 1. The ratios of prices in columns (4) and (5) are almost identical, and so are the ratios of hourly earnings of production workers in manufacturing. The remaining comparisons are mixed, but can hardly be interpreted as reflecting the effect of a substantial difference in unionization. The largest discrepancy, the much larger rise in farm wage rates in the Second World War, is certainly better explained by the correspondingly larger rise in the prices of farm products than by differences in unionization either in agriculture itself or in the rest of the economy.[10]

[8] See the collection of wage series in W. C. Mitchell, *Gold, Prices, and Wages under the Greenback Standard*, Table 5, pp. 437-512.

[9] According to Mitchell's figures (*ibid.*, p. 279) wages continued to rise after 1865, reaching a peak ratio of 1.79 in 1871. Thus the final peak bears about the same relation to the rise in wholesale prices and cost of living shown by Mitchell's index numbers as the changes in wages shown in Table 1 for the other wars bear to the rise in prices shown by the BLS index numbers. However, these changes probably understate the full rise in wages for the Second World War as well.

[10] The ratio for farm wage rates in Table 1 for the Second World War

The corrected figure for bituminous coal suggests a somewhat greater rise in the Second than in the First World War and it may be that this difference is attributable to the greater strength of the union. Unfortunately, the figures are neither entirely comparable statistically nor highly accurate, so that we cannot be sure what the actual difference in the wage rise is, let alone whether factors other than unionism may not have been responsible for it.

To avoid misunderstanding, let me emphasize that I do not regard Table 1 as "proving" that unions have no influence on wage rates or on the relative behavior of wages and prices. If the influence of unions is of the order of magnitude that I have suggested, it would take a far more detailed and thorough analysis than is embodied in Table 1 to detect it. The purpose of Table 1 is rather to provide a crude test of the general order of magnitude of the effect I have attributed to unions. If unions have a vastly greater effect on wage rates than I have estimated, this effect should show up even in so crude an analysis as is embodied in Table 1. The fact that it does not by no means shows me to be right; it does give reason for somewhat greater confidence in the suggested order of magnitude of effect.

Why the Effect of Unions on the Structure of Wages Tends to Be Exaggerated

If one accepts the crude kind of evidence presented in the preceding section, one is inclined to ask why casual observation leads most observers—even trained ones—to exaggerate the extent to which unions affect the structure of wages. Alternatively, one may seek to determine whether the effect of unions

---

is 1.46 times the ratio for the First World War. The corresponding ratio for the Second World War, computed from the index of prices received by farmers, is 1.44 times the ratio for the First World War (*Historical Statistics*, Series E-95; *Statistical Abstract for 1949*, p. 1003, Series E-95).

is exaggerated by asking whether there are any reasons why observers should, on balance, exaggerate them. The comments that follow will serve either purpose.

In a dynamic world, economic forces are always arising that tend to change relative wage rates. Shifts in demand for final products, changes in techniques, discovery of new resources, and so on, all produce changes in the demand for and supply of labor of various grades, and hence changes in wage rates. In the absence of unions, these forces will operate more or less directly on wage rates. Given unions, the same forces will be present but they will operate indirectly on wage rates through the mediation of the union. For example, a change in demand that would have led to an increased wage rate in the absence of the union is likely to do so in the presence of the union only through the intervention of the union. Strikes may be required to produce wage rises that would have occurred in the absence of the union. This change in the process whereby the underlying forces work themselves out leads to unions being regarded as causes of changes rather than as intermediaries. In many cases, so to speak, unions are simply thermometers registering the heat rather than furnaces producing the heat. This is particularly obvious during periods of inflationary pressure. It clearly must be significant at other times as well, and a number of examples illustrating this point have already been given.

A second closely related reason for the exaggeration of the significance of unions is that, like monopolies in general, unions are newsworthy. The fact that economic forces work through unions means that these forces work through a limited number of identifiable persons and thereby become capable of generating "personal" news. Moreover, since union-management dealings can only take place at discrete intervals of time and with respect to matters of some moment, forces that would work themselves out slowly, gradually, and unnoticeably accumulate until they come to a head. They must then be dealt with at one point in time and at a stage when the consequences are dramatic and obvious. On the other hand, the forces that bring about wage changes in nonunionized areas operate subtly, impersonally, and continuously, and so tend to go unnoticed.

In the third place, whereas union actions are newsworthy and call attention to themselves, the indirect effects of union actions are not. These indirect effects to some extent reflect the harm unions do in altering the allocation of resources, and to this extent lead to underestimation of the significance of unions. But more important, I believe, are the indirect effects whereby the apparent influence and importance of unions are undermined and the forces which unions bottle up find expression—whereby, that is, the demand for the services of union members is rendered highly elastic. These indirect effects work through devious and subterranean channels and attract little notice. They consist of the somewhat more rapid expansion of an industry here and an industry there, gradual changes in the kinds of workers hired, gradual changes in the consumption patterns of millions of people, the devotion of increased attention to one kind of research rather than another, and so on and on in endless detail. The strike of union typographers in Chicago, for example, attracted great attention, as did the effects of the union in preceding years on typographical wages. The slow but steady development of substitute processes of reproduction, which was undoubtedly stimulated in considerable measure by the existence of the union, attracted little or no attention. Yet this is one of the more dramatic and obvious indirect effects. Moreover, these indirect effects tend to work themselves out slowly, in the long run, and so are difficult to connect with the forces responsible for them.

These brief remarks about the factors tending to exaggerated estimates of the role of unions apply equally to industrial monopolies and serve to explain why the role of industrial monopolies tends likewise to be exaggerated. One striking illustration of both tendencies is that individuals asked to list the most important industries in the United States will practically never list domestic service. Yet the income produced through the hiring of domestic servants is year in and year out considerably larger than that produced in either the automobile industry or coal mining, and the number of employees is much greater than in the two industries combined.[11] The explanation is obvious in light of the comments above. The automobile industry calls attention to itself by the size and importance of its separate firms, by the amount of advertising it engages in, and, in the last few years, by the disputes that arise between the firms and their organized employees. The millions of domestic servants working for their separate individual employers call little or no public attention to themselves.

The bias introduced into our judgment of the effects of unions by this difference in the capacity of unionized and nonunionized sectors to attract attention is dramatized by a war and postwar increase in the compensation of domestic servants of roughly the same order of magnitude as the increase in the compensation of coal miners and much greater than the increase in the compensation of auto workers. Average annual earnings per full-time employee were 2.72 times as large in 1948 as in 1939 for domestic servants; 2.83 for soft-coal workers; and 1.98 for auto workers.[12] Yet, aside from individual grumbling, the rise in the price of domestic service has attracted little attention and has certainly

[11] See National Income Supplement, *Survey of Current Business*, July, 1947, Tables 13, 24, and 25.

[12] National Income Supplement, *Survey of Current Business*, July, 1947, Table 26; and *ibid.*, July, 1949, p. 21. The figures used for domestic servants are for the industry designated, "Services, Private households"; for soft-coal workers, for the industry designated, "Mining, Bituminous and other soft coal"; for auto workers, for the industry designated, "Manufacturing, Automobile and automobile equipment." The ratios for coal miners are not comparable with those in Table 1, because based on average annual earnings, instead of hourly earnings, of a somewhat different group of workers, and because the basic figures come from different sources. The change in the figures used as the basis of the ratios is required in order to have figures comparable to those for domestic servants.

not been attributed to the influence of unions. The comparable or smaller rises in the wage rates of coal miners and auto workers have attracted far more attention and have commonly been attributed almost entirely to union activity.

The abnormally large rise in the wages of domestic servants and coal miners, like the even larger rise in the wages of farm laborers,[13] is, in my view, attributable to essentially the same factors. All three occupations are relatively unattractive; individuals leave them gladly when alternative employment opportunities are available—and such opportunities were relatively plentiful during the period in question, so that migration from the respective industries was extremely easy. Substantial increases in wages were therefore required in all three industries to hold even as many workers as were in fact kept attached to them. It therefore seems very likely that the increase in the wages of coal miners would have been of much the same order of magnitude in the absence of the union, which implies that this is also true of the increase in the price of coal. Further support for this view is provided by First World War experience, when nonunionized coal miners experienced a larger percentage increase in wage rates than unionized coal miners.[14] Yet given the existence of a strong union, the Second World War wage increases had to take place through the medium of the union and could be obtained only through strikes, and so the general impression arose that the coal miners' union has been extremely effective in raising wage rates and has succeeded in pushing wage rates well above the level that would otherwise have prevailed.

[13] The ratio for farm labor comparable to those just cited for the other groups is 3.45. This is based on the sources listed in the preceding footnote for the industry designated, "Agriculture, forestry, and fisheries, Farms."

[14] Some of these statements are based on as yet unpublished results of research by Albert Rees to be incorporated in his dissertation, *The Effect of Collective Bargaining on Wage and Price Levels in the Basic Steel and Bituminous Coal Industries, 1945-48.*

I do not wish to argue that the United Mine Workers' Union had no effect on the war and postwar rise in wages. I do say that its effect was of the second order of importance; perhaps it was responsible for something like 10 to 30 percentage points of the 183 per cent increase in annual earnings from 1939 to 1948. Its more significant effect will probably be in delaying or preventing a decline that underlying economic conditions may tend to bring about, and this may already be in process.

Labor Unions and Economic Stability

It is frequently argued that strong unions or, for that matter, strongly organized producer groups of any kind are likely to make full employment incompatible with price stability, and hence pose a serious dilemma for economic stabilization policy. This dilemma has been suggested by numerous writers, perhaps most persuasively by the late Charles Hardy. Our experience during the postwar inflation from 1945 to 1949 is frequently cited as evidence of the existence and significance of the dilemma. In my view, this experience cannot be so interpreted. If anything, it seems to me evidence that this particular dilemma is unlikely to be serious under the circumstances likely to arise in the near future.

Unions have two rather different effects on wage determination: (1) They make for rigidity and for a lag in adjustment. (2) They make for steady upward pressure on the wage rate. The reasons why unions make for rigidity are fairly obvious. Union contracts must be negotiated at discrete intervals and tend to be fixed during the period between negotiations, so that they convert gradual movements into stepwise movements. In addition, the strong obstacles that unions interpose to downward adjustments in wage rates make employers hesitant to grant increases in response to what they may regard as short-term improvements in their position, since they fear that they will be permanently saddled with the higher wage rate. On the other hand, unions at all times doubtless seek to raise wage rates in order to keep their members satisfied and to some extent can succeed in doing so when wage rates would not rise in the absence of unions.

The reason for distinguishing these two different effects of unions is that they work in opposite directions during periods of cyclical expansion—the rigidity effect toward keeping wages from rising, the upward pressure toward forcing them up. If there is considerable pressure toward expansion from other sources, the rigidity effect is, in my view, likely to be the more significant, and the existence of unions is therefore likely to interpose an obstacle to as rapid or as large an increase in wage rates as would otherwise occur.

On the other hand, in a period when wages and prices would tend to be relatively stable in the absence of unions, the rigidity effect would be relatively unimportant and the upward-pressing effect significant. This is the case envisaged by those who pose the dilemma. Under these circumstances, they argue, rises in wage rates achieved by unions would tend to create unemployment in the union areas. Some of this unemployment might be absorbed in areas where wages were flexible, but probably not all. The result would be steadily growing unemployment that could be eliminated only by expansionary measures tending to raise prices and wages, that is, tending to promote inflation. Stable prices could be maintained only by accepting unemployment. There is no doubt that this chain of events is a real possibility. The question is how serious it would be if it did arise and how likely it is to arise. I am inclined to doubt that it would be extremely serious with the present extent of unionization, primarily for the reasons discussed above, which lead me to believe that the unemployment in the union area would be largely offset elsewhere and that a moderate amount of unemployment would constitute a pretty effective check to continued pressure for wage rises.[15] I regard the dilemma as unlikely to arise because it seems to me that the rigidity effect is likely to be more significant than the upward-pressing effect under the circumstances that stabilization policy is likely to have to face in the foreseeable future.

In my view, the most important forces responsible for the inflation of 1945 to 1949 operated from the side of aggregate money demand. Strong inflationary pressure was produced by the release of the large volume of liquid resources that had been bottled up during the war, the easy money market maintained by the monetary authorities to keep interest rates low, and the pent-up demand for durable goods. These factors led to inflationary increases in aggregate money demand that tended to pull prices up. Under these circumstances, the rigidity introduced by union determination of wages was much more important than union upward-pressingness. It seems clear, for example, that in two crucial areas—automobiles and steel—the existence of unions had the effect of making both wages and nominal list prices of products lower than they would otherwise have been. Unions or no unions, producers might not have allowed list prices to rise to the full extent justified by the immediate inflationary demand because of fear of unfavorable public opinion and perhaps of antitrust prosecution. But these factors were enormously strengthened by the practical certainty that public opinion and pressure would force price rises to be matched by wage rises and that the wage rises would prove permanent. Thus the administered prices were kept lower than they otherwise would have been, leading to lower employment of labor and a lower wage rate. In the absence of the union,

[15] My views about this have changed considerably in the last few years. See "A Fiscal and Monetary Framework for Economic Stability," *Amer. Econ. Rev.*, June, 1948, pp. 253-254, in which I attached considerable importance to the dilemma, and "A Rejoinder to Neff," *Amer. Econ. Rev.*, September, 1949, pp. 951-952, in which I indicated some change in views.

list prices would have been higher, firms would have sought to produce more to meet the temporary bulge in demand, and they would have been willing to see wage rates go up because of the expectation that wage rates could subsequently come down again. On this interpretation, the main effect, during the immediate postwar period, of the existence of unions in automobiles and steel was to transfer income from the workers to distributors, who were the chief beneficiaries of the artificially low list prices of automobiles and steel.[16] More generally, there is no evidence that, in the economy as a whole, union wage rates rose more during this period than nonunion wage rates. Indeed, if anything, they apparently rose less.

The precise circumstances of 1945-1949 will not, of course, prevail in the future. But one essential feature of this period is likely to characterize much of the foreseeable future: namely, sizable inflationary pressure from the side of aggregate money demand. The general fear of inflation that was present until the Great Depression, and that repeatedly led to a willingness to countenance deflation to avoid inflation, has now been replaced by an opposite and equally strong or stronger fear of deflation. No one really fears inflation any more—except insofar as it is regarded as likely to produce deflation. Any temporary decline

[16] A similar view has recently been expressed by Walter Morton, "Trade Unionism, Full Employment, and Inflation," *Amer. Econ. Rev.*, March, 1950, pp. 13-39, and is strongly supported by evidence gathered by Albert Rees in the study of the steel and coal postwar wage movements referred to earlier (p. 225).

Note that the lower nominal list prices meant higher free market prices since they meant a smaller supply.

Another bit of indirect evidence is the early introduction of new models. Offhand, it would seem more reasonable for the major companies to have postponed model changes so long as they could sell their old models in volume and without difficulty, and to have held the model changes in reserve to use in stimulating demand when that became necessary. Under the circumstances described in the text, however, model changes can be rationalized as a means of raising actual prices without seeming to do so and therefore without forcing corresponding wage changes.

in demand and employment, whether fated to be small or large, brief or prolonged, is almost certain to evoke strong demands promptly for rapid countering action. These demands will lead not only to reversible steps, such as easy money tactics by monetary authorities, but also to irreversible steps such as the adoption of public programs involving expenditures for a long period ahead. The lesson that a sufficient increase in public deficit expenditures will produce an increase in economic activity has been learned; the associated lesson that it is likely to be overdone and to result in inflation has not yet been learned.

The development of inflationary pressure is particularly likely because the fear of deflation is combined with such a widespread belief in and drive for a "welfare" state that there exists at all times a wide range of public projects that important groups in the community desire the government to undertake.[17] The easiest time to enact these programs will be in a period of recession as a means of offsetting and counterbalancing the downward movement. But once enacted, they are likely to prove permanent and to add inflationary pressure during the next upswing. On this view, long-run inflation will in fact be produced by the reactions to the temporary recessions that punctuate it. Such a long-run inflation will mean, at least during its earlier stages, a continuation of a situation in which the rigidity effect of unions will be more important than their upward-pressing effect. Furthermore, reversal of forces making for inflation would probably mean a general change in the attitude of the public that would produce an environment in which unions would not be so strong as they currently are, or may grow to be, and in which there would again be no real threat to the maintenance of stability in the level of income.

If this analysis is right, it means that we face a dilemma, but one that is, at least for the near future, almost precisely the

[17] For obvious reasons, I am abstracting from the inflationary pressure produced by abnormal military expenditures occasioned by war or the threat of war.

reverse of that which has been most stressed. The difficulty is not so much that strong unions will produce inflation as that inflation will produce strong unions. Inflation induced by the forces described above will mean rising money-wage rates throughout the economy. Wherever unions exist or are created, the rises in wage rates, as earlier noted, will take place through the medium of the unions, and the unions will receive credit for the wage rises. This will tend to strengthen the hold of the unions on the workers and greatly to increase their political power. Moreover, while such movements may ultimately be reversible, it is clear that if any significant fraction of the working population is involved, as it is very likely to be, the process involves serious frictional effects and dangers to political stability and security. And the movement may not be reversible if the addition of the political power of the strengthened unions to the other forces making for increased intervention by the state in the detailed conduct of economic affairs leads, albeit unintentionally, to a collectivist form of society.

If the process just sketched should occur it would tend to change the balance of forces and perhaps ultimately to justify the fear that strong unions will produce inflation. For as the inflation proceeded, the rigidity effects of unions would tend to become weaker relative to their upward-pressing effects, for two reasons. In the first place, employers would come to expect continued inflation, and so attach less importance to the difficulty of subsequently lowering wages once raised. In the second place, the increased economic strength of the unions produced by the inflation would mean greater power to force wage increases, i.e., greater upward pressure; it would not have much significance for the rigidity effect.

Conclusions for Policy

The tendency to exaggerate the effect of unions on the structure of wage rates, and similarly of industrial monopolies on the structure of product prices, has a number of possible implications for policy that to some extent are contradictory. The exaggerated importance attached to unions may make it appear that they are dominant long before they really are; or that their ultimate dominance is so inevitable that it is hopeless to seek to curb their further development. Evidence that such attitudes can readily develop is provided by the widespread, though in my view mistaken, feeling that industrial monopoly is already so important, and further extension of monopoly so inevitable, that it is hopeless to seek to reverse the alleged trend. This view about industrial monopoly not only is evidence that exaggeration of the economic importance of unions may lead to a similar view about unions, it also directly supports the development of a feeling that the further growth of unions is inevitable since unions are widely believed—whether rightly or wrongly is irrelevant for the present issue—a consequence of, or a desirable offset to, industrial monopoly.

A second possible effect, and in my view a far more salutary one, is that the exaggeration of the importance of labor unions will give rise to movements to limit their power and importance long before they have been able to achieve enough importance to exercise any significant or irreversible influence on the allocation of resources.

A third possible effect, closely linked with the first, is that overestimation of the urgency of the union problem will lead to unnecessary public policies of control and regulation that will push the economy in the direction of centralization of power. An example is the repeated proposal—made sometimes by the right, sometimes by the left—for compulsory arbitration of labor disputes.

The tendency of inflation to strengthen the political and economic importance of unions has obvious implications for policy. It adds yet another potent reason for seeking to counter the widespread inflationary bias that has been developing in our institutions and our attitudes. It increases the urgency of developing and putting into effect stabilization policies that are directed equally at the twin evils of inflation and deflation. At the same time, it calls for no action specifically directed at unions as such.

Finally, if we can curb inflation, the preceding analysis suggests rather optimistic conclusions about the possibility of developing effective policies with respect to labor unions as such. It suggests that these monopolies are likely to be weaker and less widely pervasive than one might assume offhand; that there are important economic forces working subtly and indirectly to limit their power; and that their effectiveness hinges in considerable measure on the degree of political support and assistance that they can command. It follows that it may be possible to keep in check the power of unions to affect the prices of either products or factors without any very drastic measures of a kind that are likely to be inconsistent with our general belief in personal freedom to organize. If, indeed, the current power of unions is in no small measure based upon positive acts of assistance by political authorities, the mere removal of these acts of assistance without the addition of any punitive or repressive measures might prevent any further extension of the influence of unions on the allocation of resources, and perhaps start a slow trend in the opposite direction. Once again the analogy with industrial monopolies is significant. In both cases, we are inclined to exaggerate the importance of monopoly, and to overstate its strength in the absence of direct political encouragement. In both cases, the establishment of a general atmosphere of belief in and respect for competitive forces and elimination of special privileges for special groups would go a long way toward preventing any undesirable economic growth of monopoly power.

It therefore seems to me highly desirable for policy purposes to emphasize the similarity and identity of enterprise and labor monopoly, and the importance of withholding direct political support from either. Thus, I would argue that it is highly important to have labor monopoly covered by the Sherman Antitrust Act, less because I have a clear conception of specific positive acts that could thereby be taken to reduce the power of unions than because such action emphasizes the identity of industrial monopolies and labor unions and the need for like treatment of them.

These optimistic conclusions about the possibility of keeping the power of unions in check do not imply any equally optimistic predictions that we shall do so. The economic power of unions, though exaggerated, is nonetheless already significant and important, and so is their political power. Inflation, however regrettable, seems likely, and with it a substantial further strengthening of the political and economic power of unions. For decades there has been an intellectual flight from the market toward direct state intervention in economic affairs—entirely aside from the influence of the growth of unions in this direction. There are, I believe, signs that this intellectual movement has reached its apex and has been reversed; but this may be no more than wishful thinking, or itself a temporary concomitant of postwar prosperity. In any event, it is as yet no more than a slight break in the clouds.

CHAPTER XI

Selections from the Discussion
of Friedman's Paper

KNIGHT. At whose cost do the unions get their higher wages? How do you know how many have got their wage increases by union action? It may be 10 per cent. But even so it may fall on people a lot poorer than they are on the average, and it probably does.

FRIEDMAN. I am not arguing that this is a good thing.

SAMUELSON. He says it doesn't exist.

KNIGHT. But he gives the figures 10 to 20 per cent in the paper.

FRIEDMAN. I say that perhaps 10 to 20 per cent of laborers have had their incomes raised, but of course their whole income can't be attributed to union action. Suppose their income is raised by 15 to 30 per cent on the average.

BOULDING. That figure is grossly exaggerated.

WRIGHT. How many people had their opportunities destroyed entirely? There is a great negative effect that you don't see.

FRIEDMAN. That can only be true if unions affected wages substantially. Suppose in fact that the elasticity of demand for labor of a certain type is practically infinite. That means that if wages rise a little, a lot of people will lose their work opportunities here, but they will have alternative opportunities that are not much inferior.

SAMUELSON. That is a technical question that bothers me. I ask it as a question. If demands are elastic, the unions have less incentive for wage raises. But suppose they do raise wages, not a lot—it seems to me it follows from the theory of consumers' surplus, as Edgeworth said, there is more "deadweight" harm done when demand is elastic than when demand is inelastic. Edgeworth's perfect inelasticity case you can see. How do we reconcile it with the perfect elasticity case?

FRIEDMAN. In the perfect inelasticity case, what you have is a transfer from one person to another, and that is the reason why it was said there was no dead-weight harm.

SAMUELSON. In other words, Edgeworth's proposition: The more inelastic the demand, such price increases as you do get, do rather less harm. Yet I have difficulty with that reasoning in the case of indifference—of complete infinite elasticity. It seems to me, no harm again.

FRIEDMAN. Suppose that you had perfect elasticity of demand because of another factor completely on the margin. There isn't any harm.

SAMUELSON. Is it the in-between case which has the most harm?

FRIEDMAN. There is a real problem there. I don't know. It is clear that at the two extremes there isn't any harm, dead-weight harm.[1]

---

[1] *Comment by Friedman:* Edgeworth's statement [F. Y. Edgeworth, *Papers on Political Economy*, I (Macmillan, 1925), 168-170] had to do with the effect on consumers' surplus of a given tax on monopoly. His conclusion was that the loss in consumers' surplus is likely to be greater, the greater the elasticity. His discussion is in terms of total loss, not deadweight loss. More important, Edgeworth's conclusion does not seem correct even for total loss—he appears to have judged the effect of a change in elasticity while implicitly keeping constant a magnitude that would have to change when the elasticity changed (namely, the difference between monopoly price and marginal cost). The correct answer for the total loss in the case Edgeworth considers seems to be that the loss decreases as the elasticity increases (in absolute value) if the marginal cost curve slopes positively, and increases as the elasticity increases if the marginal cost curve slopes negatively.

For dead-weight loss, in Edgeworth's case of a monopoly and a tax

WRIGHT. These arguments strike me as too static. What I am concerned with is the marginal efficiency of capital. If you raise wages, you may discourage investment very considerably so that you destroy a great many more investment opportunities. I don't think you can argue in terms of a given elasticity. You have to consider the effect on expectations.

FRIEDMAN. Once again, these effects depend on how much wages in fact rise.

WRIGHT. Also a great negative effect on confidence. It may depend on how violent the strike may be. To go back to the

---

of a fixed amount per unit of product, the correct conclusion seems to be that the loss is zero for infinite elasticity of demand, increases as elasticity initially declines (in absolute value), reaches a maximum for an intermediate elasticity, and then declines as elasticity declines further. Professor Samuelson, in correspondence between us on this point, wrote that, more generally, his impression is that "to put things roughly, the dead-weight-loss-per-equivalent-dollars-worth-of-tax is proportional to the 'net-elasticity' derived from both demand and supply curve," which implies that, given the supply schedule, the dead-weight loss for a *given* tax revenue is greater, the greater the elasticity of demand.

For the present problem of the relation between the damage unions do and the elasticity of demand for their services, however, neither Edgeworth's monopoly model nor the model just discussed, which keeps total tax revenue constant, seems the relevant one. Presumably we want to determine the effect of the elasticity of demand per unit of "power" (power over supply of laborers or power over employers) possessed by the union— where power must be measured independently of the elasticity. It hardly seems sensible to interpret equal power as the ability to extract equal total sums. Neither does it seem sensible to interpret equal power as the ability to extract equal wage rises with different elasticities of demand. Surely the more elastic the demand for services, the more "power" will be required to extract the same wage rise. A more satisfactory definition of equal power is the ability to force a given reduction in employment (though I am not sure even this definition is entirely satisfactory). In this case, the dead-weight loss in consumers' surplus is less, the greater the elasticity of demand—the conclusion implicit in the paragraphs in my paper to which the discussion refers.

Comment by Samuelson: Professor Friedman and I cleared up this point by correspondence after the conference.

question you made before, in the attempts to force a higher wage rate, you can do so much damage, scare everybody to death—

KNIGHT. And the effects on morale. I think we are letting something go by. A lot of industrial leaders who are entrepreneurs in the old sense—men who want to do their job—are just exasperated because they are not allowed to do it, because they have to put in all their time and energy placating labor, even though the public does not hear about it or see any visible effect of it.

SAMUELSON. The countering forces do come into play, but they only do it through the dead-loss harm having been done.

HABERLER. You could also argue that unions are important but that they could be scaled down in their power by mild reforms only, as you suggest later on.

FRIEDMAN. If they were really important, then I doubt that mild measures could be highly effective.

SAMUELSON. If they have no effect, there is no reason for change to regulate unions or anything else.

FRIEDMAN. There is still reason to do so because of their political importance, and the extent to which their receiving credit for changes that would have occurred anyway builds up their power and enables them at a later date to have a greater effect.

WRIGHT. It seems to me your paper, though you did not mean it that way, read rather like an appeasement paper. You say they are not important now and therefore we don't have to worry too much about them. That is not what you mean to say, but that is what it reads like.

FRIEDMAN. That is not the impression I wanted to give. Unions, I argue, have not had an extremely important effect, to date, on the structure of wage rates. It does not follow that they raise no social problems now or in the future.

HABERLER. And if it were true that unions could not affect wage levels significantly, say, in the coal field, then I would say let us abolish them. I would draw exactly the opposite conclusion from what you say is the logical one because certainly unions are destructive.

BOULDING. The economic aspects of unions are not the important ones.

HABERLER. It is the economic aspects we are discussing. If you say the union is not worth while because wages would rise anyway to the same level, then I say, "Let's abolish them."

FRIEDMAN. I don't disagree with that.

HABERLER. I thought you did. If we assume they are very important, I thought you would say we should use drastic measures; if not, then we should not use drastic measures.

FRIEDMAN. Whether their effect on economic activities has so far been important or not, it seems to me that like all other monopolies labor monopolies are undesirable. This goes back to my fundamental belief in a competitive society. What I intended to say, in my earlier remarks, is that if they were extremely important economically, then I think it would take drastic measures to abolish them; and I wouldn't be very hopeful about easy measures. If they are not terribly important, then maybe there are some mild measures of a kind that would not seriously raise problems of political freedom.

SAMUELSON. This is uncertain strategy, a strategy of uncertain validity.

FRIEDMAN. Yes.

SAMUELSON. I think you made that clear.

WRIGHT. You mean importance for what?

FRIEDMAN. Every time I use the word "important" here without qualification I mean it to refer to the structure of real wages.

WRIGHT. I think that is a *non sequitur*.

CHAMBERLIN. I don't think any conclusion follows from that. If they don't influence wages substantially, they are neutral so far as wages go.

WRIGHT. Isn't it a *non sequitur*, first to say they are not important in raising real wages, and then to say they are not important, period? What you are talking about is whether they are important socially, politically. You say they are unimportant in fixing wages, and then you jump to saying they are unimportant in disturbing things. You were criticizing Professor Clark for saying—that is you implied that he said—that the unions are so powerful we have got to take them. Now, it seems to me that you could well say that they are so powerful we have got to take them, even if their economic effects in raising real wages are very small. They might be a tremendously important political pressure group.

CHAMBERLIN. Do you think that in the absence of the union the level of wages in the coal industry would be what it is, and with only two hundred days work a year?

FRIEDMAN. At the moment, the present level of the coal miners would not in my view be much lower.

SAMUELSON. One hundred days of unemployment would exist?

CHAMBERLIN. If there were no collective bargaining, why would not wages go down? There is plenty of labor in the coal areas.

FRIEDMAN. Is there? If you look at evidence from the First World War, you will find the wages of coal miners in non-unionized areas rose by the same ratio.

WRIGHT. You are a bit inconsistent. You say the union was going strong until 1920.

FRIEDMAN. The point is the union then only covered part of the coal territory. There was a large nonunionized sector.

WRIGHT. I notice in Dwight E. Robinson's book [2] he points out that although the ILGWU raised wages, employment fell steadily in the industry.

FRIEDMAN. My argument is that it would have happened anyway because of the cessation of immigration and the fact that—

---

[2] *Editor's note: Collective Bargaining and Market Control in the New York Coat & Suit Industry* (Columbia University Press, 1949).

SAMUELSON. How do you solve these terrible problems of empirical identification, concerning which analytic effect you are observing, by these simple historical comparisons?

BOULDING. Do you think that a union-generated or advocated inflation policy is in any way comparable to the kind that comes out of a war? I would question it very much.

SAMUELSON. Why can't you look forward with alarm to a much larger deficit than at present if the cold war continues?

FRIEDMAN. Let us leave out the cold war. And I would argue that the expectation is still for substantial inflation. Why? I think our differences will be clarified if we go on to the next step. It is not simply because of pressure for a welfare state. Economists have known two propositions for one hundred years or more. They have known that by printing and spending enough money you can produce any desired level of activity; and, second—

WRIGHT. What kind of activity?

FRIEDMAN. I want to use the word "activity."

WRIGHT. I don't think you can do that. If you spend as much money as you want you can always get some sort of churning around. But by activity do you mean real income or what? [3]

FRIEDMAN. That is why I want to use the word "activity" and not real income.

BOULDING. Say money income.

FRIEDMAN. Say money income if you wish. The second thing is that there is great danger that in the process you will produce inflation. Now, the public, it seems to me, has learned the first thing; it has not learned the second; and it is likely to learn it only by precept. People are now very much more worried about deflation than they are about inflation. Every time you have a recession—and you will have some recessions—there

[3] *Comment by Wright:* In the German inflation after the First World War, industrial activity and employment began to decline while the inflation was still continuing. See Bresciani-Turroni, *The Economics of Inflation* (London, George Allen and Unwin, 1937).

is going to be an atmosphere created in which people will be willing to cut down taxes and raise expenditures. That alone might not produce a long-run inflation, if it were not backed up by welfare demands, which always involve long-run commitments to spend money. That is the argument.

SAMUELSON. The orthodox members of the community, say the businessmen, who don't approve of the purposes for which the government is spending money, usually think of the power of the purse, not as the power to control the printing press, but as the power of not voting taxes. In Congressional hearings the CIO and A.F. of L. are not against taxes any more than the Chamber of Commerce.

BOULDING. Haberler is the only one here who has personally gone through inflation. He is the only one who thinks inflation will produce any political effect. We learn this lesson once every so often, very few have done so nowadays. A generation is growing up now which knew not 1929, which did not know the depression, and which has no fear of inflation.

FRIEDMAN. From the testimony before Congress two or three years ago about inflation, one would gather that there was only one thing wrong with inflation, namely, that it was bound to produce deflation. There wasn't anything wrong with it, in and of itself. It was a fine thing.

HABERLER. I think that is deceptive. I will give you one indication. You would say probably that Alvin Hansen has nothing against inflation, but you remember during the war he wrote an article wherein he said inflation was worse than deflation.[4] I thought that was a little too much for my taste, but it shows how quickly people change their minds when they are confronted with the real thing.

SAMUELSON. Once the high cost of living starts higher and higher, it will be a source of great churning about and activity. It takes more than good intentions to stop an inflation.

[4] *Review of Economic Statistics*, February, 1941, pp. 1-7.

FRIEDMAN. It is more than that, Paul. It seems to me your remarks would be more pertinent if the inflation proceeded gradually, say, 5 per cent a year, year after year. But with this particular mechanism of producing it, what happens? An inflationary movement starts by accident or otherwise. At about the time people start getting worried about the inflation, a recession occurs. The recession produces something of a fall in prices. The attempt to get out of the recession now produces another surge of inflation. The worry which people were formerly developing about the rise of prices is deadened. Now people say, "We have to watch out that we don't have a deflation." This time the process may go a little bit further before people get worried again about inflation. Then they may put on the brakes or do something. And then the process can be repeated, it seems to me, for quite a long time.

SAMUELSON. What about inflation *cum* unemployment?

FRIEDMAN. If my argument is valid at all, it argues strongly against that.

SAMUELSON. I thought there was that prediction implicit in your argument—unemployment will police inflation and will not arise unless already aggregate demand is insufficient.

FRIEDMAN. I accept the latter part of your statement but I don't know what you mean by saying unemployment will police inflation.

SAMUELSON. That there can't be inflation from the supply-cost side in the face of unemployment.

FRIEDMAN. I don't deny for a moment the logical possibility of inflation from the cost side in an economy of strongly organized producer groups. It is not only labor unions. The same argument applies for strongly organized farmers or producers of automobiles. It is logically conceivable that you could have a situation in which strongly organized groups would push up their cost prices. Let us not argue whether to call it inflation or not. But the phenomenon of higher prices plus unemployment, that is logically possible. What I deny is that it is an empirically important possibility. The empirically important possibility is inflation pulling up wages.

HABERLER. I think you argue too much from American experience. I think you are perfectly right that inflation promotes unions, and that unions in the United States have become strong in an inflationary period. But I do not think it follows from that that when inflation stops they will disappear again, or that the history of the twenties, as you put it, will repeat itself. I think there is very little chance of that. Therefore, you are confronted with a new situation; and, therefore, your historical analogies are not very conclusive.

FRIEDMAN. Let me see what the implication of that is. Let us suppose that you have a noninflationary policy, somehow produced, and that you really otherwise would have a stable price level. I don't want to argue that unions would disappear overnight. I want to argue that their tendency to grow stronger and more important politically would be checked and reversed; and relatively mild measures of the kind I was suggesting here—a change in the general public attitude toward unions, reduction in the political support of them, subjecting them to the antitrust laws, etc.—would probably be adequate to keep that decline in the power of unions continuing.

HABERLER. I am not sure, I have strong views on that, but I do not think it necessarily follows that from what I said you must rush in with very drastic measures. I think it is possible that you are right, that mild political measures, say, stiffening of the Taft-Hartley law, might be sufficient; or maybe comparatively mild unemployment would be sufficient. After all, if you look at the situation last year, that did put a certain damper on unions, even though the recession was really mild. Of course, if you follow a full employment policy, if you want, say, full employment in the sense of Beveridge, not more than 3 per cent unemployment at any time, then you get into trouble. If you allow, say, up to 10 or 15 per cent of unemployment, that would probably be sufficient.

FRIEDMAN. But the question is, do you get into trouble because of the unions or not? Because it seems to me that makes an important difference. One of the implications which people have been drawing—in my view, erroneously—is that "full employment" policy—the policy of increasing Government expenditures whenever unemployment threatens—would be perfectly all right if it weren't for these "wicked" unions, and that if only we would get around to knocking these unions on the head we could go ahead and print money.

BOULDING. I am quite confident that the main effect of unionism is to hold down money wages and to prevent them from rising faster than they otherwise would. What does monopoly do? It introduces stability in the price system. Stability in the price system is wonderful from the point of view of fiscal policy. It is exactly what you want. It enables you to get away with it. If you had a flexible price system, you could not get away with fiscal policy at all because prices would always catch up. Of course, monopoly does raise these long-run questions as to whether you get away with it if it involves you in the necessity of a perpetual inflation. That is the thing the labor people have not faced up to.

I think these discussions of the allocational and the economic-progress effects of unions are not very significant. Unions are the opiate of the people under capitalism. That is why you have got to have them. That is the public relations line.

SAMUELSON. They are also a stimulant to the people. I think there is a double-barreled effect, namely, when you get high inflation, you up your demand. The effect of unions may be to slow down the rate of increase of prices. Nevertheless, as we approach full employment it may touch off increases. We may get some testing of these hypotheses.

FRIEDMAN. With respect to the slowing up of prices, once again I doubt very much that the unions slowed up the rise in the prices of final products. Their major effect was to cause all kinds of redistribution—to shift incomes from workers to distributors, for example. I don't believe they slowed up the rate by which prices rose.

KNIGHT. Milton, what has become of the doctrine that you create purchasing power by forcing up wages? Has that died all of a sudden? It was in the A.F. of L. bulletins not long ago— John Fry's doctrine.

FRIEDMAN. If you want to see the effects of unions, my point is don't go and look at what they say. Go and look at what they do. They still hold this doctrine. The question is, does it have any influence? And it seems to me these doctrines are all convenient rationalizations for policies they want to pursue for other reasons. Whether they are able to pursue them or not depends on the demand for and the supply of labor.

KNIGHT. Is it true that with unemployment last year the unions mitigated their demands for higher wages or is it only that they couldn't get away with it?

FRIEDMAN. The actual wage increases during the course of the recession were certainly less than they had been in the preceding two years.

KNIGHT. Which was it, that their demands were less, or they had less power, met more resistance?

FRIEDMAN. They are both the same thing.

SAMUELSON. *Pro forma*, they would ask for the sky.

CLARK. I think the demand was less because they knew the resistance was greater.

HABERLER. May I ask a specific question here. On pages 222 and 223 of your paper you list three reasons why people are inclined to exaggerate the importance of unions, and the third one does not make any sense to me. You say some influences are devious and slow and hard to follow—are very gradual; I should think that would make one underrate the importance of unions.

FRIEDMAN. You are quite right.[5] The indirect effects of unions are of many kinds. There are those which have the effect of

---

[5] *Comment by Friedman:* I have revised the paragraph in question in the light of Professor Haberler's comment.

eliminating the unions' force, of finding ways around them, which means that they essentially consist of new ways to label old things. So that if you are really going to say what happened to the wage rate of this and that thing—

HABERLER. You mean, a shock effect?

FRIEDMAN. Substitution. It may only be that the people who would be hired under the title of typographer get hired under another name in another industry.

SAMUELSON. Unions guard their grade classifications. You don't get away with that in a plant. I fully agree with the argument of Professor Chamberlin, which is an old argument of Hutt and the Webbs, that it is not a question of unions limiting the supply of labor and thereby raising wages, but it is just one of setting a higher rate and making it stick. Now, you deal with these large companies, and they set a pattern for everybody. I wonder if the unemployed rank and file—who are mostly "abortions" rather than "stillbirths" or "deaths," as a result of the union policy—if they do keep the wage demands reasonable?

FRIEDMAN. They certainly do.

SAMUELSON. How? What is the *modus operandi* by which they do?

FRIEDMAN. Because the larger the discrepancy between the wage rate of the people employed in the automobile industry and the wage rate of similar people elsewhere, the larger the incentive for some employer to establish a plant or firm there or somewhere else which will enable him to benefit from this wage differential; the larger the incentive of the existing firms to change, to buy stuff from parts people, to change their form of organization. What will happen is that instead of Chrysler or General Motors producing certain things themselves, they will now depend on other parts manufacturers who will produce it with people who are not called automobile workers.[6]

[6] *Comment by Wright:* This supposes that parts manufacturers are not also organized by the union. In fact small parts manufacturers have often

SAMUELSON. And Walter Reuther will realize this and he will be moderate in his wage demands?

FRIEDMAN. I don't care whether he is moderate. If he isn't moderate, he will discover his union people are now suffering considerable unemployment.

SAMUELSON. You think there will be a soup kitchen at union headquarters serving as a warning to him? Has any political observer of the UAW found any such lines of influence? There ought to be some objective evidence, such as at union meetings a feeling of unrest and booing and hissing; and there ought to be letters written.

FRIEDMAN. I think if Reuther were to disregard these effects and if he were to seek—and for the moment let us suppose he is temporarily successful—very radically raised wages, and if that had the effect of grossly reducing employment within the automobile industry you would find opposition building up that would break the union down. Knowing that in advance and being as smart as you and I, he would avoid such action.

SAMUELSON. Suppose over a given period there is a tremendous turnover. No one is made explicitly to appear as unemployed. So the victims would be the hillbillies in the hills of Kentucky. Professor Chamberlin seems to be much more realistic as to the motives of the participants.

FRIEDMAN. Consider what would happen under those circumstances.

SAMUELSON. You think it hasn't happened?

FRIEDMAN. It seems to me that the wages in the automobile industry today are certainly less than they would have been in the absence of the union.

---

proved more vulnerable than big companies to union action, and have been forced in some cases to pay higher wages.

Comment by Friedman: This only means one has to go still farther afield. The feeling of necessity that unions have to organize parts industries is itself testimony to the importance of the indirect effects mentioned above.

SAMUELSON. I wonder.

CHAMBERLIN. He says the coal miners would gladly leave, on page 225.

WRIGHT. How do you work out this idea that automobile wages are lower now because of union activity?

SAMUELSON. How are you sure of it?

FRIEDMAN. You are never sure of any interesting proposition. If you are really sure of it, you can certainly be sure that it is an unimportant and uninteresting proposition. It seems to me that it is related to the pricing policies that the automobile firms have used. In the postwar period, in the absence of a union, there might have been some tendency for the well-known automobile manufacturers to have held nominal manufacturers' prices down anyway, the usual tendency for monopoly people not quite to exploit short-run possibilities to the fullest.

WRIGHT. This word monopoly bothers me.

FRIEDMAN. I will leave it out if you want.

WRIGHT. How is Ford a monopoly?

FRIEDMAN. I really think that is going to lead us off on a sidetrack; let us stick to the main argument. In the postwar period there was an exceedingly strong demand for automobiles. The demand was such that equilibrium manufacturers' prices would have been considerably higher than the actual list prices charged. What explains that differential? I want to argue that two things explain the differential: one, the desire on the part of Ford, for example, to keep good public relations for the future, together with the fear of antitrust prosecution, which might have caused them in any event to hold the list price slightly under the equilibrium price. I think this factor is not very important if only because it is hard for me to see how Ford's public relations advanced very much from having his distributors "gouge" the public instead of doing so himself. I use the term "gouge the public" in the sense that the public understands it. It seems to me the existence of a union made an additional extremely strong reason for holding the list price down. Given the general state of public opinion and the union bargaining situation, any rise in the list prices would have had to be matched by a rise in wages, and Ford might have thought that the strong demand for automobiles was temporary.

SAMUELSON. I don't understand on the basis of your theory that he should have felt he has to share, any more than that the oatmeal in the barn had to be shared with laborers.[7]

FRIEDMAN. If there were no union at all, I say Ford would have raised prices to the market level—all the automobile people would have done so. They would have tried to bid for more labor in order to produce more, and would have been willing to hire more labor at a higher wage rate because they would have expected that the wages would decline again when the demand for automobiles declined.

SAMUELSON. They would not have had to raise wages. The automobile unions as a whole face a very elastic demand because the supply of other laborers is very great. That is your essential position.

FRIEDMAN. They still would have had to pay a higher rate of pay to attract a larger fraction. You may argue how much higher.

SAMUELSON. I understood the schedule is elastic.

FRIEDMAN. The long run highly, the short run less so, but still elastic; and in the process wages would have gone up in order to attract labor. Now, what happens when there are unions? Automobile companies keep nominal list prices down because they figure that if they allow the prices that they charge to go up, employ more labor, and allow the wages of labor to go up, then they are going to be stuck with those higher wage rates permanently.

CHAMBERLIN. That is the essential argument—where you have a case.

[7] Cf. footnote 4, Professor Boulding's paper (chap. vi).

FRIEDMAN. That is what my argument rests on essentially. Because of the process I have sketched, their marginal revenue from raising the price of cars has to include a negative allowance for the higher wages or wage rates they will pay in the future. So the result, it seems to me, was that they kept the nominal prices of cars down, employed fewer workers than they otherwise would have, and kept the wages down below what they would otherwise have been. If you want some kind of empirical evidence on that, let me note first that the wage rates of automobile workers and steel workers went up less than the average wage rate of all workers in manufacturing, and that the wage rate of steel workers in this war and postwar period went up less than the wage rate of steel workers in the First World War when they were not unionized.

SAMUELSON. Some auto industry executives have said that is what they have done.

FRIEDMAN. That is not evidence. I can't rely on that evidence when it supports me and object to it when it does not support me. I do not care what they have said.

SAMUELSON. They have said this off the record.

FRIEDMAN. I don't care whether they said it on the record or off the record. Because Mr. Jones said he lived to be a hundred years old because he smoked a package of cigarettes a day, does that mean you accept his theory of longevity?

HABERLER. You really assume more than simply that there would be no union. You assume prices would have been free to go up. And I say in that period, it would not have been reasonable.

FRIEDMAN. Why wouldn't automobile prices have been free to rise?

HABERLER. There was still a possibility of price control.

FRIEDMAN. That might have kept it down somewhat, but it would not have kept it down as far. There was an additional factor.

HABERLER. We all agree that if there were no unions and no monopoly and no controls the general level of income would be higher and probably the income of workers would be higher too. We can't be sure about every group.

FRIEDMAN. No, that is a question of real income for altogether different reasons. If we consider just the automobile industry for a moment, I believe the wage rate of labor was lower and the income of distributors higher than they otherwise would have been. As for the consumer, the fact that the manufacturers kept their list prices down meant that the price of automobiles to the consumers was higher than it otherwise would have been.

WRIGHT. Why?

FRIEDMAN. That meant they produced a smaller total of cars, which implies a higher price. The differential went to the distributor in the form of under-the-counter payments or low trade-in values or things like that.

HABERLER. You say that what restrained them from raising the prices was that they were afraid that once they let wages go up they could not push them down. I think that there were other considerations. Public relations, of course, that is also somewhat connected.

FRIEDMAN. I am not denying that. The fact that I have more than one reason for an event does not mean that each reason does not contribute to it. These reasons might have kept the nominal price 5 per cent below the equilibrium price. The effect of the union may have been to keep it another 5 per cent below the equilibrium price.

SAMUELSON. This is my feeling about the UAW. I feel that over the last twenty years, including the war period, there have been in the country an awful lot of people of the same skills who could do the job that the automobile workers do and be delighted to do it, if there was no feeling of class consciousness or unions or anything else, for a lot less than we have been getting our automobiles produced for.

FRIEDMAN. I don't believe that to be true.

WRIGHT. Since I more or less come from the hillbilly section, that reference to the hillbilly who is still down in Tennessee is very pertinent. I do think that the effect of union actions, to a large extent, is to keep a great pool of disguised unemployment in the South.

KNIGHT. In the country, in the rural areas, not just the South.

SAMUELSON. Even in cities of New England.

FRIEDMAN. During the period of the twenties, the automobile industry expanded drastically; and there weren't any unions; and they did attract a good deal of labor from the South to the North; and they had to do it by a substantial differential in wage rates; and that is the way they did it. And it is obvious that the migration from the South kept the wages from rising as much as they otherwise would have.

SAMUELSON. I did not say it was just unions. I said the feeling of class consciousness and all the rest so that a man has no way of going to Detroit and saying: "Give me the job; I will do it for less." In fact, once he gets in the plant, he immediately changes his attitudes and won't do it for less. This will all exist even when there are no unions.

BOULDING. If you went to the University of Michigan and said, "I can do Boulding's job for less"—?

FRIEDMAN. I am not denying the existence of forces of this kind. If you go back to the Civil War period again, when there weren't any unions at all, you will find that wages in the post–Civil War period fell less than prices. You had the same kind of rigidity then that you have now. But look at this particular period—the period since about 1935. This is a period when money wages and prices throughout the economy have been rising, when a decline in real wages can be perfectly consistent with a rise in money wages. This is precisely the period when you could have had a decline in relative real wages in the automobile field without a decline in money wages. In point of fact, I am under the impression that there was such a decline, that over the seventeen-year period from 1933 to date there has been a decline in the real wages of the automobile industry relative to manufacturing in general.

BOULDING. You must realize that the labor market is like the marriage market; it is as if some woman said, "I will be your wife cheaper than your wife." It is preposterous to suppose that you can have this economic model.

SAMUELSON. This does happen in a perfect supply and demand market.[8]

FRIEDMAN. This is just a general methodological question of what you mean by realistic. It need not be realistic in detail. The question is whether it gives you the right answers, and I would argue that it substantially does.

SAMUELSON. When you put a microscope on any labor market, almost all observers say in the big companies the people get more than in the small companies. The big companies do not adjust their rates to the number of people at their gates; and this all has something to do with the fact that they are big plus, and it is only part of the story, the fact that there is a union there. In a big company where there is no union, there is a situation recognizable to any observer very similar to what there is when there is a union. Discharge for cause, for example, is almost impossible, like the Civil Service. You can't easily get rid of a man if he is incompetent.

FRIEDMAN. Obviously no one can deny there are elements like that. The question is an empirical one of their relative importances compared to other forces. The important point is that forces which bulk large when you look under the microscope at the individual case, but which vary from firm to firm and industry to industry, are likely to bulk small when you look at it in the aggregate.

[8] *Comment by Wright:* And if job transfers are not permitted, do we not regress to an economy of status? See my paper on "Conflicting Standards" (chap. xii).

SAMUELSON. Ross's study of the over-all problem? [9]

FRIEDMAN. My impression is Ross's study is marred by a statistical fallacy. He classifies workers by their wages at the beginning of a period and then argues that you find larger percentage increases of low-paid workers than of high-paid workers.

SAMUELSON. Suppose he works it backward?

FRIEDMAN. My guess is he would find the opposite—that if he classified by wages at the end of the period, he would find smaller percentage increases at the bottom and higher at the top.

SAMUELSON. What he does is he compares unionized trades with the same income level as nonunionized, and he asks what are the gains for the people who started out even.

FRIEDMAN. He is taking them from different occupations and different parts of the distribution. What he would have to do in order to eliminate this regression fallacy effect is take the top 10 per cent and the bottom 10 per cent, not equal incomes.

SAMUELSON. I don't understand that. It seems to me he has controlled for that fallacy.

FRIEDMAN. No, he hasn't. If the average income in the two classes of pursuits were equal, he would have controlled for it.

[*Editor's note:* At the end of the discussion of Dr. Friedman's paper there was a digression on medical training. In view of the numerous references to the medical profession in Dr. Friedman's paper it is included.]

WRIGHT. There is one point I would like to discuss with you. But I didn't want to break into the discussion. I don't agree with your statement that the medical profession is deliberately re-

[9] Arthur M. Ross, *Trade Union Wage Policy* (University of California Press, 1948); "Forces Affecting the Interindustry Wage Structure" (with William Goldner), *Quart. Jour. of Econ.* (May, 1950), pp. 254-281. Joseph W. Garbarino, "A Theory of Interindustry Wage Structure," *Quart. Jour. of Econ.* (May, 1950), pp. 282-305; "Unionism and the Wage Level," *Amer. Econ. Rev.* (December, 1950), pp. 893-896.

stricting its numbers. It seems to me that with the terrific cost of educating a doctor, and with rapidly rising scientific requirements, we just haven't got the money to educate as many doctors as we need as well as we want.

FRIEDMAN. This is partly a cyclical phenomenon. Restrictive practices of this type always become important in depressions. If we want to find out whether the medical profession has restricted numbers to raise incomes, we must examine what happened in depression periods. There the evidence is overwhelming. In 1934 or 1935, for example, the Council on Medical Education of the American Medical Association issued a statement to its member medical schools saying that in the opinion of the Council schools were admitting more persons than they could give adequate training to. In fact, as I recall the figures, they were admitting only a slightly larger number than they had been admitting five years earlier. The next year the number admitted fell sharply, and it continued to fall in each of the succeeding four years.

WRIGHT. I happen to be a lawyer as well as an economist. When I was a lawyer I came into contact with some work in connection with raising legal standards in Georgia. It was sought to get through the requirement that lawyers have the "equivalent" of a high school education. And that was vetoed. It does not seem to me that the statement that the schools were admitting too many men to educate them adequately needs to be taken to mean any more than what it said. The students were not being prepared adequately. I happen to know something about the financing of medical schools in connection with our State University at Virginia; and I know that the requirements, the standards of medical knowledge which are being required of a graduate, call for an immensely expensive plant.

FRIEDMAN. Let me by-pass this and give you evidence to which these questions do not apply. What you say should lead the medical profession to welcome with open arms physicians who have been trained abroad and who are bringing their capital here—if they are good physicians. The fact is, during the thirties the American Medical Association was so successful in putting up barriers to the admission of foreign physicians that, despite the extreme pressure of refugees, the actual number of foreign physicians admitted to practice in the United States was approximately the same from 1933 to 1938 as in the preceding five years. That incompetence was not the primary basis of exclusion is clear from the fact that one of the ways foreign physicians were excluded was by imposing citizenship requirements. If anybody will explain to me the relationship between being a citizen of the United States and being an efficient and competent doctor, I will admit there may be some merit in your point.[10]

HABERLER. Everybody knows that only a certain fraction can pass such an examination. A man may be trained as well as you like. If there are too large a number, two-thirds will be flunked.

FRIEDMAN. In many, perhaps most, cases they did it more subtly than that, by requiring that the examinations be taken in English. That was enough.

WRIGHT. Don't you think it is a sensible requirement?

FRIEDMAN. A man may come to New York and practice in a Puerto Rican neighborhood where it is important that he speak Spanish and not English. In any event, he ought to be able to converse with his patients, but not necessarily answer complicated questions.

WRIGHT. Working the thing out in terms of cost, you will see that if we want better health service for our people we have to have a lot more doctors, and that is going to cost millions and millions, or, rather, billions and billions. Emotional and romantic people would much rather say that it was due to monopolistic practices by the medical profession.

[10] *Comment by Wright:* We should, in my opinion, distinguish between the effect of an antiforeign prejudice—general and to be deplored in American life—and the basic economics of the medical profession.

FRIEDMAN. This is not a random remark. This is a field in which I have examined the evidence in some detail.[11]

WRIGHT. If you are going to maintain a high standard of medical training, if we really want to get better health services, we have to train more doctors; and that is going to cost enormous sums.

FRIEDMAN. I see no reason why society should subsidize the training of physicians. I would like to see medical tuition fees raised to cover the marginal cost of training additional physicians.

WRIGHT. If you or somebody else raised them, then the same people would say you were cutting down on the supply of doctors.

FRIEDMAN. I would like to see society make it possible for everyone to have free access to capital to be able to meet the expenses of becoming a trained physician. I have a special gadget of my own, that I won't go into, for doing this, but you see my point. I would argue that what we ought to do is make the individual bear the capital cost of getting his training and then let down all barriers. And my guess is that we would have more physicians.

WRIGHT. You are thinking about the students and not who is training them. The point is, you can let in twice as many students, but how are they going to be trained?

FRIEDMAN. In at least one or two notable instances in the thirties it has been said by responsible persons that the American Medical Association refused to approve new medical schools for which philanthropic funds were raised.

WRIGHT. Have you any evidence that it was a desire to keep down numbers other than your inference?

HABERLER. It depends on how the various states excluded doctors trained in another state. Of course, in some cases, it may have been because of poor training. It is a very common prac-

[11] See footnote 5, chap. x.

tice, isn't it, that even doctors from states where medical education is best are not allowed to practice elsewhere?

FRIEDMAN. There are always mixed motives in cases like this. I don't mean to argue that physicians are malicious or that they are deliberately going along these lines. Of course, there are a great many physicians who honestly believe that standards have to be raised and that the various restrictive measures are called for by the necessity of raising standards. The point is that this belief can be used for other purposes, or that particular measures can have other effects entirely unintended by many who support them. The only reason similar success hasn't been attained in law is because of the somewhat accidental factor that state legislators in large measure have been trained in night law schools. That is an important reason why you haven't more restrictions in law. Restriction would involve ruling out many if not all night law schools. The Bar Association has few if any part-time or night law schools on its approved list. The state legislators are not going to vote against the night law schools that they themselves have been trained in.

CHAPTER XII

Conflicting Standards
in Union Action [1]

BY DAVID McCORD WRIGHT

"ONLY through sympathy and not through hatred do we achieve understanding," said Charles A. Beard. If people seem to us to be behaving shortsightedly or wrongly it is not enough to condemn them. We must find why they are acting that way. A "bad" act is not necessarily bad in intention. Nor can we ever rule out the possibility that by standards other than our own it may be both just and sensible. Thus to understand the American labor movement we must go beyond economics. Analysis of social goals and social values is also indispensable.

If a man really believes in democracy and tolerance he must be prepared to put up with a great deal. If he comes to find that most people are beginning to have different ideas than he does as to the right way to live, then—provided they are not trying to destroy the fundamental values of tolerance and democracy themselves—he will be obliged largely to go along. He can, it is true, continue to dissent and try to persuade, but that is about all. Thus if, for example, the majority of people should come to believe in a world of secure "poverty," I do not see how I could expect to impose my values upon them.

But suppose the people involved don't really believe in the

---

[1] *Editor's note:* This paper was prepared for the institute and distributed, but not delivered. It is nevertheless included in the report because it deals with an important aspect of the union problem which should be mentioned if the problem is to be seen in proportion.

ideas they think they do? Or suppose, to put it more clearly, that while the various aims for which a group is pushing are all understandable enough in themselves, they nevertheless contain, when combined, a serious hidden conflict. Suppose that if the conflict were really known or understood by the group involved they would drop that particular combination of aims: In such a case it seems to me no more than right to point out the hidden weakness. One does not deny the right of ultimate choice merely by trying to help make the choice an intelligent one.

2

Any single simplified list of union aims for the United States today is bound to be inaccurate. Some groups are interested in some problems, others in other problems. Furthermore, the passage of years brings many shifts in emphasis. But perhaps we can approximate an acceptable statement if we group some of the major union slogans from "right" to "left." That is, we begin with the more generally accepted views and then go on to those which are more "radical," or, at the moment, anyhow, less widely stressed.

Following the order suggested, I submit that some of the major ideals avowed by sections of the American labor movement today are: (1) to raise the living standards of the worker; (2) to give him greater "opportunity"; (3) to give him more "security"; (4) to create a more "democratic" world; (5) to give the worker a sense of "participation"; and (6) to try to create a world free from coercion, rivalry, and conflict. Not one of these aims is objectionable in itself. Yet my thesis will be that, if they are literally interpreted, all of them are more or less in conflict, and that until the labor movement recognizes these conflicts and is prepared to allow for them there will always be a danger that, however unintentionally, the labor movement may bring American economic life to a full stop.

3

Let us begin by exploring the problems hidden in the aim of raising living standards. One can hardly read a paper today without seeing some glowing forecast of the "abundance" which could be ours, or at any rate our grandchildren's. Some people are so optimistic that they feel we could get this abundance merely by using the knowledge we have now. Others put their confidence in a series of great new inventions. But the one thing generally overlooked today is that whatever form the idea takes it inevitably means *change*. Men have got to be moved from one place to another, certain skills will become obsolete while others will become more valuable, and so on. If you doubt this, think what sort of living standard we would now have if we were restricted merely to efficient use of the techniques known in 1870.

But the problem is not merely one of reorganizing methods of production. The fact usually overlooked is that—whether we are dealing with a socialist, a generally planned, or a capitalist society—if we want higher living standards, and if we want to make some effort toward giving the consumer approximately what he wants when he wants it, we will immediately have a forecasting problem. As long as output is not growing, past experience is a fairly reliable guide. But as soon as we start to expand, it will be necessary for those in control, whether they call themselves commissars, bureau chiefs, union officials, or businessmen, to go beyond mere repetition, and to draw up estimates of the pattern of wants during the next planning period. Then, if they guess incorrectly, there can be great dislocation. For example, if a planning board thinks consumers are going to want lots of sewing machines and allots numerous materials to that industry only to find housewives buying vacuum cleaners instead, there will probably be considerable disturbance, shortages, and, without control, price adjustments and employment adjustments.

There is, however, a further point usually overlooked in most planning literature but overwhelmingly important. This is the variability and unpredictability of consumer wants in an *expanding* and unrationed society. Those who think about the problem at all usually assume that during an expansion the demand for each good will grow up in approximately the same proportion. For example, it may be supposed that a planning board could order, say, a general 20 per cent increase of output by all industries and leave it at that. Thus Dr. Albert Lauterbach of Sarah Lawrence College in his *Economic Security and Individual Freedom: Can We Have Both?* [2] after first describing quite correctly the over-all budget procedure needed for a comprehensive economic plan, goes on to say: "There is no reason why such a procedure should necessitate any consumer rationing or allocation. If, as we assume, the national consumption scheme follows closely the long-range pattern of consumer preferences *which is known from experience* [italics added], if the production scheme is flexible and designed to serve the consumer, and if this policy is integrated with broad facilities for consumer education on a voluntary basis, then compulsion on the consumer level can be avoided." [3]

But if we examine the specific statistics and historical records on this problem we will find that Dr. Lauterbach's statement is far too optimistic. Publications, for example, of the National Bureau of Economic Research clearly indicate that symmetrical and predictable expansion is largely impossible in an unrationed world. In some industries, for instance salt, a 20 per cent increase in output would probably pile up a great surplus inventory. In other cases so small an increase would be quite inadequate. A good statistical indication of some of these divergencies will be found in an article in *The Survey of Current Business*

[2] (Cornell University Press, 1948.)
[3] *Ibid.*, p. 65.

for January, 1950, on the income sensitivity of consumers' wants.

Some people feel that any changes in wants which are actually observed to occur must be the work of businessmen and of advertisers. This is, unfortunately, not at all correct. The mere fact of increasing income and output, in and of itself, will change the pattern of wants—even though there is no advertising whatever. For example, a man who has been in the habit of drinking a bottle of beer a day is not simply going to drink a barrel of beer. A man who has lived in a small house is not going to live in two small houses. A businessman may, it is true, influence the direction which the new expenditure will take, but it cannot be successfully denied that there would have been change anyhow.

Summarizing then the problem of social growth, we find that both on the production and the consumption side growth inevitably entails a number of adjustments in method and in work teams. Even if we leave out new inventions, the mere fact of increasing output will necessitate some redesigning of equipment and relocation of men and factories. Furthermore, unless new inventions are introduced, the law of diminishing returns will probably soon bring expansion to a halt. On the consumption side also, the consumer, as he becomes better off, will inevitably shift his wants and shift them in a manner which will be frequently both disproportionate and unpredictable. Thus growth involves change, and if we are to try to cut off change, then we must be prepared to cut off growth. This is the fundamental challenge which the desire for rising living standards presents to the union movement.

4

Many people are willing to accept without protest the account of the growth dilemma which I have just given. Indeed, it cannot be successfully disputed. But they have maintained that these sociological frictions of growth and the resulting pressure group problems can be met by various changes in economic organization. First of all it may be argued that the matter can be handled by comprehensive planning for full employment plus equal or nearly equal distribution of money income. In such a case, it will be said, there will no longer be any resistance to growth adjustments—for the only way any man will be able to increase his income will be by helping to increase total income. This argument is prima facie very persuasive.

Again it may be argued that "industrial democracy"—the control of management by the vote of the workers—will create such changed morale conditions that there will no longer be any pressure toward restrictivism.

The writer would be the last to deny that appropriate economic measures—unemployment insurance, fiscal policy, welfare expenditures, etc.—can help to mitigate insecurity. Also some sort of small-unit, guild, industrial-democratic organization of industry might certainly reduce the feeling of "aloneness" or sociological "anomie" of the worker. What I do deny is that either of these types of planning can wholly remove the pressure group problem. Indeed the second—the "industrial-democratic" type—in the matrix of values in which it would probably appear—would increase it.

We have already seen that mere planning for full employment, even with government ownership of everything, would not remove the physical necessity of reorganizing work teams, relocating factories, redesigning machines, and so on—*if growth is to take place*. Now the notion that giving equal and secure money incomes would remove the pressure group problem in these circumstances is, I submit, the direct bastard offspring of "economic man."

An "economic" man is only interested in consuming income. But this is not necessarily the case with a real man. Let us run over some of the "noneconomic" pressures toward sabotage which would survive in the planned equalitarian state:

In the first place a man may like a given community, a given house, a given view, and may not want to leave them. In the second place he may be attached to a given group of friends, a given organization, or a given team of workmates. Thirdly he may have a special love of his work and a special pleasure in it. Finally he may love power and prestige, and his particular source of power may be some line of activity which change threatens to make obsolete.

The love of friends and of places does not require much explanation. The love of one's work, however, does need a bit of elaboration. Under the nineteenth-century ideology men were looked upon as balancing a certain amount of work (disutility) against a certain amount of enjoyment, or leisure, or consumption (utility). Work therefore was conceived of as drudgery and the aim of progress was to enable us to do as little of it as possible. The whole creative instinct of the human race was slurred over. In a healthy society, however, work is not to be thus sharply set off against enjoyment. It is true that we can get tired from doing *too much* or too unpleasant work—just as we may get tired of eating too many bananas—and we may have to supplement the pure instinct of workmanship to get as much work out of a man as we wish. But this is not ground for making the sharp division between labor and consumption which is usual in economic and Marxian thinking. Work is still frequently one of a man's satisfactions. Just because a man gets tired of eating bananas, if he has too many of them, we can't jump to the conclusion that it will make no difference to him whether he eats bananas or oranges. Just because he gets tired if he works too long at one job, we cannot jump to the conclusion that he would just as soon work at any other job.

As Krech and Crutchfield put it in their *Theory and Problems of Social Psychology,* "The worker whose painfully acquired skill has suddenly become useless and meaningless by some new invention or improvement in production methods finds himself facing very serious psychological problems. Not only must he learn new skills and routines of work, but his feeling of *personal worth and self-esteem* [italics added], based in many instances on his mastery of the now obsolescent skill, is threatened." [4]

When we add to frictions like these the love of power which many people have, the problem of finding a perfect solution becomes insuperable. It is all very well for Lenin to say that in the Marxist utopia "the authority of the government over persons will be replaced by the administration of things and the direction of the processes of production." [5] The trouble is that one cannot direct and (more important) redirect the processes of production *without* directing people.

The trouble is that in shifting resources or altering technical methods we also alter work relationships, and in altering work relationships we also alter *power* relationships among the human beings who make up the work teams of the organizations involved. "Retraining" some men—especially young ones—could certainly *help* to minimize friction. The same would also be true of removing the fear of starvation, or indeed of any reprisals on the consumption level of an individual. But though the sources of friction are *helped*, they are never wholly removed. What does a guaranteed consumption level mean to a politician, compared to the loss of office or power, or to a physicist if balanced against the loss of his laboratory? A man who loves a special community may value contact with friends much more than a guaranteed ability to buy beer. Similarly a man who loves a special job (or art) may value it more than a mere fixed income.

But it may be objected that we can "compensate" the individuals whose skills are made obsolete, or who have to do un-

[4] (McGraw-Hill, 1948), p. 540.
[5] *State and Revolution* (Vanguard, 1929), p. 124.

pleasant work. Again, however, infinite possibilities of disagreement are opened up. There are some people whose love for their work, or power, or friends, or community, may be such that *no* money could compensate them for their loss. Would Mr. Truman resign from the presidency for a million dollars? I doubt it. Would Stalin move to Monte Carlo for the sake of a guaranteed income? It scarcely seems likely. But even on a more mundane plane, and even if there was some money sum which might induce many of us to leave our employment willingly, still the amount demanded by us, as individuals, to compensate our *subjective* valuations might appear utterly ridiculous to the rest of society and be far more than they would be willing to pay. Hence, unless those inconvenienced by change are to be allowed to levy unlimited blackmail, many conflicts still remain possible.

Again there is a suggestion contained in some of the Marxian literature that everyone could be trained simultaneously to do anything and everything. As Dr. Bober puts it, "In a joint work in 1845 the two young revolutionaries [Marx and Engels] irresponsibly declare that under communism the worker will hunt in the morning, fish in the afternoon, rear cattle in the evening, and criticize after dinner." [6] But it does not take much thought to see that even if everybody was intrinsically capable of being trained to do everything (which is surely a doubtful proposition—can the tone-deaf man be trained to sing?) the immense amount of time needed to train *everyone* to be *at once* a doctor, lawyer, physicist, actor, railroad engineer, truck driver, painter, sculptor, chemist, etc. etc. and etc., in one lifetime, would speedily use up the whole national income.

[6] *American Economic Review* (May, 1949), p. 37.

5

Against this background let us next, however, try to evaluate the guild-socialist, industrial-democratic solution. Here we will find that the problem is if anything accentuated. In the first place there is the possible great loss of efficiency from breaking up industry into small technological units. (If we try to keep big units then the sociological frictions still survive.) A man can be just as "lost" in a big union as in a big industry. For example I may again cite Krech and Crutchfield: "Some unions, whose battles are in the far past, no longer offer their members an exultant sense of progress . . . other unions operate as a tight bureaucracy." Also "Labor unions *deepen the depersonalization of worker-management* contacts." [7]

Also the *London Economist,* commenting on the dock strikes of 1949: "This union has the worst record of unofficial strikes because its enormous *size* [italics added], wealth and power place its leaders in a position so exalted that only an exceptional man can keep in close touch with the rank and file. Consequently the Union had, in the minds of its members, become an entity as remote as the government *or the employer* [italics added]." [8]

But even if we have only small unions there remain two problems in connection with growth. First there is the problem of quick, energetic, and adaptable managerial decisions. Next there is the problem that each individual union may have reasons for trying to block change. For change may affect the union's routine, or relative position.

On the managerial point the *London Economist* writes: "The main argument against the direct control of industries by those who work in them—whether the doctrine is christened syndicalism or guild socialism—is that it does not work, any more than the various experiments that have been made throughout

[7] *Op. cit.,* pp. 549, 537.
[8] Vol. 154 (June 26, 1949), p. 1055.

history to run an army by delegates from the ranks have ever worked." [9]

One should see also, and from a very sympathetic observer, the following remarks by Lord Lindsay of Birker (made a peer by the Labor government): "One of the most persistent ideals of early trade unionism was that of the 'self-governing workshop,' in which the distinction between the management and the managed had entirely disappeared. Unfortunately experiments made of setting up such workshops have always, or nearly always, been inefficient. It is interesting to note that the Russians started with the same idea—that the worker, the ordinary simple worker at the bottom, should run the business—and they have had, in the interests of efficiency, progressively to give up any such notion." [10]

Again on the question of the combination of industrial democracy with general planning, Lord Lindsay writes: "What I am concerned to point out is that the making a business in itself democratic is not the same problem as making the management of an industry responsible to the community as a whole. Either of these problems could be solved without solving the other. . . . Discussion *for* us is not the same as discussion *by* us." [11]

Finally, while one must grant a good deal to the "anomie" argument, it is necessary to protest the view often implied that the union is the *only* group within which a poor man can possibly find help, intimacy, and shelter. In every American city there are dozens of nonunion, "benevolent and protective" organizations, fraternal, civic, and religious, eagerly looking for members. The man who keeps himself an "isolated" cultural or economic unit in this country must be responsible in large part for his own isolation.

[9] "Old Boss Writ Large" (June, 1948), p. 1001.
[10] *Ideological Differences and World Order*, F. S. C. Northrop, ed. (Yale University Press, 1949), p. 261.
[11] *Ibid.*, pp. 262, 265.

6

I do not like to weaken the force of the entirely noncontroversial argument I have given so far by adding more personal theories. Nevertheless I think it important to touch upon another point. What we said at the beginning about the need for continuing invention implies even deeper problems in connection with social growth. Not only does growth cause change, but also it comes about through change, and change is the work of independent minds, either the independent mind of the reseacher or the independent mind of the manager, government official, or worker who sees the new possibility and puts it into action. Professor Alfred North Whitehead has remarked that the great invention of the nineteenth century was not any particular invention but the invention of the method of inventing. Using Professor Usher's classification of the stages of invention, we find three steps: (1) the consciousness of need; (2) the setting of the stage; and (3) what he calls the saltatory act, or the final act of synthesis which produces the invention.

Now, as Whitehead says, the great invention of the nineteenth century was the invention of the idea of setting the stage: the accumulation in a given laboratory of all the various possible things and methods which the researcher thinks may conceivably have some bearing upon his particular problem. Some people have gone so far as to think that the "invention of the method of invention" makes all previous social institutions obsolete and that we may consider science from now on as self-creating and self-implementing. This seems to me entirely mistaken.

No matter how elaborate a laboratory may be, no matter how many materials we assemble in it, still there remains the necessity for creative, bold, and independent imagination on the part of the research worker. If he is to be tied down to a particular party line, or if he is held back under a bureaucratic organization which puts more emphasis upon agreeable conformity than upon experiment and adventurous thinking, then the new inventions will not be forthcoming in the quantity which they once were.

But we cannot stop even with the laboratory. Whenever a new invention or method is introduced, we have seen that it inevitably entails certain insecurities, and that these would not be eliminated even if everyone received the same income. This being the case, it will always require a certain amount of energy and leadership to break through the accepted methods and to establish new ways of doing things. Today in England a great deal of propaganda is being issued regarding the need for more work and longer hours, but this is not really the basic difficulty. It is not so much *more* work as better work. It is not so much longer hours of working as longer hours of thinking. It is a willingness to shift around, use new methods, work in different ways, different places, which is the essential problem of economic growth.

As I see it, it is these two problems—the need of change *when* growth takes place, and the need for independent minds *if* it is to take place—which furnish the key to some of the basic conflicts inherent in the modern union ideology. These problems are, furthermore, closely related to some of the most important standards of union action, namely, the urge for opportunity, for security, for democracy—and to some extent for "participation." The economists have talked of social security, and most of them realize that that is all the security they can give, but to the general public security means *personal* security. People are more and more being encouraged to understand the word "security" as meaning that nobody will ever have to change jobs unless he wants to move to one he thinks is better; that nobody actively at work will ever have any changes in wages except increases; and that nobody will ever be fired except for the most egregious misconduct. But the more nearly we think of security in this way, the more we will have to cut down on expansion. Eternal stability in the same kind of employment cannot be guaranteed if there is social growth also. Job security and social growth can never wholly be reconciled.

The basic problem is that it is absolutely impossible to have a society in which expansion will not inconvenience some people. No private business, unless it is part of a system of ironbound monopolies cutting off all further change, can guarantee to its workers eternal security or unbroken routine. But what is much more important, no socialist or communist bureau could do the job either. The communist ideology of a world in which "the free development of each would be free development of all" is an impossibility. Space is lacking to analyze its hidden inadequacies. I discuss some of them in my book on *Capitalism*.[12] But the tragedy of economic life, no matter whether it be under socialism or under capitalism, is that change which benefits society as a whole virtually always implies, at the very least, serious inconvenience to certain work groups within society.

It may be that people will come to prefer, as I began by saying, a world of secure poverty. It may be that they will feel it better to stop the drilling of oil wells in order to keep the coal workers prosperous; to stop the invention of airplanes in order to keep the railroad workers prosperous, and so on down the line. But where would we be today if our great-grandfathers had made a similar decision?

7

Yet we must not overstress the problem we have before us. While it is true that some men are obliged to lose relative power, or prestige, or satisfaction in the process of growth, nevertheless, as the total output rises relative to the population, the basic level of consumption for all may be increased. I remember a Hungarian friend who remarked to me in the depths of the depression of the thirties, "In my country this would be

[12] (McGraw-Hill, 1951.)

considered wildest prosperity!" Furthermore, while some industries may disappear absolutely, it is often the case that some of the older industries merely stop growing and that the change may be relative rather than absolute. With growing total wealth and unchanged proportionate distribution suffering, in physical terms at least, is replaced by inconvenience. Yet one thing is certain. While it is true that we cannot say in any *given* instance that supply will necessarily create its own demand, it is also true that if every man is taught to hang back and withhold his labor until he is perfectly certain that there will be a market for it, then the total of expansion will be cut down or enormously reduced. A society which does not insist upon absolute security, and which encourages individuals to go ahead and expand, is likely to be a far wealthier and more rapidly growing society than one in which each man waits and holds back until a complete general agreement has been reached.

In this connection it seems to me important to remember that rising standards of living are not to be valued merely for their own sake, but also as *by-products* of other more deeply prized values. We may decide that growth is a delusion and that the static state would be better. But if we do so we will have to set up a sort of technological inquisition to suppress invention or to turn scientists into miniature painters. I refer you to Samuel Butler's *Erewhon*. Our dilemma, as I have put it elsewhere, is that if we make men "free" they will become creative, and from their creations will spring the probability of growth and the certainty of trouble. In any event we can be sure that the price of the static, job-secure "laboristic" state must be the elimination or castration of the pursuit of new knowledge and new invention.

Much has been written about the "hectic civilization of capitalism." But what about the flaccid civilization of a mature, job-conscious unionism? In this connection the writer has found few more just and thorough statements than that by an English writer, Honor Croome, writing in *Lloyd's Bank Review* (July,

1949). The whole essay, especially its distinction between the "classless" state and the "one-class" state, is warmly recommended. But I wish only to quote the following: "The oppression-born, depression-fostered degeneracy of the wage earners' attitude to service . . . can, with some effort, be dismissed as a passing deformity of the social sense, certain of cure under the therapeutic influence of social justice. But there remains something more permanent; the profound dislike of the good trade-unionist, however public-spirited, for the free lance and his methods. Action should be collectively determined; benefits should be collectively assessed; the norm should be collectively established; and the individual's only business is to share—of course on a footing of democratic equality—in the taking of these decisions and loyally to co-operate in implementing them. Solidarity is the supreme working class virtue, and individualism is correspondingly open to condemnation in all its manifestations. Excellence is suspect; he who excels might constitute himself a pacemaker. Resourcefulness is suspect; it may lead to the cutting of collectively sanctioned corners. Imaginative innovation is suspect, no less because it is rarely the outcome of collective action than because it may threaten a vested interest in the obsolete. All must travel in convoy, at the pace of the slowest; whoever follows a privately charted course is, almost by definition, a pirate." [13]

But finally, and again to introduce a more personal, controversial point, will the decisions necessarily be reached on a basis of "democratic equality" just because the rank and file have a vote in the management of the union or the business? Not only is opportunity involved but also democracy. Neither democracy nor the feeling of participation is derived merely from the right to drop a piece of paper in a box. Hitler after all let the Germans vote *Ja* and Stalin does the same. Democracy implies the chance to choose and to reject. But how much democ-

[13] "Liberty, Equality and Full Employment," pp. 20-21.

racy will there be—how independent will the voters in a union election be—if their jobs depend largely upon the O.K. of the union leaders themselves? And, as we have seen, may not the feeling of participation be at least as much a function of size as of labor organization? Again to quote Krech and Crutchfield: "A number of unions are dictatorial in their procedures and are not averse to using violence and goon squads to silence their members who would participate in free speech. Other unions operate as a tight bureaucracy and opportunities for leadership are limited to a selected and self-perpetuating few." [14]

This final democratic problem may not be an inevitable concomitant of universal unionism, though I strongly suspect that it will be, especially as the right to shift jobs without inordinate sacrifice progressively disappears. But the sabotage of change and production would unquestionably be an inevitable result of a program giving everyone absolute job security.

8

Since what I have said may be so easily misunderstood, let me summarize it carefully. I do not mean to imply that the only choice is between the Yogi and the Jitterbug. I do not mean to imply that my values are the only values. What I am anxious to point out is merely that there is a hidden conflict here; that while some compromise may indeed be reached, it can only be reached at the cost of some sacrifice regarding one quality or another; and finally that unless we *know* our problem we can scarcely hope to solve it.

Thus, to return to our starting point: if secure, stratified "poverty" is what the people want then there is little that can be done. But if that is what the unions and union leaders really believe in let them say so. What is being done instead is to whip up a constant demand for "more" at the same time that

[14] *Op. cit.*, p. 549.

demands for "security," seniority, and so on progressively hamper growth. True, this combination may end capitalism, but what comes after that? When the union leaders themselves are confronted with the task of running society then they will face the same dilemma they have created for the capitalist. The masses will call upon them to give constant rising living standards *and* a tremendously high degree of personal security. And since the masses will inevitably be disappointed, will not the way be paved for still more extreme leadership?

Let me run over my points:

(1) A fair amount of aggregate stability can be managed by appropriate fiscal policy and other methods. But this does not meet the basic conflict of *personal* security with *social* growth.

(2) Some unions may be called the prime apostles of the *indignity* of labor. For by encouraging a "hold-back" philosophy they progressively diminish the general instinct of workmanship.

(3) By their seniority and security schemes many unions are destroying opportunity and growth alike.

(4) By wage demands in excess of productivity it is possible to bring the process of investment to a full stop and cause unemployment.

Are we not justified, then, in treating many unions by the same techniques as those we apply to other restrictive power groups? Wherein do unions differ? All that I ask of the unionist is that he apply his own values to himself. If unionists do so I feel sure that many of them will be forced to revise their polcies.

CHAPTER XIII

Concerning Aggregate Wages [1]

BY DAVID McCORD WRIGHT

WHEN an economist says that we have "no theory of wages," he must, I submit, be referring to the theory of aggregate wages. There is, I believe, a fairly adequate theory of the differential reward of particular wage groups. Marginal productivity, plus a study of training costs, plus the theory of bilateral monopoly and cross-elasticities of demand, seems to me to be adequate to explain particular wage differences as we find them at any given time, either under unionism or not. To be sure, such a theory of bilateral monopoly and so forth leaves many indeterminacies, and this is particularly the case when we add to it the usual difficulties concerning a joint product or "common" costs. Nevertheless the recognition that, once we depart from wages more or less market-determined, the matter *is* largely a matter of bilateral "monopoly," constitutes in itself an important advance in the understanding of the problem. And in this connection I think it important to remember that the orthodox theory of particular wages is not a theory of what *cannot* be done, but a theory of consequences. In other words, the orthodox theory does not deny that an embattled union by surrounding, as it were, a given piece of equipment with a barbed-wire fence can divert to its members a great part of the return from such equipment. What the orthodox theory does say, however, is that such action is likely to be attended by con-

[1] *Editor's note:* This is a revision of the speech actually given at the institute.

sequences which may be unfavorable either to the growth of output as a whole or to the opportunities of certain members of the laboring class.

2

In the present paper I do not propose to develop the elaborate problems involved in the theory of particular wages and wage groups. Rather I wish to ask what economic theory has to say concerning the general movements of aggregate wages—and here I think it will be advisable to distinguish between wages set according to the pure theory of a self-adjusting market and the actual wage movements in a cyclical and not completely self-adjusting society.

Concerning aggregate wages, my thesis will be that while marginal productivity is capable of describing the *results* which will be achieved under an aggregate equilibrium, nevertheless it does not, standing alone, constitute a very meaningful theory of aggregate wages. This is especially the case if we bring in the problems of effective demand. For example, it is conceivable, under some circumstances, that a reduction in real wages would, for a time anyhow, induce a fall in capital's share also. I do not think that this is the most important possibility to keep in mind, but it *is* a possibility under certain very restricted assumptions. However, let us in this section concentrate instead upon the problems which are not tied up with effective demand. In other words we will assume for the moment that consumption and investment are mutually self-adjusting and thus that prolonged cyclical unemployment is impossible.

Clarity of reasoning demands that we start with the concept of the stationary state, very rigorously defined. Here, however, it is necessary to make a methodological digression. I agree with Professor Frank Knight that there is no spontaneous *economic* tendency toward stationary equilibrium. In other words, unless special forces intervene, the process of change and expansion has no end. There is a constant spontaneous shift in the pattern of wants and of technique to which no foreseeable limit can be assigned. However, this does not mean that, as a practical matter, the stationary state is an impossibility. On the contrary, sociological forces externally applied—for example, in anthropological language, a shift of the "culture concept" toward serenity rather than activity—could serve to bring the whole process to a full stop. Thus, while the stationary state finds its main importance as a theoretical concept and a tool for the clarification of thought, it is nevertheless not a practical impossibility, given certain shifts in social attitudes within a particular historic conjuncture.

Now, assuming the existence of a stationary state as the result of sociological resistances to change, then I submit that aggregate income would be distributed between wages and rent only. And by "rent" I do not mean quasi rent. That is, my stationary state would not show a *net* return at the margin to durable but not everlasting instruments of production.[2]

Many economists—in fact probably a majority of economists—believe that it will prove necessary to retain in such a stationary society an impatience rate of interest—time preference, or something of that sort. I do not personally feel that this result necessarily follows and I have discussed the paradoxes implied, in my *Economics of Disturbance*.[3] However, this issue seems to me to be of far greater theoretical complexity than practical value, and therefore I believe we will do best to leave it to one side. In other words, those who wish to put into the stationary state a minimum impatience rate of interest, needed to prevent people from eating up the capital stock, are free to do so. It would still remain true, however, that the major portion of the

[2] Any "net" return could exist only under the very special circumstances mentioned below in the remainder of this section, especially the last paragraph.

[3] (Macmillan, 1947), chap. iv.

distinctively entrepreneurial incomes, that is to say, the special rewards for owning capital, would tend to disappear in a stationary society, and that is the important point. The best way to raise real wages is by increasing output.

Again it must not be supposed that something called profit might not survive.[4] But these profits, so called, would be predominantly differential rents or wages of management rather than pure profit. Also there might be "profits" needed to offset certain uninsurable risks, such as those Professor Knight has spoken of. These risks also might give rise to certain elements of "profit." But there would be very little else, and so we find ourselves once more with the conclusion that pure profits would have a tendency to fall to zero, and that barring the special risk cases the national product would be divided between wages, including wages of management; rent on everlasting sources of income; and, if one wants to save argument, a minimum interest rate. Rent, furthermore, could not be successfully attacked by wage increases, but would have to be seized, if at all, by taxation.

3

Our analysis leads to the conclusion that the major portion of the typical capitalist incomes are the product of growth and change. This is at once their explanation and their sanction. If at any given point of time society ceased to change and to grow, and if the problem of effective demand did not arise—that is, if changes in consumption and investment offset one another, then I submit that society would settle down into a stationary state in which income would be divided as sketched in the preceding section. But from this conclusion we may say that in a stationary state which has otherwise adjusted itself—that is, a state in which there would be no net growth either in population or in capital—the existence of any important entre-

[4] See my *Capitalism* (McGraw-Hill, 1951), chap. v.

preneurial income would depend upon a race between "innovation" and "imputation." Of course it is difficult to conceive of a society in which large-scale innovation was taking place which did not have net growth in output and in the capital stock. Nevertheless, a situation is *conceivable* in which there would be no net growth in capital stock and no net change in population, but which nevertheless, because of the effect of innovation, could show a net share going to entrepreneurs.

A critical theoretical case concerns the behavior of the economy if we suppose population to recommence growing, but the stock of capital to remain initially unchanged. Under the marginal productivity theory this would be considered to lead to an increase in relative aggregate entrepreneurial income. I do not quarrel with this conclusion, so far as the beginning of the process is concerned, but unless some independent explanation is adduced, it seems to me that, under the assumptions of pure competition and so on normally made in problems of this sort, the effect of such a population increase would be to raise once more the *marginal* profit incentive for the expansion of capital.[5] The capital stock, therefore, would "automatically" be increased until the net marginal reward of capital would once more be reduced to zero, subject to the qualifications already stated.

If one denies such a tendency toward growth of the capital stock, one will have to bring in special assumptions regarding increased risk, or hostile institutional environment, which would keep entrepreneurs from carrying the process of investment as far as it could go. The total net effect of the population increase mentioned, barring some such external institutional interference with the investment process, would be to raise rent, but not to give any permanent increase in entrepreneurial income—aside from the minimum interest rate often thought necessary. Thus, while the marginal productivity theory can always describe what has happened, it nevertheless, if used uncritically, can give a

---

[5] I am indebted to Professor Friedman for correcting certain errors in my initial statement of this point.

very misleading impression. There is first the unlikely fringe-end case of an otherwise stationary state in which the process of innovation maintains certain entrepreneurial incomes. Secondly, in a growing society the entrepreneurial incomes cannot merely be explained by aggregate static physical productivity functions, but must also be explained by the rate of innovation. Finally, although the productivity theory yields results which are technically correct in the case of an increase in population with capital stock initially unchanged, such results are apt to be misleading if taken too literally. The initial rise in entrepreneurial incomes could not be consistent with an equilibrium situation under our assumptions.

4

But the theoretical interest and complication of the analysis just given far exceeds its practical importance. The major conclusion which emerges from our analysis is that effective *practical* analysis of aggregate wages has to be in terms of growth and change. Let us proceed in this section, therefore, to analyze the effect of aggregate wage movements upon growth, change, and employment. We will drop the assumption that the propensity to consume necessarily moves in an offsetting manner with the inducement to invest, and we will come to grips with the problem of effective demand as well as with the problem of the business cycle.

The kind of analysis for which I contend runs in terms of two margins. First of all, there is the margin of net new investment—the proportion of gross national product which goes into net new capital instruments. This is the most delicate part of the total national product and furnishes what might be called the "setscrew" of the economic system.

The second margin which I think it necessary to bear in mind is the margin of profit to be derived from increasing the output of a given plant, or from building an entirely new plant. This second margin I find it convenient to analyze in terms of a distinction between "total" profit and "marginal" profit. "Total" profit means the profit which one happens to be making from a plant already built and operating at a predetermined production schedule. "Marginal" profit refers to the profit which one expects to make either from working existing plant more intensively or else from building additional plant. It thus corresponds pretty closely to Keynes's "marginal efficiency of capital." From the point of view of general employment, the margin of net new investment is kept occupied when there is an adequate expectation of "marginal" profit. It is in terms of these two margins that the question of wage increases must be discussed.

Now the really vital consideration and the one which is almost wholly left aside in much modern discussion is that a money- (or real-) wage increase which seems to leave to the entrepreneur a quite "fair" or even "excessive" amount of "total" profit may nevertheless have the effect of cutting off all "marginal" profit expectations. It is true that statistics have been gathered which would indicate that at certain stages of the cycle the (short-run) marginal cost curves are practically flat and far below average costs. But I submit that these statistics are misleading as statements of universal behavior and that the nearer we get to full employment, the more "orthodox" in shape the cost curves are generally apt to become. For everybody will be drawing on the same pool of labor and, as it is exhausted, individual cost curves will tend to rise more steeply as an attempt is made to increase relative output.

Under such circumstances an increase in average wage rates may have a more than proportionate impact on marginal cost and thus may destroy marginal profit incentives.

It is, for example, often thought that if during an inflation prices rise more than wages as a result of a wage increase, or if profits go up by a greater percentage than wages, this must indicate some sort of monopoly action. Such an attitude may be entirely mistaken. Under inflationary conditions the public may have the funds to buy as much of a given product as before, but if marginal costs are affected disproportionately by a wage increase it would be necessary, even under pure competition, for prices to go up faster than wages in order to cover the extra cost of the marginal increment of product.

Before going further, however, I should like to call attention to what I consider to be a serious defect in many theoretical treatments of the problem of bargaining. It is not only the marginal profit incentive of the *particular* firm that counts but marginal profit incentives throughout the entire industry. For example, a man who because of some temporarily favored position is making a very large total profit, may nevertheless not have *any* "marginal" profit expectations because he is already equating marginal costs with marginal revenue on his plant. But this will not mean that there is necessarily no "long-run" marginal incentive in the *field*. On the contrary, other people, seeing the abnormally high profit which the individual in question may be making, may feel it worth while to construct a new plant paralleling the old one. This increase in total "long-run" capacity may have the effect of bringing down the rate of profit throughout the whole field.

"Long-run" analysis of this sort has important implications for wage theory. The modern tendency to consider that the only adjustments are those between a *particular* union and a *particular* company seems to me very unfortunate. It overlooks the fact that the most healthy way to bring down profits is through construction of a number of *additional* plants. Such construction occurs, however, because of the lure of abnormal profits.[6] If, *before* new investors have had an opportunity to enter the field, the union has forced up wage rates, cutting off marginal in-

---

[6] To cover special risks of expansion. See my "Toward Coherent Anti-Trust," *Virginia Law Review* (October, 1949), p. 665.

centive, then society loses a potential margin of increased opportunity, and an increased output most of which in the long run would go to labor.

5

Let us, however, leave to one side analysis of particular margins and pass on to the crucial problem of the effect of a general money- and/or real-wage increase upon employment and social growth. If such an increase takes place in a society operating, let us say, on the basis of 100 per cent money, and in which MV is not allowed to increase, but may fall, then the wage demands come up almost at once against the ceiling of a limited money supply. *Ceteris paribus*, therefore, a large wage increase will cut off "marginal" profit incentives, in the manner just analyzed, and cause a state of unemployment in the investment goods industries. General deflation will be likely to begin.

The effects of the wage increase may under some circumstances, it is true, be offset, even though MV has not increased, by the simultaneous introduction of an exogenous new invention forming a new investment outlet—some great cost-saving invention, let us say, which gives a source of profitable investment despite the wage increase. Such an invention could recreate the marginal incentive to invest in spite of the fact that, had it not occurred, the money-wage increase would have *ceteris paribus* cut off investment. Thus, even in the case of a limited money supply, the possibility cannot be ruled out entirely that a general large-scale money-wage increase, under some very special circumstances, might not result in unemployment. But while this case is possible, it is not likely, or at any rate cannot be relied upon.[7] It belongs in the class with the infant industry

[7] It may be argued that the high wages, by creating a special premium for labor-saving devices, will actually have a *net* stimulatory effect upon

argument and many other theoretical problems which economists have recognized for generations, but which they have not
considered important enough to affect practical conclusions. And
it remains true that if the money supply or rather *MV* cannot
rise, then an important rise in money-wage rates is likely to
cut off the marginal inducement to invest and cause unemployment.

A more important case, in the light of modern attitudes
toward fiscal policy, is the case in which the government inter-
venes to underwrite the new price level made necessary by the
increase in costs. It may be asked why the government would
intervene. The answer, it seems to me, lies in the sequence indicated by Professor Haberler in chap. ii: (1) a money-wage
increase; (2) an observed faltering in the production and employment indices; (3) public clamor for deficit finance; (4) a
consequent increase in the money supply.

Now under such circumstances it is often argued that the
money-wage increases would have no effect upon marginal investment incentives and upon employment. It should of course
be observed that likewise, however, they would have no particular influence upon the general proportionate share going to
labor. But that is not our particular point at the moment.

---

total investment. Thus the unfavorable effects of the wage increase upon
marginal incentive in some lines will be offset by an artificially created
net incentive in others. Professor Clark's paper mentions this possibility,
pp. 11, 12.

But there are two points to be remembered here. First of all the process
of innovation, if one follows Schumpeter's analysis, can introduce a "discontinuous" change in production functions. There is a temporary but
nevertheless real, independent value-creating source derived from the individual saltations. Thus there is no need for as much "labor" to be demanded in building *and* designing the new machine as is displaced by
the machine. The changes in outlay need not be offsetting.

Secondly, and perhaps still more important, even if aggregate income
is maintained there will probably be created a growing class of semide-
pressed unemployables due to the artificial stimulus to labor-saving devices
and the artificially high price of crude labor.

I do not, however, feel that this so-optimistic statement is correct or that if the government underwrites the increased money cost there necessarily will be no unemployment. Entrepreneurs continue to have certain long-run expectations concerning normal prices, expectations which may change relatively slowly. Accordingly, even though there has been an increase in MV, financed by the government, and even though the higher labor costs are being matched by higher prices supported by government-created money, still this does not necessarily mean that the climate of opinion will be favorable to investment; for the entrepreneur may feel that the present level of prices will not last, and therefore he may be reluctant to commit himself to long-range investment projects undertaken at a time in which the cost level is in his opinion inflated. Consequently, even if all industries were to have similar money-wage increases, and even if the government might stand ready to increase the money supply sufficiently to underwrite these increases, nevertheless this would not mean that the whole process would not affect investment adversely. On the contrary, the cultural atmosphere engendered, particularly if there had been a number of strikes and so on, might be such as seriously to deter investment incentives and even to cause unemployment, in spite of the inflationary tendencies—unemployment which in the last analysis could only be avoided, under the circumstances assumed, by direct government investment.

Putting the analysis now into reverse for the case of general wage cuts, it is of course often argued that a cut in wages restricts demand as fast as it cuts costs and therefore gets us nowhere. I do not think it necessary in this paper to analyze the numerous complicated sequences of price reduction, cash balance shifts, and so on, which are often worked out to show that there may be some net increase in total real consumption, even though money wages are falling. I leave these constructions to one side because they do not seem to me to be very fruitful, practically speaking—at least not so far as cyclical stabilization is concerned.

The main point, as I see it, is that, other things being equal, there are apt always to be a certain number of *"autonomous,"* exogenous investment outlets which can be used whenever there is a general upturn in confidence.[8] Now, just as the entrepreneurs have an idea of normal prices which may make them unwilling to invest when prices are higher than this supposed normal level, so also they have an idea of what constitutes normal prices when prices fall. Thus though prices and perhaps even income are falling, the entrepreneur may nevertheless feel that prosperity will return, and he may start on autonomous investments in order to take advantage of what he conceives to be bargain rates. This is a case explicitly recognized by Lord Keynes but generally ignored by his more self-conscious disciples. It will be recalled that Keynes said that a wage cut may strike through a vicious circle of "unduly pessimistic" expectations and, by inducing a feeling of confidence, cause a renewal of investment.[9]

It must be remembered that investment in our society is not necessarily made in any fixed, rigid, mechanical relationship to the movements of the level of consumption. Indeed I consider

[8] As to the word "autonomous," compare J. R. Hicks, *A Contribution to the Trade Cycle* (Oxford University Press, 1950).

[9] *General Theory*, p. 264. Keynes wrote: "A general [money-wage] reduction . . . may also produce an optimistic tone in the minds of entrepreneurs, which may break through a vicious circle of unduly pessimistic estimates of the marginal efficiency of capital and set things moving again on a more normal basis of expectation."

Again he said (p. 265): "When we enter on a period of weakening demand, a sudden large reduction of money-wages to a level so low that no one believes in its indefinite continuance *would be the event most favourable to a strengthening of effective demand*" [Italics supplied].

I mention these passages merely to remind the reader that Lord Keynes was not himself a "streamlined" Keynesian and that the analysis of the *General Theory*, especially as to wages, interest, and investment "outlets," is much broader and more catholic than usually understood. Cf. my "Future of Keynesian Economics," *Amer. Econ. Rev.* (June, 1945), which was approved in essentials by Keynes himself.

the idea of a fixed relationship to be the basic fallacy of crude Keynesianism.[10]

6

What are we to conclude, as a matter of practical policy, from the foregoing analysis of general wage increases in relationship to employment and unemployment? It must be conceded that, just as we cannot rely upon an exogenous invention which might conceivably offset the effects of an otherwise unreasonable money-wage demand, so also, in the same way, we cannot, as a matter of practical policy, rely upon the immediate existence of autonomous investment outlets which will be exploited as soon as a general cut in money wages is made. I believe, therefore, that the proper policy, so far as unemployment is concerned, would be that worked out by Professor Haberler in his *Prosperity and Depression*.[11] In other words, we should maintain aggregate demand within reasonable limits by appropriate fiscal policy. Thus we avoid the pessimistic expectations which a general wage decrease and general unemployment might cause. But at the same time that we are maintaining relative stability of aggregate demand, a reduction of money wages in many lines would serve to give a special added stimulus to investment. Thus, as I see it, a policy which combines the relative maintenance of aggregate money income with a program of selected money-wage cuts or even, in some cases, of general wage cuts, gives us the best

[10] Even if consumption is falling, investment may be made for any one of the following reasons: (1) a new product which is expected to be very popular; (2) a new technique so cost-saving as to be profitable even though demand is falling; (3) a feeling that business will soon turn up, which state of confidence *can* (though not necessarily) be self-verifying; (4) a long-run project geared to, say, a twenty-year expected trend rather than immediate consumption; (5) modernization of facilities merely to hold one's own.

[11] (United Nations, third ed., enlarged, 1946.)

of both worlds—both Keynesian and orthodox. It will, further-more, serve to start investment going once more and thus stimu-late that process of growth upon which in the last analysis all important variations in the level of real wages depend.

One final word of warning should be given. I have argued as if it were possible to distinguish sharply in real life between *aggregate* real- or money-wage movements and particular money-wage movements. Actually of course the problem is exactly like that of the price index: large-scale individual move-ments may also affect the aggregate. Therefore we can only divorce the aggregate and the particular by doing some violence to reality. Nevertheless I believe that the outline of an aggregate theory sketched herein will be valuable even though it is no more than a first approximation.

CHAPTER XIV

Selections from the Discussion
of Wright's Second Paper

FRIEDMAN. I wish there were some way to have this argument without having it involve the theory of capital and yet I don't see how we can. I hate to see us have to argue about the theory of capital.

It seems to me utterly fantastic to suppose a stationary state would be one in which interest would conceivably be non-existent.

WRIGHT. That is the point which I argue with one of my colleagues three times a week, as I told you. He often maintains that capital has to have an infinite value under my concept. Now so far as noneternal durable capital is concerned it only has to have a price, and that price will merely cover its cost of production—which does not include interest if you are assuming the automatic replacement of capital.

FRIEDMAN. In your society, can people borrow money?

WRIGHT. Nobody wants to borrow money.[1] If they want to borrow money, you would get—

SAMUELSON. Only with the intention of repaying.

FRIEDMAN. They can borrow at 6 per cent?

SAMUELSON. The man who has no intention of repaying is delighted to borrow at any percentage, even the infinite. They must have an intention of repaying.

[1] *Comment by Wright:* In other words my model assumes no net new investment, and a "marginal efficiency of capital" of zero.

WRIGHT. There would be no incentive to borrow. If you want to put time preference in, you can.

SAMUELSON. It would simplify this discussion if you would.

WRIGHT. To put it in?

KNIGHT. It would make it unintelligible from that moment to me.

WRIGHT. Leaving aside time preference, I conceive of interest theory in this way. You have a certain number of people constantly saving—i.e., not consuming—and then you have a certain number of people constantly borrowing, and if more people want to borrow "capital disposal" than want to save, interest will go up. This is a "real" theory. Under "full" employment, and without inflation, the money saving is simply the tickets, so to speak, to the free resources that are being constantly freed by the act of current saving. The borrowing is to make new investments, and the motive power for the new investments is the hope of marginal profit. You do it in other words, because there is a marginal efficiency of capital [MEC]; and as the MEC rises, the rate of interest rises; and as the MEC falls, the rate of interest falls. This "classical" scheme can be interrupted by all sorts of speculative and liquidity disturbances. But, leaving aside sudden liquidity panics, as at the downturn of the cycle, or the special Keynesian case of a minimum liquidity preference rate, if the MEC fell to zero, the rate of interest would fall to zero too.

FRIEDMAN. On your own logic, then, your stationary state is a real state, stopped by a camera.

WRIGHT. Professor Knight convinces me there are no limits to the use of capital.

SAMUELSON. And that, by the way, is to be considered a technological fact.

WRIGHT. I think the matter something more than a static technological statement. I hold it to be true that people automatically form new wants as they get richer; and that the pattern of consumer's choice spontaneously changes, as output rises; and that theoretically, therefore, if there was no friction and if the businessman could read off the future wants of the consumer there would always be enough obsolescence to maintain an inducement to invest.

SAMUELSON. Is there any reason why there should be any positive net investment due to obsolescence? The obsolescence of old instruments satisfying old wants could balance the creation of new instruments.

FRIEDMAN. It is a technological fact in the sense that if it weren't true we would have a society in which all goods were free.[2]

WRIGHT. Leaving the stationary state for a moment, the really important practical point, so far as Dr. Samuelson's question is concerned, is that there is not any close mechanical relationship between the consumption level and the demand for investment goods, and that you can't use the Marxian model in which the demand for investment goods is rigidly related to the stock of investment goods—in which it is assumed that for each level of consumption there is a certain pile of investment goods, and that net investment gradually eats away that pile until you either have a stationary state with a zero rate of interest or else a social crisis. That model may possibly hold for short intervals, as I say in my paper. It may hold for short intervals, but there are so many other sources of capital demand, so many autonomous changes that occur, that the question of investment outlets is one that cannot be discussed in those terms. The question turns on all sorts of sociological forces, cost-price relationships and that sort of thing.

Now, I do think, however, that practically speaking these sociological frictions are so great from time to time that we

[2] *Comment by Wright:* We have here the basic difference between Dr. Friedman's views and my own. I do not believe that because the marginal efficiency of capital is zero all goods must be free. Compare Irving Fisher's *Rate of Interest* (Macmillan, 1930).

can temporarily reason in terms of the stationary state. It is not therefore wholly meaningless.

HABERLER. Concerning that stationary state, is this discussion necessary? It is very interesting, but I wonder whether it is necessary for our wage question.

WRIGHT. Well, the reason for bringing it in is that it shows that if capitalism loses its dynamic character at any given level of output, then, first of all, the immediate consequence may be unemployment—that is, if you cut off the flow of net new investment without a rise in the propensity to consume. But supposing the thing works more slowly and that the propensity to consume rises slowly as the flow of net investment declines. Then, under the Ricardian model, as the rate of interest falls, the urge to accumulate declines, and society slowly merges into a stationary equilibrium. Suppose it goes that way. Then you are left with the theory of the division of the national income between wages and rent.

SAMUELSON. Why at the zero level? I would like to be a peacemaker and not get into asymptotic questions. If that fails, I am willing to argue that it has been mathematically rigorously demonstrated that you can conceptually have a zero rate under proper self-consistent technological assumptions. But, in any case, Schumpeter's "theory of economic development" would be absolutely no different if he had not had a zero theory, but instead a 2 per cent theory. People live a definite length of time, and at some level, such as a 2 per cent rate, they would on balance, in a stationary population, consume in their lifetime all their wealth, bequeathing nothing behind them; and, therefore, Schumpeter's model would be the following: Economic development comes along, plucks the violin string, the rate of interest rises above 2 per cent, then gradually through time, with no more innovation, it sinks back again, not to zero rate but 2 per cent, and the income then is divided between wages, rents, and this very moderate 2 per cent interest rate. There is nothing different for his business cycle theory if that was the lower asymptote instead of the zero asymptote.

WRIGHT. It might save a lot of trouble to take that as my model. Switching to marginal productivity, for a minute, the point I do not like is the assumption that, given things otherwise fixed, you can compare a fixed amount of capital with a fixed amount of "labor." How are you going to measure capital? That is one of the big questions.

I never have been able fully to accept Paul Douglas's theory of wages as a theory of aggregate wages. The theory of partial wages, yes. For aggregate wages, it seems to me, if there is no change and no entrepreneurship, then the total product is eventually divided between wages and rent; and if you want to put in this minimum interest rate, that is all right.

FRIEDMAN. There is no contradiction between the so-called theory of partial wages and the theory of aggregate wages. What is the contradiction? I am going to assume a stationary state and make it exceedingly rigid, by assuming it contains only permanent capital instruments. There is nothing that wears out, and we will beg the question of the interest rate by supposing that there are no purchases or sales, no interest rate, no borrowing or lending. In such a society all of current income will be divided between payments for wages and payments for rent on durable capital goods of various kinds. That which determines a particular wage rate or rent per unit of capital goods determines also the fraction of the total which goes to one kind of factor of production.

WRIGHT. Take a given plant. They are going to buy a dynamo. They have to pay for it.

KNIGHT. Why do you have to pay for anything with interest free?

WRIGHT. My model didn't say there would be no purchase of capital goods.

FRIEDMAN. I assume no purchase of capital goods because I want to try to eliminate the interest rate problem.

WRIGHT. You are assuming the problem.

SAMUELSON. No interest problem for nonperpetual yields.

FRIEDMAN. I want to discuss the issue without assuming either that the interest rate is zero or that it is not, and that is why I am eliminating this altogether. I would rather have no purchases of capital goods.

WRIGHT. Let's go back to J. B. Clark's stationary state. You remember that there the entrepreneurs are automatically putting aside depreciation quotas, which they use to buy new equipment as fast as the old equipment wears out. That is what I have in mind, and I don't see why you necessarily have to bring in the interest rate.[3]

SAMUELSON. If it is there, you bring it in.

FRIEDMAN. Again, let's avoid the interest rate. All I want to argue is it seems to me that this marginal productivity theory gives you all the answers in the aggregate. I don't know what you say is missing.

CHAMBERLIN. What is missing? I quite agree.

WRIGHT. If you have this J. B. Clark's stationary state in which you are paying for your machinery, you replace what is wearing out and automatically provide for it by depreciation allowances, this equilibrium would have been reached through marginal adjustments in which the marginal cost of that machinery had been balanced against the marginal product—the price of labor, the marginal product, and all the rest of it. There would be a gross return to capital, but not a net one. And part of the gross would go to rent, the space, you see, and part of it would go to depreciation, and that would be all there would be. But you would have made the usual calculation here, the machine would cost a certain sum.

---

[3] *Comment by Wright:* In other words the firms pay for their replacements with depreciation quotas. The price of the new machine covers its costs but no interest. Regarding perpetual yields see my *Economics of Disturbance,* chap. iv.

FRIEDMAN. What is missing? What do you need a theory for that the marginal productivity theory doesn't give you?

WRIGHT. The marginal productivity theory is excellent in this setup for the wages of this or that group, but where it goes wrong, or perhaps, to speak more accurately, where it is often misunderstood, is in giving the idea that if you had an increase in population, other things being equal, that that increase in population would result in a *permanent* rise in the interest rate or in the rate of profits. I don't think it would.[4] In the long run, it could only result in the increase of rent.

SAMUELSON. Suppose you took a balanced increase in population of every grade. I think some generalized statements could still be made. Given the historical endowment of durable goods, not necessarily of perpetual life, but possibly with some of them having perpetual life, I think it is likely that this would pluck the violin string, in the same way technological change would, and transiently there would be a higher net productivity of existing stock of capital. Depending upon people's net saving habits over time, this transient increase in interest rate might be whittled down to the previous long-run equilibrium level of interest at 2 per cent or *k* per cent where *k* might equal zero if we get away from certain contradictions.

CHAMBERLIN. You are increasing the supply of capital. You are increasing the supply in response to the higher interest rate. What is there about that which is contradictory to the marginal productivity theory?

FRIEDMAN. These propositions can be demonstrated or proved or disproved by the marginal productivity apparatus. You [Wright] seem to be saying that you accept the marginal productivity theory, but you don't accept the conclusions to which it leads. Then you are required to show there is something wrong with it.

[4] *Comment by Wright:* Barring special assumptions. See my paper, "Concerning Aggregate Wages" (page 282).

WRIGHT. I take the idea that at any given level of national income if you stop change, but accumulation continues for a time, as Professor Samuelson suggests, your profits would tend to disappear and that you would only get the minimum interest rate, or zero, whichever assumption one makes.

FRIEDMAN. What are profits? I don't understand. Again, we are using this word "profit" in two senses—one in an accounting sense; a second in Knight's sense of a form of income produced by industry.

WRIGHT. There would be wages of management and risk premiums, because both of these could survive. Wages of management; and if you want to put in this minimum interest rate, you can.

FRIEDMAN. There would be an equilibrium rate.

WRIGHT. I can't see an equilibrium rate if nobody wants to expand.

FRIEDMAN. You don't have to have expansion. You need it to make people willing to hold the existing stock of capital and neither increase it nor decrease it.

CHAMBERLIN. That is precisely what J. B. Clark says about the interest rate in a static state.

BOULDING. If we are going to talk about interest, we ought to talk not about real capital but the financial system. The purpose of the financial system is to separate ownership from control, and interest is the price we have to pay for it.

WRIGHT. Does it give any independent—

FRIEDMAN. I think the point Professor Boulding is making now is an important one, that we get ourselves confused by treating interest as if it were comparable to a wage rate. It isn't at all. Interest is comparable to the wage rate of unskilled labor divided by the wage rate of skilled labor, not either one alone.

BOULDING. Not even that. Interest is a rate of growth.

FRIEDMAN. It is a price.

BOULDING. No, it isn't.

FRIEDMAN. It is a relative price.

BOULDING. Interest is not a price; it is a rate of growth. It is a thing like 5 per cent per annum, which is a rate of growth.

FRIEDMAN. We can express it that way. It is a price that I pay this year to get a dollar next year.

WRIGHT. I think of it as a price you have to pay for capital disposal; and if you don't want capital disposal, you wouldn't pay anything for it.

FRIEDMAN. You still want capital disposal. You want to prevent the other people from eating up the capital.

WRIGHT. Suppose that nobody has any opportunity for profitable new investment? You assume that sociologically you somehow cut off change and you are settling down on fixed preference scales, and that you 'have carried investment out to the point where there is no longer any net profit incentive from increasing output, nobody wants to borrow, nobody has any desire to increase output. Why should they pay interest?

FRIEDMAN. In that case you won't stop where you are. In that case, you will eat up your capital and move to a lower level of capital.

WRIGHT. You assume that. That is an assumption. It may be true or not. It is an independent assumption.

FRIEDMAN. It is not an assumption. It means that otherwise, when things are scarce, there is one thing for which people don't get paid. Therefore they are going to substitute other things for it. Goods are scarce.

WRIGHT. Well, as I say, *if* you assume that people do have such a psychological propensity, that they can't be trusted to replace their equipment, and they have to be paid to keep them from consuming their capital, why, then you do bring in a rate of interest. And that may be true, but I don't think it is a necessary assumption.

CHAMBERLIN..Why is it necessary not to assume it? Isn't it a natural assumption?

WRIGHT. It seems to me you see this particularly clearly in a modern large-scale corporation where there is almost perfect foresight as to the need to keep the institution going. The people in charge would desire to maintain the continued existence of this entity, and they will "automatically" and without interest or profit expectation put aside the necessary depreciation.

CHAMBERLIN. Why should you *assume* they want to maintain the thing at the existing amount automatically? As a matter of fact, whether they want to maintain it at the existing amount is tied up with the question as to whether they are getting an annual interest return.

WRIGHT. To the salaried manager the interest is not important. He is interested in his salary.

CHAMBERLIN. But here the decision would ultimately be taken by those who had provided the capital. Of course, you do have problems of separation of ownership and control in the corporation, but you can't separate them completely.

FRIEDMAN. To get the marginal productivity theory going again, you can surely have a society in which there is no borrowing and lending, or no buying or selling of capital goods. So if you have a firm, all it can buy is services. It rents the use of land; it rents the use of a perpetual machine for so much a year; it rents hours of labor from people. Now, the Walrasian system or whatever assumption you want to make—

SAMUELSON. That isn't the Walrasian system. He has a theory of capitalization.

FRIEDMAN. The Walrasian system minus the theory of capitalization. Given the volumes of these various capital instruments, technology, and tastes, there would be some equilibrium wages, some equilibrium rents, some equilibrium—if you want to call them so—wages of management or whatever you want to call them. All the prices of the services of factors are determined and so the proportion of total income which goes to each factor is determined. Do you change anything by suddenly saying we will call some of these incomes, interest or not interest, instead of "rents"? In such a society, what does the marginal productivity theory not give us? Why do we need a new theory?

WRIGHT. I just don't think that the theory as applied to the aggregate is very meaningful. It is true by definition that whatever aggregate wage share you get in the stationary state can be explained by marginal productivity, but I don't think that you, practically speaking, can make predictions according to some production function.

SAMUELSON. It does not say much. That is true.

FRIEDMAN. It says a great deal.

HABERLER. I think you ask a little too much of the theory. That brings me to the point that the marginal productivity does not tell us whether wages will be above the subsistence level.

SAMUELSON. It does tell you after a while.

HABERLER. If you ask something like that of the theory, I would say it is simply too much. If you have a general theory, you must still make what philosophers call initial assumptions. You must say what the shape of the production function is. But you are asking for something which a theory, in the nature of it, cannot give you. The theory gives you only relationships, and now you have to put in the concrete, technological factors; and it is conceivable that our world is such that the marginal productivity of labor is so low that people couldn't live; and that would be inconvenient. That is not excluded by the theory but, from experience, I think we can conclude that it just would not happen so.

WRIGHT. Well, I think that there is not a great deal of point in arguing the very abstract question here. I think what we do all agree upon is that in the stationary state, barring a minimum interest rate, labor and rent would get most of the income. I can't see that there would be anything but wages and rent.

SAMUELSON. Interest would be a way of looking at rents.

WRIGHT. So the subsistence theory is simply a statement that the population has got to increase down to some subsistence level, which is a totally unnecessary assumption; and as far as any aggregate theory is concerned, you just say that whatever the rise of national output may be, that most of it is going to labor anyhow if we cut off change. Practically speaking, however, if we want rising living standards then we must remember that the entrepreneurial incomes which induce change and growth may be very easily cut off; and labor in trying to grab for more than its share, and thus cutting off the marginal expectation of profit, will be likely in the beginning to cause unemployment in the very important and very vulnerable net new investment sector.

HABERLER. You are assuming a deflationary spiral or something like that.

WRIGHT. Yes. Raising the level of money wages, if you have an MV that cannot rise, may well cut off the marginal expectation of profit and immediately induce unemployment. It doesn't necessarily have to because, by the grace of God, somebody may make a remarkable cost-saving invention, or there may be some change in wants which may create a very fine new investment opportunity and high yield. Then if that happened, a sufficient inducement to invest might remain to keep investment flowing in spite of the wage increase.

HABERLER. Remains independent of the rise of wages.

WRIGHT. Yes, but if the two things, wage rise plus invention, should happen simultaneously—it is very unlikely but possible, the fortuitous combination of increased money-wage demand and a big new invention lowering costs—you might still have enough net yield surviving to keep full employment; but there is always the risk that in pressing for money-wage increases you may cut off the net marginal profit expectation and induce unemployment, immediately, particularly if MV cannot rise.

FRIEDMAN. You are just using the marginal productivity theory, that is all. Your statements are merely a translation. If the selling price is fixed, and the money-wage rate rises, then the money-wage rate will exceed the marginal value product of that number of employees and, therefore, each employer will have an incentive to discharge employees. On the other hand, if something else is changing—

WRIGHT. It can certainly be put in a marginal productivity language. I am doing something a little different from what most people do in that I am throwing the thing into expectations of the marginal revenue products to be derived from starting something new. I can easily see wage changes which would still leave a considerable total profit, something that would look pretty nice, and which yet might cut off all marginal profit expectations whatever, so that they also cut off investment, and cut off growth—even though at first, while there might be some retrenchment on existing equipment there would still be a substantial yield on it.[5]

FRIEDMAN. I don't like your use of "marginal" in some sense other than "derivative," but that is all right. Your conclusions are all right. We have no quarrel with them. They are simply an application of marginal productivity analysis.

CHAMBERLIN. What is meant by saying it is not meaningful— it doesn't say anything? It seems to me it says a very great deal; and, as a matter of fact, as has just been shown, it is useful in saying all the things that Dave Wright wants to say. He says it all, using this theory. It seems to me it is exceedingly meaningful. What do you mean, Paul, when you say it isn't meaningful?

SAMUELSON. I say it is empty.

CHAMBERLIN. But why? It means that each of the factors receives an income which corresponds to what it adds to the total for a very small change in its amount, the derivative of the total with respect to the factor.

SAMUELSON. Take von Wieser's book, *Natural Values*, written in the 1880's. He explicitly omitted, if he did not reject, the marginal productivity theory; he worked with completely fixed coefficients of production; yet no conclusion either for welfare economics or anything else was changed.

CHAMBERLIN. Well, Taylor has shown that even if you use these Wieser equations and fixed coefficients you can still get a

[5] *Comment by Clark:* I have tried to say something about marginal productivity, in this regard, in my concluding statement (chap. xvii).

marginal significance of factors because the factors are used in different proportions in different products. That is in F. M. Taylor's *Principles*.[6]

SAMUELSON. This reinforces my point; it doesn't change it. The fact of substitutability, the thing that was added after 1878 by Walras in the second edition, in the late eighties, and what J. B. Clark and other marginal productivity theorists are supposed to have added, was *intra*firm factor substitution; and that changes not at all the problem of general equilibrium. It just requires that certain of the schedules be more elastic than they otherwise would have been.

FRIEDMAN. That does not mean that marginal productivity is an empty theory.

SAMUELSON. I say it added nothing. Which are you talking about?

FRIEDMAN. The theory of general marginal productivity.

SAMUELSON. What it says is all prices are determined in a simultaneous general equilibrium system.

FRIEDMAN. The theory is simply a restatement of part of the general theory in terms which are relevant to the particular problem we are interested in, which is the pricing of factors of production.

SAMUELSON. Yes?

FRIEDMAN. It has implications that are easily capable of being contradicted—such as the rise in the wage rate of a particular brand of labor. It would be contradictory if such a rise were associated uniformly with an increase in employment of that particular brand of labor.

BOULDING. It can't do more than that.

SAMUELSON. That is just what I said there in my paper [chap. xv]. If you are willing to assume, even prior to the wage fund, as economists, that there is elasticity for the demand of labor,

[6] Ronald Press, 1921.

the marginal productivity within the firm adds the presumption of the degree of elasticity and nothing else.

FRIEDMAN. That is all right.

BOULDING. It can't answer the questions we are concerned about.

FRIEDMAN. What questions are you concerned about?

BOULDING. What happens if there is a general rise or fall in money wages? Does that result in an equal, greater, or smaller rise in the price of wage-goods? Does that result in a decline or increase in unemployment? Does it result in changes in consumption and investment and the rest of it? I would say the general equilibrium theory does not say anything about that.[7] Maybe it ought to.

SAMUELSON. I think one could establish a few presumptions that would result from a real substantive change in wage rates of one grade. I think that it could be shown under a wide set of plausible conditions that the demand was negatively sloped.

BOULDING. For all wages, you mean?

SAMUELSON. For any category, any single grade that you take.

BOULDING. We agree about that. We all agree.

SAMUELSON. Then take all grades together, holding other factors constant.

FRIEDMAN. I must say I find it hard to see why anybody is interested in the particular figure of the percentage of aggregate income that goes to wages.

BOULDING. I am interested in it.

CHAMBERLIN. We have a half-hour yet. I was suggesting that we might have another half-hour on Dave Wright's paper or hear Paul Samuelson's and then discuss both together.

WRIGHT. I am quite willing to stop now. I do want to say one thing. The first part of my paper seems to me pretty academic and not to be of very great practical importance. What does in-

---

[7] *Comment by Wright:* But marginal productivity language may help to clarify dynamic considerations. See my "Aggregate Wages" paper (chap. xiii).

terest me is what happens when we throw the question of the general wage level or wage increases into terms of its effect, not on the profit earned from existing instruments of production, but on the expectation of profit from new instruments of production, in other words its effect on marginal incentive; I am very much interested in showing that it may leave enough to keep people going on what they have already built and yet cut off the margin of growth. I am also interested in showing that a reduction in wages may have a direct effect on confidence because a businessman will assume certain customary levels of price value; and, therefore, if the wage level falls below them, so that he thinks that there is going to be a spread between costs and prices, it may stimulate confidence which in turn may stimulate autonomous investment which could be self-justifying. On the other hand, if you have an increase in money wages, even if you have an increase in money supply to underwrite it, I am interested in showing that if the businessman does not expect the change in values to last, the rise in money wages—compared to his idea of customary values—may cut off his inducement to invest even though the state does try to underwrite it with increased money.

BOULDING. Could I add one word on the third point on this innovation question? I suppose that we would all agree that if we take the model of perfect mobility, I mean the most completely perfect competition you can think of, there would be no innovation because any profits of innovation would immediately be imitated away. In order to get innovation, you must have some degree of immobility in the system. And in our system we provide that by the patent law and the copyright law and all the rest of it.

FRIEDMAN. No, I disagree completely with that position.

BOULDING. What Wright wants to say is that if you have an aggressive labor movement it will operate in somewhat of the way that imputation does, so that the profits of innovation, instead of being squeezed out by other imitators, will be squeezed out by the workers who are working for the innovator; then again you won't get investment. Is that what I understand?

WRIGHT. Yes.

BOULDING. Which is a proposition I should question very substantially, but it is a proposition which, at least, isn't nonsense.

WRIGHT. I am therefore a little worried about this standard of raising wages as fast as "productivity" rises. Of course, you can define productivity in various ways. That would take care of it. But it seems to me that if a businessman introduces a new method, it will be in the expectation of unusual profits, which are temporary, to pay for risk. Now if before he has gotten any unusual profits to compensate him for his risk a wage increase is expected to take them away, and if that is the expected pattern, it will tend to cut off innovation because people simply won't bother.

BOULDING. I would argue that unionism isn't necessarily a hindrance to innovation, because one of the great impacts of unionization is to establish uniformity in wages over a given class and a given unit. And it would be extremely surprising if a union pushed up the wages in a successful plant much above those of others. It would raise terrific internal strains within the union. Suppose that Mr. Tucker had been successful in the automobile market and suppose he had produced an automobile which was much better than anybody else's and the UAW had organized him right away. Do you suppose the union would have doubled the wages in his plant and then left the others unchanged?

WRIGHT. They would go over and try to double them in the other plants too.

BOULDING. They can't; they don't.

WRIGHT. The union is operating as a strong monopoly. They had a higher wage level in Ford than Chrysler or vice versa for some months. They will strike a given plant and get a concession and insist upon a higher wage from it; and then when the contract falls due in the next plant, they will insist on its matching the concessions they got from the first people.

BOULDING. And that has nothing to do with whether Ford is producing a better automobile or Chrysler.

CHAMBERLIN. When you speak of doubling the wage in the Tucker plant, you are distorting what a labor union could do at one time. I tried to explain in my paper how such changes could come about slowly. Evidently if they proposed such a patently absurd thing as to double the wages immediately because Tucker was making a lot of money, they would have no support from anybody; and they would not succeed in doing it; but they might succeed by smaller gradations and possibly get some slice of it.

BOULDING. That is all right. That is exactly what the competing entrepreneurs do. They proceed by smaller degree; that is, the profits of innovation will be eliminated, but as long as they are not eliminated too abruptly, innovation is possible.

FRIEDMAN. The question there is, of course, whether you are going to include perfect foresight in your prerequisites of perfect competition. In that case there isn't any possibility of innovation; there isn't anything to innovate. But the implication of your remarks is that an increased degree of competition tends to reduce innovation, and this implication I do not accept.

SAMUELSON. Professor Boulding's qualitative theory is possibly correct. Increased certainty of perfect competition might hamper *ex ante* incentives. There are extreme external economies in the field of innovation through which other people can get by imitation what you have got by painful costs. Even where conditions are appropriate to it, laissez faire cannot be expected always to lead to an "optimal" rate of innovation. And Schumpeter argues with some convincingness that just as monopolies and patents are an artificial island of monopolies, so the big corporations—

FRIEDMAN. Let me start from patents. I grant that an intellectually defensible case for patents can be made, but I would be in favor of abolishing patents and copyrights also. I refer you to the classic articles on that—the two articles by Arnold Plant on the economic theory concerning patents and copyrights. The harm that has been done by patents, in particular, greatly exceeds the social benefits from them, and exactly the same thing is true for monopoly in general.

BOULDING. There is an optimum amount of monopoly which is not zero. Whether the amount you get by leaving things alone is the optimum or not, I don't know. I am not prepared to argue that. You may have to intervene in one direction or the other in order to produce the optimum, but you cannot say the optimum is zero.

SAMUELSON. I agree.

WRIGHT. "If the system worked 'perfectly,' it wouldn't work at all." What I meant by saying that is that, since these net investments are stimulated by special profit incentives which cover their special risk, if you had pure and perfect competition that would immediately impute away those special incentives— why, then, nobody would make the investment.

SAMUELSON. Only impute it by free enterprise, no automatic imputation; but the point is that knowledge spreads and the man who has invested his money in knowledge has a—

FRIEDMAN. Two different points, aren't they? One point is the social and one point is the individual benefits of innovation.

SAMUELSON. *Ex ante* effect.

FRIEDMAN. I have no quarrel with that, but it does not follow from that that innovation would cease.

SAMUELSON. His qualitative theory is all right, but not his quantitative theory that it would necessarily be zero.[8]

WRIGHT. Say you are a banker and some businessman comes to you and says, "I have a new invention which under the existing level of costs and wages will yield a 30 per cent profit

---

[8] *Comment by Wright:* I do not say innovation would *necessarily* be zero. But I think that likely, under highly "pure" and "perfect" competition.

within five years." And the banker says, "That is fine, I will go ahead and lend the money." And then he thinks that I am taking what will seem an outrageous profit. Then he thinks the union will probably strike for higher wage rates the day after the new plant is finished. So he will think: I have got to make my calculations on a basis of 15 per cent rather than 30 per cent in order to allow for the fact that wages are going up by union action, and that the union may make its wage demands stick at a higher figure than the mere competitive market would do. But 15 per cent may not be enough in view of the risk. Then the loan may be stopped. So growth can be cut off if the thing is thrown into expectations.

FRIEDMAN. I have no quarrel with that statement but that is a different statement from the statement—

SAMUELSON. That is Wright's point.

Professor Boulding commented on the latter part of this discussion as follows:

> We all agree that state and nation
> Will benefit from innovation.
> The question we must answer later
> Is, Will it help the innovator?

CHAPTER XV

Economic Theory and Wages

BY PAUL A. SAMUELSON

Introduction

WHEN an economic theorist comes to write an *apologia pro vita sua,* he writes certain chapters at great speed and in considerable length, knowing full well the worth of his contributions. The theory of comparative advantage in its applications to practical problems of international economics may perhaps be cited as an example. But I fear that when the economic theorist turns to the general problem of wage determination and labor economics, his voice becomes muted and his speech halting. If he is honest with himself, he must confess to a tremendous amount of uncertainty and self-doubt concerning even the most basic and elementary parts of the subject.

It is not that there is a shortage of wage theories. Indeed there are many: too many and too mutually contradictory, so that they obscure rather than point up important truths. And for all his self-doubts and humility, the economic theorist knows as he surveys the bouquet of wage theories that, thorns, blossoms, and all, they are the creation of economic theorists living or dead. The practical man of labor affairs has always acted by instinct, and to justify his behavior he has shopped around to choose the most suitable economic rationalizations; but their fullest articulation has almost all been the product of fairly academic writers.

In the present paper I propose to sample unsystematically

some of the theories bearing on wages and labor economics. My task is not to explain their content, since fairly widespread acquaintance with their general features can be taken for granted. Rather my efforts can go toward evaluation of the elements of validity and error involved in the various theories and toward identifying those areas in which our existing knowledge seems inadequate.

Over-All Wage Theories

The language and concepts of economics have evolved over centuries, with much of the development being accidental rather than inevitable. Since language is not neutral in its influence on thought processes, we can guess that the classification of productive agents into land, labor, and capital prepared the way for separate theories of rent, wages, and interest. But so long as no member of the triology was treated very differently from the others, the problem was not much more than reformulated.

To writers of earlier centuries it was apparently too dull to treat all productive agents alike, and so we were provided with ingenious figures of speech and analogies to demonstrate that work or something else is the true source of value or of something-or-other. "Labour is the Father and creative principle of Wealth, as Lands are the Mother," or alternatively, land is the source of all *produit net*. Today such romantic distinctions leave us a little cold and we are inclined to wonder how their lack of real content could, for good or evil, have had much effect upon the understanding of economic happenings. But this is to overlook the persuasive role of language in forming people's perception and interpretation of what it is that they see in the world around them. Even at the present time it is a provocative statement to affirm that labor is merely a commodity.

By the time of Smith's *Wealth of Nations* (1776) economic analysis had not yet emancipated itself from the influence of its historical terminology—indeed it has not been able to do so since. Still the terminology had become so varied and ambiguous in meaning that the classical writers could both pay lip service to a labor-theory-of-value (whatever that is) and disregard it whenever it became convenient for them to do so in the course of trying to explain some part of economic reality.

In the last century and a half at least the following general wage theories are commonly distinguished by economists: (1) the *subsistence* theory of wages; (2) the *wage fund* doctrine; (3) the *indeterminacy* or *bargaining power and exploitation* theory of wages; (4) the *marginal productivity* theory of wages; (5) the *purchasing power* theory of wages.

Such a list is of course a logical monstrosity. The various categories are overlapping. They cut across each other logically and their number could easily be expanded or contracted. Nonetheless each involves a catch phrase around which arguments have been marshaled and concerning which writers have felt strongly, both pro and con. For the purpose of the present unsystematic sampling of views, the classification will do.

Subsistence Theory

The world must have been ripe in 1798 for Malthus's population theory because its impact was immediate, substantial, and lasting, while at the same time its facts were inconclusive and its simple reasoning by no means completely new. The dismal iron law of wages deduced from it can be sufficiently epitomized in modern terminology.

Human fertility is such as to cause the long-run supply curve of labor to be horizontal at the minimum level of biological subsistence; because fixity of natural resources brings the law of diminishing returns into play, the general demand curve for labor is a downward-sloping schedule. Although technological change tends to shift the demand schedule upward, fertility can override all; so that equilibrium will (or can) only take place at the very low intersection of supply and demand where the wage is low enough to choke off lives and births so that the population is just replacing itself.

Despite the fact that the next half century was one of rapid increase in life expectancy, in total population, and probably in real wages, this subsistence theory nevertheless remained an important influence on political thought. As a statement of tendency about what would happen, or would have to happen, in a limiting state of equilibrium, the theory was practically immune to any factual attack: indeed, a critic wishing to attack it would have had trouble deciding which facts to play up and which to soft-pedal, and a defender might have faced the same dilemma.

The highly specific content of the doctrine—its exact quantitative character, rooted in the physiological level of subsistence—would have delighted the heart of an ancient Pythagorean or a modern econometrician. But by the time of Ricardo and the late classical writers the horizontal long-run supply curve of labor had been permitted to rise to whatever *conventional* level of wages workers were taught to insist upon prior to their reproducing themselves. Labor then differed not at all from capital, which too had its conventional level of "subsistence interest rate"—or "effective rate of accumulation"—below which all capital growth was thought to cease.

For America and Western Europe the crude subsistence theory of wages possessed no empirical validity, even though it continued to be appealed to in controversies over unionization and governmental aid to the poor.[1] It is an irony of history

---

[1] Yet as late as the mid-nineteenth century so judicious a writer as John Stuart Mill was led by his preoccupation with the birth control movement to make a famous utterance stating how doubtful it was that the technological improvements of all history had "lightened the toil" of suffering humanity. And he seriously argued that unions should disregard the depressing effects on the wages of others that would follow from raising their own, on the ground that in any event the general class of

that so unrealistic a theory should have given economics so bad a name for so long a time. And as is so often the case with intrinsically weak arguments, every victory it brought to those who used it was ultimately dearly purchased: critics of classical economics and of the existing social order were enabled to make a completely unjustified identification of competition with minimum subsistence wages.[2]

The Wage Fund Doctrines

Discussion of the so-called wage fund doctrine constitutes one of the most sterile chapters in that dreary gap between the classical age and the revolutionary neoclassical discoveries of the last third of the nineteenth century. If the subsistence theory had been true, it would have been important. Even if the wage fund theories were correct—it really would have made no great

---

unskilled labor could always be expected so to change their numbers as to keep their wage level constant.

One grain of truth in Malthus remained truly applicable to Europe in the last century: the great reduction in death rates was not accompanied by an immediate and contemporaneous decline in birth rates, so that population grew tremendously; and to the extent that statical diminishing returns was then operating to counter dynamic technological innovation and cheapening of American food, Europe can be said to have been "spending" some indeterminable fraction of her gains from progress on mere increase in numbers.

[2] Karl Marx replaced the devil of biological fertility by the "reserve army of the unemployed." Their downward pressure on wages was supposed to lead to the same iron law of subsistence wages. Except for the overlaps between this notion and the later-discussed bargaining or exploitation theory, there is no validity in this Marxian notion: in simple competitive models, unemployment causes the real wage to fall to the equilibrium intersection of supply and demand, which for modern nations would presumably have no connection with physiological minima of subsistence. With the same logic Marx could have promulgated the golden law of wages: Unfilled job vacancies will cause wages to reach the level of bliss.

difference, since the controversy was largely over empty words.

It is one of the characteristics of the history of economic doctrines that whenever Adam Smith let fall a casual remark—perhaps defining a desirable canon of taxation, or extolling the superiority of short-term credit, or pointing out the dependence of wages on capital—then throughout subsequent history these casual thoughts have gone reverberating down the corridors of time, ending up in the strangest places and in the strangest forms.

Even before Smith,[3] Turgot had noted a dependence of employment and wages on capital. Smith, Ricardo, and the earlier classical writers gave a prominent place to such considerations. But only in the time of Senior and Stuart Mill, when the subsistence theory was fairly played out, did the doctrine of the wage fund begin to have attention focused on it. Around the middle of the century it ruled triumphant, but in the late 1860's it came under attack by Leslie, Thornton, Longe, Walker, Jenkin, and others. And when Mill made his famous recanta-

---

[3] Smith's view that "industry is limited by capital" is well expressed in Book IV: "As the number of workmen that can be kept in employment by any particular person must bear a certain proportion to his capital, so the number of those that can be continually employed by all the members of a great society, must bear a certain proportion to the whole capital of that society, and can never exceed that proportion." If such an extreme degree of technical complementarity between capital and labor were to hold in each small line of production, and this seems doubtful, still it would not have to hold for society as a whole. Yet this notion dies hard: in a recent U. N. Full Employment Report by able economists, deviation from full employment in backward countries—and not simply low wages and productivity—seems to be attributed to capital scarcity. Few will deny that a disturbance of the supply of raw materials in a country like Italy could cause temporary unemployment; but who can agree that this condition is remediable in the long run only by a restoration of that same flow of materials? I will concede that backward countries do have special disguised unemployment problems, and that the process of their awakening is interrelated with capital formation, but all this needs careful and critical spelling out.

tion in a review of Thornton, there followed for thirty years an era in which the economic theorist was thought to have withdrawn his former objections to the attempts by unions to raise wages. The whole episode represents much ado about practically nothing, and so I may be very brief in my summary.

Just as the subsistence theory was a special theory of the supply curve of labor, the wage fund doctrine was a special theory of the demand curve for labor. In its strictest (meaningful and nontautological) form, it held that the total wage bill is approximately a constant, being predetermined by the money funds of the capitalists set aside for wages, or at the deeper level, by the predetermined total real-wage bill of goods and services to be advanced by the capitalists to the workers. Dividing this constant numerator by the volume of employment would yield by simple arithmetic the average money or real wage. Of course, the issue was rarely stated so clearly and simply as this.

Now if this strange notion had been empirically valid, it is not at all clear that this would have constituted an argument against unionism. On the contrary, the short-run case for workers limiting their numbers would be an especially strong one in this rigid case of *unitary elasticity* in the general demand for labor. And, as a matter of fact, Mill with his weakness for good causes actually used the doctrine as a justification for birth control and as a reason to implore the capitalists to increase their saving and investment.

Union wage increases could be expected in the longer run to lower the profit incomes of the wealthier and thriftier classes, and therefore, to result in less saving and in what Mill and the other classical believers in Say's law of markets regarded as exactly the same thing—less investment. A slower growth of capital would result in lower wages in the future than would otherwise have been the case. Hence for workers to accept lower wages was regarded as equivalent to their putting money in the bank, which would return to *them* with interest in the form of higher wages in the future. Thus Senior's defense of capital and interest by appeal to the saver's real cost in the form of *abstinence* could now be reinforced by the view that investing by the rich involved an act of altruism as well as of self-interest.

Today we would agree that there is an important element of truth in the view that a rapid growth of real capital can be expected to increase labor productivity and real wages. But just as the wage fund theory came into the limelight because of its absurdities, it met its doom for the same reasons. To explain wage rates by the wage bill is to put off an answer and to raise the problem of what it is that determines the wage bill. If we regard wages as a flow per unit time, what factors shape and limit the total of this flow? Today we may provisionally answer that labor's total consumption is limited by the total flow of national product; but even this is not strictly true in the short run, since for a time a nation can enlarge its consumption at the expense of capital.[4] If we grant that 100 per cent of the national product is an upper limit for wages,[5] then we are

[4] In the 1890's Taussig and the Austrians came to the defense of the wage fund using arguments more subtle than those of Mill, Fawcett, and Cairnes. Taussig's *Wages and Capital* (1895) describes the time dimension of the capital process; but as he pointed out in the 1932 reissue, it would have been better to have omitted the name of the wage fund altogether. In this modified form the wage fund has almost nothing to do with any of the issues involving unionization; if anything, a realistic view of the capital process increases the *short-term* gains that a labor monopoly might capture. It might be added that the Taussig view of the capital process is divorced from any dependence upon a numerical average period of production and gives a desirable counteremphasis to the J. B. Clark abstractions of an almost automatically self-renewing capital stock.

[5] The nebulous doctrine of noncompeting groups in consumption, if ever relevant, is so no longer. In this country, workers consume the same articles as anyone else. But even if this were less the case, as in Europe in an earlier century, we could still rely on a free pricing mechanism to put each and every consumption good (including paintings and stickpins) into the hands of those who have the highest monetary demand—and all

granting all that the most avaricious trade unionist could desire;
and if we look for exact quantitative principles to determine
some more limited fraction, we look in vain in economic books,
modern or ancient.

Indeterminacy, Bargaining, and Exploitation Theories

The wage fund doctrine was a weak argument to use against
labor unions and it inevitably boomeranged against its users.
For ,once it had been cast in doubt and discredited, the sup-
position grew up that there was nothing in economic theory that
was at odds with the attempts to raise wages by collective bargaining. The sole importance of the wage fund doctrine, if true,
would have been to establish a general demand for labor with
negative elasticity, so that higher real wages would mean lower
total employment. We can believe in the fact of negative elasticity without the wage fund doctrine. Consequently the falseness
and emptiness of the wage fund doctrine impresses a modern
observer as irrelevant.[6] Yet the floodgates had been opened to
economists' views more sympathetic toward collective bargaining; and not until the later, scarcely more relevant, marginal
productivity theory became known were theorists shunted back
to their earlier opposition.

In the last third of the nineteenth century the apparatus of
geometrical supply and demand curves was coming into use.
This had been implicit in older writers; explicit in Cournot but
inaccessible to the unmathematical, which is to say to practically
everybody; and all but explicit in Mill's *Principles*, particu-

---

this regardless of the distribution of income. The short-run changes in consumer surplus, it is true, might be smaller than the long-run changes.

[6] W. H. Hutt, one of the modern theorists most uncompromisingly opposed to all collective bargaining, makes this point very strongly (*Theory
of Collective Bargaining* [P. S. King, 1930], pp. 2-10). As compared to
later quantitative estimates of elasticity of labor demand, — 1.0 is a gross
understatement.

larly in the numerical tables relating to international trade. In conjunction with the rediscovery of marginal utility Jevons and Walras were motivated to perfect the analysis of supply and demand. Marshall too—probably from his study of Mill's international values—developed his geometrical cross of supply and demand. Probably a little earlier than Marshall, Fleeming Jenkin, an Edinburgh engineering professor, was led *by his studies of the labor market* to a formulation of supply and demand which appears to me to have *all* the *essential* features of the Marshallian analysis, including an independent rediscovery by Jenkin of Dupuit's consumer surplus and tax incidence analysis.

I mention this history because of the following paradox: During this same thirty years of perfecting of the tools of supply and demand, the labor market was by special dispensation considered to be an exception to supply and demand. The special features of the labor market and the peculiarities of labor as a commodity were dwelt upon at great length, perhaps even at excessive length, with the result that some of the most enlightening comments on the labor market go back to this period.[7]

Loopholes in the laws of supply and demand were eagerly sought out. Thus, Thornton pointed out that if there was a

[7] Fleeming Jenkin, *Papers*, Vol. II (reprinted as a London School of Economics Scarce Tract, 1932) contains the interesting essay, "Trade Unions: How Far Legitimate" (pp. 5-75), written in 1868, a year or two before his paper on supply and demand. This has a most modern air about it and would be worth quoting at length, since it deals with many of the issues debated in connection with the Taft-Hartley Act. The 1870 paper on "Graphic Representation of the Laws of Supply and Demand, and their Application to Labour" (pp. 76-93, 93-106) is a little disappointing in its applications to labor: instead of stating simply that a monopoly can travel up the demand schedule for labor by restricting employment, Jenkin couches the process in the language of cost of production, reserve price, standards of comfort, etc. A. Marshall, *Economics of Industry* (Macmillan, 1899), has an interesting chapter on trade unions (Book VI, chap. xiv. See also Book VI, chaps. iii, iv, v).

coincidental complete inelasticity of both the supply and demand schedule, then competitive price would be indeterminate within that range. To the extent that economic goods or services are discrete and lumpy rather than perfectly continuously divisible, something like this is bound to be true on a small scale at least. Later Böhm-Bawerk, with his tedious horse market, was to exhaust the patience of subsequent theorists by his inordinate dwelling on this point. Consequently modern theorists tend to regard these early discussions as rather piddling.

But in doing so, we must not forget something infinitely more important than the coarseness of the units in which labor comes: namely, the tremendous differentiation of abilities and attitudes as between workers, so that no two are alike—and so that no person can accurately ascertain their differences. This, plus the fact that the performance you get from a man is not something that exists independently of his wage, the wages of others, his past employment experience, and the performance of others, pulverizes the labor market into separate but highly interrelated segments. If each morning people could be hired in an organized auction market, the world would be a very different one—not a slightly different one, but a substantially different one, in my judgment.

Whatever its merits, there came to the fore in this period the endemic notion that the wage bargain was indeterminate, depending much on relative bargaining power, and that the individual workingman would by himself be inferior in bargaining power to the more wealthy employer who was possessed of greater financial resources to outlast a strike and who in any case could almost always be regarded as being in an overt or tacit combination to keep wages down.[8] In its crudest form this view

---

[8] Most of these doctrines go back at least to Adam Smith, that alleged apologist of the bourgeois class. Labor was supposed to be at an additional disadvantage in that its services were perishable, in the sense that the work you don't do today, you can never do; also the cost of maintaining the workers' families was regarded as a recurring overhead cost that went on

pictured each helpless worker as being picked off by a powerful employer and having his wage forced down to a minimum necessary for existence.

Either in defense or for offense, a subgroup of workers by banding together and bargaining collectively could hope to raise their wages. That any reasonable economist should have denied that a monopoly of labor in one given market can affect supply and raise the price above the competitive level, today appears strange. Scarcely less explicable was the factual assertion that trade unions would not be able to make their monopoly power stick and would find their attempts to raise particular wages as unavailing as attempts to stop the ocean's tide by oral exhortation. Those who argued in this way were bad political and market analysts.[9]

In economics it takes a theory to kill a theory; facts can only dent the theorist's hide. Edgeworth in his *Mathematical Psychics* (1881) came forward with an elaborate analysis of two-sided monopoly, thereby giving geometrical content to the old examples of dickering between buyer and seller of unique objects such as musical snuffboxes. One of the most important applications of this theory of bilateral monopoly was felt to be

---

independently of employment. It has been truly pointed out that some—but not all—of the services of capital equipment are also forever lost if not used today; and in many industries today it is simply not true that the days lost on strikes represent a full net subtraction from the days that will ever be worked. (Cf. the Chamberlin paper and discussion, chaps. viii and ix.)

[9] If unions do not raise certain wages relative to what they would otherwise be, it is hard to understand much of the criticism of organized labor. Nonetheless, it is not possible to document the view that unions have substantially raised their wages relative to others. Such is the character of economics! Contrast the views of union power (for good or evil) set down in the Chamberlin and Clark papers and the Friedman paper (chaps. i, viii, x); of course more than the effects of unions on money and real wages must be taken into account.

the labor market. The general conclusion of Edgeworth was that the amount of employment and the wage would under imperfect competition be indeterminate rather than uniquely determinable as under perfect competition. By agreement both contending parties might be expected to leave certain mutually disadvantageous settlements; but this would only narrow down the field of battle to (the so-called Edgeworth "contract curve") a point where the interests of workers and of employers were diametrically opposed. An infinite continuum of final settlements could thus eventuate from collective bargaining, depending upon some kind of vaguely defined bargaining power exerted by each side.[10]

Doctrines of inevitability oust issues of morality; doctrines of free will raise questions of norms. When economic theory began to give its blessing to the notion that organized labor might be master of its fate and wages, interest was rekindled in the old question of what is the fair or normal share of labor. Where does exploitation begin? Where are workers organizing defensively to recapture what is rightly theirs, and where are they beginning to go too far?

The term "exploitation of labor" has, of course, myriad meanings. In recent years some economists have tried to give this

[10] Marshall and his pupil Berry tried to define a determinate price even in the case of bilateral monopoly. If the income that employers are bartering against workers' labor has "constant marginal utility" to both parties, then every point on the contract curve will represent the *same* amount of employment, and the final marginal rate of substitution of work for income will be everywhere the *same*. But even under the bizarre conditions assumed, note that the settlement is still highly indeterminate, and that the well-being of workers and employers depends completely on the outcome of the bargaining. See A. Marshall, *Principles of Economics* (8th ed.; *Macmillan*, 1920), Appendix F and Note XII. Recent theorists, such as Leontief and Fellner, have attempted to apply the tools of bilateral monopoly to exposition of some problems of collective bargaining; and in 1932 Hicks set forth a theory of strikes. In my view disappointingly little has yet come from theorists in this field.

concept certain precise and technical meanings representing well-defined deviations from optimum welfare conditions. Thus, Joan Robinson, *Economics of Imperfect Competition* (Macmillan, 1933), follows Pigou and defines two kinds of exploitation of labor. The first kind exists when the employer is an impure competitor or monopolist who equates marginal revenue rather than price to marginal cost—or what is the same thing, who hires inputs until their extra cost to him is balanced by their "marginal value or revenue product" rather than by the "value of their marginal product"; the second kind of exploitation occurs when the employer is a *monopsonist* in the labor market and equates to marginal revenue product the extra cost of a worker, calculated as his wage *minus* the additional amount previous workers must thereby be paid. These definitions are somewhat misleading since the workers in question are not the ones being exploited: a worker employed by a large corporation in a company town will *probably* be getting higher rather than lower than the average wages paid by small nonmonopsonistic firms; and impurely competitive firms probably pay higher wages than purely competitive ones do. As Mrs. Robinson indicates, it is the community that is being exploited, in the sense that there are two kinds of deviations from optimum welfare economic conditions.[11]

[11] In the oral symposium Professor Chamberlin and I discussed at some length whether the first kind of "impure competition exploitation"—i.e., the equality of wages with marginal revenue product rather than with value of the marginal product—did truly represent a deviation from the optimum. I affirmed that it did, and this he questioned. The discussion was continued in correspondence and the area of disagreement was, I think, narrowed. The following summary represents my own personal view and is not at all binding on Professor Chamberlin.

If outputs and inputs have not reached the position compatible with prices everywhere equal to 1.00 times marginal cost, then there is a deviation from the optimum in the following sense: *everybody* can be made better off by some theoretical rearrangement of resources. The equality of P and MC, which is the same thing as the equality of factor prices with

It is not clear that these new meanings are at all what earlier observers had in mind in using the word "exploitation." In fact, I doubt that any one thing very definite lay in the back of the minds of users of the term. "Exploitation" is a general word of opprobrium, and anything that strikes the onlooker as a bad thing seems to deserve this label—whether it be wages low enough to keep a worker thinking about his stomach, or quite high wages paid by a man of great wealth to a poorer man. There is always a latent feeling that it would be nice for us all to live at the level of, say, the upper eighty-fifth percentile of the income distribution; and since most of us must necessarily fall short of such a level, it is clear that wages generally can always be regarded as too low. And this will remain the prevailing attitude even if it can be pointed out that median wages in this country are a multiple of general wages elsewhere; so long as median wages are less than average national income, wages tend by many to be regarded as too low—and among those not well versed in arithmetic this may persist even after the median has been brought up to the mean.

---

the value of their marginal products, may be inconsistent with $p =$ average cost and may require ideal "lump-sum taxes and subsidies" if a perfectionist's optimum is to be reached. These marginal relations are *necessary* conditions for an optimum that must hold *whatever* the ethical norms prescribed. But they are definitely *not* sufficient conditions. To determine which commodities are to be produced at all requires "total conditions" in addition to the marginal ones—as Dupuit, Hicks, Lerner, Meade, Henderson, Chamberlin, and others have shown. See my *Foundations of Economic Analysis* (Harvard Press, 1947), chapter 8.

At the level of workability or feasibility, the above paragraph needs careful qualification. Lowering prices to marginal costs in some subsector of the economy alone may *worsen* rather than improve the situation. And since ideal lump-sum taxes and subsidies are not feasible, the actually feasible optimum is consistent with some degree of both kinds of "exploitation."

Marginal Productivity Theory

A historian of industrial life and of economics books cannot neglect people's attitudes toward the rightness and wrongness of wages. But he must also not forget that the importance of a proposition in this sphere is often independent of its intrinsic logical merits or its empirical validity as a description of what goes on in real markets.

After 1900 the marginal productivity theory of wages became increasingly popular among economists. Its recognition and assertion of substitutability among inputs within the firm does provide one extra reason for elasticity in the sloping demand curve for labor. But except for this I cannot see that this theory is particularly relevant to the question of whether competition will result in low or high wages, or of whether collective bargaining can hope to raise wages. Within the realm of economic theory itself, marginal productivity relations are one subset of the conditions of general equilibrium; and if the existence of the partial derivative postulated by this theory contradicted technological fact, the status of labor economics would be in no significant sense altered.[12]

---

[12] George J. Stigler, *Production and Distribution Theory* (Macmillan, 1941), is the indispensable reference to the genesis of this theory. Anyone who thinks that marginal productivity analysis adds to the ethical merits of competitive wages should recall that v. Wieser's *Natural Value*, which antedates the theory, gives a full teleological defense of competitive pricing. Cf. also F. M. Taylor, *Principles of Economics* (8th ed.; Ronald Press, 1921), or the modern "nonmarginal" theory of "linear programming." Pareto, it will be recalled, disbelieved in marginal productivity but nevertheless was one of the first to set down the optimizing character of competitive pricing under capitalism or socialism. Between the first and third editions of his *Éléments*, Walras adopted a marginal productivity theory of production: nonetheless, even back in the 1870's he held firm views about the optimum character of general equilibrium pricing. In 1925 in the *Journal of Political Economy*, Professor Knight showed that even in the case where there was no substitutability because of "fixed coefficients,"

A subsistence theory of wages is quite consistent with marginal productivity, and for that matter so is a meaningfully stated wage fund theory. Under appropriate conditions of demand and technology, a marginal productivity theory might impute 99 per cent of the national income away from labor, which would be exploitation enough in the eyes of radical agitators; or it might impute 99 per cent to spendthrift workers, which would be bad indeed in the eyes of those who strain for progress.

Perhaps the importance of the theory is to be found in the use made by it to rationalize the *correctness* of wages as determined in relatively competitive markets.[13] True the theory is too complex ever to have percolated down to the noneconomist public; but then it was never needed at that level, since the earlier mentioned general discontent over low wages has always been matched by an elaborate set of doctrines to explain why this condition must prevail.

J. B. Clark, one of the many developers and expanders of the marginal productivity theory, clearly thought that its importance lay in its demonstration of the ethical merits of competitive wage determination. In his *Distribution of Wealth* he speaks again and again of having identified the "natural law" of wage determination, whereby labor received *its* "normal," "ideal," "specifically produced," "traceable" fair share of the

---

the competitively determined wage would equal the addition to the value of total product resulting from the addition of a single worker (the evaluation of product being at the previous set of prices).

It is in view of these facts that I make the statement that there is nothing in the marginal productivity doctrine as such that adds to the normative significance of competitive pricing.

[13] Even to this day one reads in important economic writings such statements as: If workers get less than their marginal product there may be underconsumption and a crash; or, Workers can be expected to be given their marginal product in good times but not in bad times when profits are under pressure. Not only does some moral connotation still cling to the concept of marginal product, but also there is fuzziness on how this condition of equilibrium comes about or is departed from.

product. Indeed Clark seems to have felt that his most important contribution beyond the earlier work of von Thünen lay, not alone in a different or better description of the facts of the market place, but in the demonstration that the marginal productivity theory is a theory of *justice* and not, as von Thünen believed, of *exploitation*.[14]

[14] *Distribution of Wealth* (Macmillan, 1902), preface; pp. 321-324.

Comment by Clark: I feel I should not let this question go entirely by default. As to the terms in which J. B. Clark's marginal productivity theory was formulated, it was first publicly presented in 1889, by a non-mathematical economist, in the light of prevailing issues far different from those raised by 1950-brand mathematical-welfare theory. On the general horizon, von Thünen bulked less large than Marx, under whose theory any share capital gets is outright robbery. As against this, the marginal productivity theory asserts that the rewards of both labor and capital are in exchange for productive contributions. They embody the (limited) ethics of mutual exchange, as against the nonethics of robbery, just as any sale of a commodity does.

I do not know anyone who has seriously claimed that either settles all ethical questions: certainly not the question whether the unequal distribution of inherited property or innate ability is just, or the more practical question whether one whose innate abilities enable him to produce five times as much as another, should justly receive five times as much (before or after taxes). But the idea that of two who have equal abilities or command of property, the one who uses his to render twice the useful service has a claim to twice the reward (less taxes)—this accords with a widespread feeling that this is *one* important element of fairness, in addition to the obvious elements of expediency and incentive which it involves. I hope that such criteria are not going to be discredited on the ground that they are partial and limited, because I am sure that perfect and all-embracing ethical formulae for concrete actions are impossible, and that limited and partial ones are the only kind we shall ever have.

As to "specific" productivity versus "partial derivatives," the idea J. B. Clark wished to convey was that of the amount of added product dependent on the presence or absence of *any one* of a number of interchangeable productive units, in the setting represented by the presence of the other interchangeable units, and the other factors. If it is wrong to attach the idea of specifically traceable causality to such a relation, I am

J. B. Clark stated his position clearly and strongly, but it is now commonly regarded as such an ethically arbitrary one that he has become somewhat discredited in the eyes of modern economists.[15] Still, this all took a good deal of time and was aided by reinforcement from later social developments. We must not deny, therefore, that the marginal productivity theory did—rightly or wrongly—serve the purpose of refuting the notion that wages are simply a matter of workers' aspirations backed up by organized collective bargaining.

In concluding this section, I should like to add some reflections occasioned by the oral discussion of the significance of marginal productivity. Assuming the absence of uncertainty and of market imperfection, and assuming the existence of continuous partial derivatives of all the production functions in the eco-

---

puzzled as to what causal relations may generally involve which is different from this.

By all means, let us modify the formulation of this principle, for present use, in the light of current methodological attitudes. And let us distinguish more systematically between positive analysis and terms of ethical appraisal.

[15] It is not clear to me that J. B. Clark ever meant what he seems to have meant. Why should a man of his general sentiments have cared to identify the functional distribution of income with the personal distribution of income? Once he agrees to their separation, marginal productivity ceases to be an ethical doctrine and becomes a theory of production (and possibly of incentive). T. N. Carver, among others, pointed this out a half century ago; but I do not know whether Clark ever changed his public position.

Comment by Clark: As to the relation between functional and personal distribution, I had construed the principle as stating that the personal owner of a factor receives the share functionally attributable to the factor he owns. This seems to describe a pretty close relation, compounding the ethical problem of ownership with that involved in marginal imputation. Accordingly, I would not "agree to the separation" of functional and personal distribution in any sense that would completely destroy whatever (limited and partial) ethical implications there may be in the theory, and I doubt if my father would have done so.

nomic system, the Walrasian conditions of general equilibrium (which include a subset of marginal product conditions) *do* determine a configuration of relative prices. In the absence of detailed quantitative knowledge of the production functions, and of consumer supply and demand functions, we cannot state what the quantitative pattern of resulting prices will be, nor how it will quantitatively change when certain changes impinge on the system. We can perhaps formulate a few qualitative laws of behavior simply from our knowledge of the conditions of returns and maximization, yet admittedly we would be happier if the "empty boxes" could be filled with detailed quantitative knowledge. Yet no one should expect to make bricks without straw, and the theory in question should not be blamed for the complexity of the facts and our ignorance of them. Under the above simplified conditions, the general equilibrium theory is the *only* valid description and any competing valid theory must turn out to be identical with it and hence no less complicated.

A more serious accusation against the marginal productivity theory resides in the failure of its assumptions to be realized. Here the problem becomes one of deciding how far the facts depart from the theory's implications, and how good a first approximation is provided by the simplified version of the theory. I personally think it does provide us with some insight but that—especially where imperfections and impurities of competition are concerned—where uncertainties and feed-back influences of wages on management and worker productivity are concerned, and where the uncertainties associated with cyclical investment and technological changes are concerned, the simplified version of the theory needs to be amplified by successively more realistic theories.

But suppose we were to waive the fact of our empirical ignorance, and suppose we were to grant that reality faithfully matches all the premises underlying marginal productivity and general equilibrium theory. There still would remain the question of its normative significance. Does it then simply tell us what will happen if nothing is done? Or does it go further and tell us that what will happen *ought* in some sense to happen? This is the welfare economics aspect of the problem, and to my astonishment I find that the arbitrariness of J. B. Clark's views on the deservingness of competitively determined rewards is not universally recognized, as I had earlier declared. I must refer the reader to the oral discussion and to my own concluding remarks on welfare economics.

Purchasing Power Theory of Wages

For a long time Henry Ford shared with the A.F. of L. the conviction that high money wages helped to create and preserve prosperity all around. While economic outlaws such as John A. Hobson had long preached a doctrine of underconsumption due to inequality of income distribution as lying at the root of depression and the trade cycle,[16] until recently respectable economists regarded such doctrines with some amusement and threw them to their fledgling pupils as exercises in avoiding sloppy thinking.

Then suddenly J. M. Keynes's *General Theory* (1936) reopened the question of the efficacy of money-wage cutting in curbing a depression. In the first years after 1936, the bulk of the discussion emphasized the lack of connection between autonomous changes in general money-wage rates and the resulting real-wage rates. It was often believed that to a first approximation a general change in all wages would be accompanied by an

[16] Wm. T. Foster and Waddill Catchings in *Profits* (Houghton Mifflin, 1925) and in numerous other books published during the 1920's proclaimed an underconsumption doctrine, but pinned their hopes for a remedy on unorthodox government monetary and fiscal policies. The Brookings Institute also placed early stress on the consumption effects of the skewness of our income distribution, but advocated lowering of prices by industrial statesmanship.

equivalent all-around change in the price level, with no appreciable change in real wages.

Keynes himself in one of his early chapters enunciated a peculiar definition of "involuntary unemployment" that hinged on an alleged myopia on the part of workers and unions toward a decrease in money wages as against an equivalent increase in the price level. The author and his readers were misled into thinking this an important concept; actually it later became clear that the concept of involuntary unemployment was only used by Keynes to explain rigidity of money wages in the face of unemployment—a rigidity which can be amply explained by a great number of other factors, such as legislation, trade union activity, imperfect competition in labor markets, general attitudes, etc.

Also, as Keynes came later to realize, he at first put too much emphasis on changes in the level of employment as being finally determined by somehow brought-about changes in real wages *along a fixed real demand schedule for labor, downward sloping by virtue of the classical law of diminishing returns.* Actually the essence of his theory was that fluctuations in total investment demand would, in a regime of fairly invariant propensity to consume, represent *shifts* in the total demand schedule so that even at the same real wage employment might change. When it was pointed out to him that the most careful examination of all known facts could not rule out the possibility of increasing rather than decreasing returns, he was delighted and gladly dropped forever the notion that saving and investment could influence income *only through* their differential effects on money and real wages.[17]

This also opened the way—although in truth that way had never been closed—for considering whether a completely bal-

[17] Even with diminishing returns, if real saving and investment propensities are not changed by extreme changes in money wages and prices, attempts by collective bargaining to accept lower real wages would not

anced hyperdeflation brought about by a fall in all wages accompanied by a proportionate fall in all prices might not have substantive effects on employment. Early it was agreed that so long as the monetary system was not infinitely elastic, the hard-money and fiduciary issues of currency would form a "nonhomogeneous" element which would not necessarily shrink proportionally with the price and wage level. Thus, a policy of hyperdeflation brought about generally by wage-cutting would be one way of making the volume of money redundant, and one roundabout way of engineering low interest rates and easy money. *Unless* the liquidity preference schedule of people is so completely elastic as to make lower interest rates impossible—or unless the general demand schedule for investment is so completely inelastic as to make lowering of interest rates of little potency in promoting recovery—a policy of hyperdeflation was early conceded to be capable of having favorable *statical* effects on employment.

But in the 1930's when the potency of an easy money policy was so widely discounted, to say that an all-around deflationary policy might contribute to easy money was to damn such a policy with faint praise—especially since the authorities had ample powers to ease money far beyond those they were using. Therefore, it was a matter of some interest when Pigou [18] and other neo-Keynesians began late in the 1930's to emphasize a new avenue whereby hyperdeflation could add to the level of real effective demand: namely through *the stimulating effect upon the propensity-to-consume schedule of the increased amount of (real) money wealth created by the process of wage-price cuts.*[19]

---

necessarily lead to full employment but perhaps instead to an endless hyperdeflation. I am not here arguing that such a model is realistic, but rather that such a model can be rigorously defined—a logical fact which has been repeatedly denied in the recent literature.

[18] Haberler's 1937 *Prosperity and Depression* (United Nations, 1946) has already emphasized this aspect of the matter.

[19] Since the numerical importance of hard money and fiduciary currency is limited, the asymmetrical character of the public debt was brought

In the absence of much factual or theoretical knowledge about the potency of this "wealth effect," it was seized upon by those who favored wage-price flexibility and minimized by those who did not; and no doubt over the next decades the numerical importance of this effect will continue to be argued in the journals. According to many, including Pigou himself as he tells us in the preface to *Lapses from Full Employment*,[20] deflation is not necessarily to be recommended as a cure for unemployment: real wealth can be put in people's hands more easily and equitably by other measures; other expansionary policies are also preferable. Nonetheless there are undoubtedly some modern economists who believe the wealth effect to be substantial so that deflation need not become hyperdeflation; and who believe that expansionary central bank policy can simultaneously mitigate the money-income-depressing effects of wage cuts; and who believe that the necessary adjustments of relative wages and

in as a substantially equivalent factor. As a people, we both owe and own the public debt; but we recognize the debt we own and tend, so it is persuasively argued, to forget about what we owe. Therefore, all-around hyperdeflation will not have canceling-out effects on public debt as it is supposed to have on private debt. Instead the government bonds, in people's hands or in their financial institutions, will be a nonhomogeneous item just like hard money.

Be it noted that open-market operations of the conventional sort *are not by themselves* capable of bringing about the same real expansion in the community's total of *government bonds + cash*. Only to the extent that open-market operations are capable of inducing secondary expansions or contractions of commercial loans—a smaller category relative to total bank assets than it used to be—can they have effects similar to those brought about by hyperdeflation, hyperinflation, or cumulative treasury surpluses and deficits. When a low interest policy has reached an impasse due to interest-elastic excess reserves by commercial banks, interest-elastic cash holding by individuals, or interest-inelastic investment demand schedules, then central bank operations do not have the wealth effects of the other policies named. These latter may be potent even when the central bank is not.

[20] (Macmillan, 1945.)

relative prices that a dynamic economy always requires are more desirably brought about by permitting some wages to fall, whenever unemployment develops in a given sector of the market, rather than by giving the system an inflationary bias through requiring that all relative-wage changes take place as a result of differential increases alone.

In a sense a compromise doctrine has emerged from the combination of classical, neoclassical, Keynesian, and neo-Keynesian analysis. A legitimate and convenient name for this common core is, I suggest, "neoclassical." Neoclassical analysis permits of fully stable *under*employment equilibrium only on the assumption of either frictions or a peculiar concatenation of wealth-liquidity-interest elasticities; and this is in a sense a negation of the more dramatic claims of the Keynesian revolution. On the other hand, this neoclassical doctrine is a far cry from the old notion that unemployment is simply the consequence of imposing too high real wages along a sloping aggregate marginal productivity demand schedule for labor: it goes far beyond the primitive notions that by definition of a Walrasian system, equilibrium must be at full employment; and beyond the view that the same analysis which demonstrates a drop in price will equate supply and demand in any small partial equilibrium market will also suffice to prove that a drop in general wages must clear the labor market. It rejects the question-begging gobbledygook of Say's law of markets, whereby supply creates demand and the flow of purchasing power automatically conserves itself—regardless of saving and investment decisions. Perhaps the cream of the jest is the final vindication of the classical belief in full employment *by means of a mechanism which leans heavily on indirectly destroying thriftiness and on the matching of full-employment saving and investment* so ardently desired by the underconsumption denizens of the academic underworld.[21]

---

[21] *Comment by Wright:* Regarding the doctrinal history implied in this passage compare chap. xiii, especially pages 289, 290.

All the above is a fairly far cry from the older mechanism by which wage cuts were supposed to lead to increased employment, for it will be noted that if the above process results in extra employment, it does so without necessarily diminishing real-wage rates and almost certainly by increasing rather than decreasing real consumption. Professor Wright has very properly asked whether there is not also *a more direct effect* of wage cuts on employment through directly favorable effects upon investment incentives, the marginal efficiency of capital, or autonomous investment.[22]

That wage cuts may directly stimulate investment is an important possibility; and we must also consider possible unfavorable effects upon net investment. In which direction the final balance is to be struck will depend upon many quantitative crosscurrents. While I do not feel competent to evaluate the empirical magnitudes of the conflicting tendencies, I am prepared to listen with interest to those who do have definite hypotheses on this point.

The problem would of course be a much simpler one to analyze if we were talking about cuts in particular relative wages. No one can doubt that such a cut might, other things being equal, result in some increase in the particular line of employment involved. But when it is a question of a change in all wages—or even more generally of a change in *all* cost items—then the argument must be a quite different one. To take only one example: We often read that increased money-wage rates will favor mechanization and *increase* the propensity to invest. This cannot be uncritically accepted—though, to be sure, there are theoretical models in which exactly this does happen. But there are also models, Leontief's elaborate one, for example, in which a universal increase in wages will raise the price of machinery by exactly the same proportion, with no substitution taking place.

[22] The next few pages addressed to this problem were added to my original paper as a result of the oral discussion.

Similarly, except in terms of the earlier described "indirect influences," we cannot decide whether a decrease in wages will involve any change in the interest rates relevant to investment decisions.

Moreover, it becomes important to distinguish between changes in real wages and changes in general money wages. To the extent that general wage changes result in proportional, more-than-proportional, or less-than-proportional changes in prices, the leverage of the direct influence may be zero, unfavorable, or favorable to aggregate employment. If we try to avoid this difficulty by working with sliding-scale real-wage formulas of the 1950 General Motors type, the result—in many relevant monetary models—may simply be cumulative deflation or inflation. (Denmark, Finland, and other nations have had not altogether favorable postwar experiences with such devices.) If on the other hand one makes certain other monetary assumptions, so that changes in real wages do result in changes in employment, the mechanism by which this is brought about— whether it is expressed in terms of the consumption-investment propensities of modern income analysis or in terms of the conventional quantity theory of money—is of the "indirect" rather than "direct" type, as I have classified these terms.

In all of the above I have made no mention of "expectations" generated by transitionally *changing* prices and wages, but have concentrated on *levels* of wages and prices. Realistically, these dynamic transition stages with their expectation patterns are very important; but, as Professor Haberler points out, almost anything can be proved by some appropriate assumptions about expectations. Thus, a once-and-for-all wage cut followed by expectations that wages will be higher in the future might be favorable to current employment, whereas the same wage cut regarded as part of a continuing deflationary trend might have opposite effects.

As far as the moving trend of wages and prices is concerned, and assuming that prices and wages do move together with no change in any real relations, we would typically suppose that a rising trend favors investment and employment; and that a falling trend inhibits real investment and encourages attempts to hoard. More realistically, all the quantity theorists since Hume's time have recognized the transitional expansionary effects on investment and employment of rising price and wage levels: A shift toward profit and an increased propensity to invest could be expected, along with "forced saving" resulting from the price rise and the delay in spending income. However, if the question is one of a price rise induced by prior autonomous wage increases, some of the above conclusions need to be modified: businessmen may still not be slow to spend their cash, but there may be a shift *away from* profits in this case of wage-price rather than price-wage inflation.

In all of the above, I have shown what scientific caution suggests must be said on some of the pros and cons of wage increases and employment. But now suppose we take a bolder view and set up the hypothesis—which I understand Professor Friedman to doubt and Professor Wright to affirm—(1) that unions do stand by vigilantly to capture increased real wages from a firm's *ex post* profitable operations, and (2) that this fact or fear operates as one of the important elements in the firm's *ex ante* deliberations. Then the following result seems reasonable: the motivation and ability of firms would be adversely affected and the propensity-to-invest schedule would be shifted downward. The above real-wage change can be expected also to shift the propensity-to-save schedule downward; hence the final effects on employment and inflationary gaps will be in either direction and will be qualitatively different at different times. But whatever the final effect on income, there will probably be a lower rate of real capital formation [23] and hence a lower rate of growth of the future productivity and real wages in the system.

---

[23] This is a probability, not a certainty: if (1) the shift in income distribution has very adverse effects on thriftiness so that (2) income greatly

The preceding paragraph gives my version of the important issue raised by Professor Wright. The point's importance goes beyond any issues of unionism or nonunionism; it directly involves the possible clash between the present and the future. As the verbatim discussion concerning competition and innovation brought out, the wage-price configuration that would result under vigorously competitive or under union monopoly conditions might very well result in a slower rate of progress than under some other system where wages were, so to speak, "taxed" in order to subsidize entrepreneurial profits.[24]

From the above discussion it will be clear that the analysis of purchasing power aspects of wages remains in a fairly primitive state. Certain dogmatic conceptions have been found to be complex and uncertain, even under simplified assumptions. But the reality of these simplifying assumptions is still very much an open question: Will militant raising of money-wage rates all around succeed—for good or evil—in raising real hourly wage rates? Will the relative share of real income going to labor improve? Will higher wages decrease thriftiness more or less than it will decrease the desire to invest? Will strategic changes in relative prices brought about by wage changes increase or decrease over-all employment, welfare, and effective demand? [25]

---

expands, and (3) if the induced marginal propensity to invest is very substantial, then, paradoxically, real-wage increases are a way of increasing capital formation.

[24] *Comment by Wright:* The semantic connotations of this sentence seem a bit unfortunate. *De facto* I suggest it should rather be put that the *new* wealth created *by* entrepreneurial saltations should not too soon be seized by other groups. Cf. my *Capitalism*, chap. iv.

[25] Bergson and Bissell have shown that increasing the costs of investment projects—such as housing—may in some circumstances add to the total value of investment and consumption spending, and in other cases have opposite results.

I think one must entertain the hypothesis that for a large sector of American industries the relationship between prices and labor costs elsewhere is determined by the institutions and mores of modern business. Competition is real; but for the group as a whole the predictable limits

Our ignorance on all these questions, even at the deductive level, is almost as great as the intensity of our convictions.

Conclusion

The final impression of my historical survey of wage theories must, to a careful reader, be a feeling of their emptiness and irrelevance. But they should not be lightly dismissed: if one were to make an equally careful survey of the pieces of theory that modern economists draw upon to answer these same questions at the present time, one would find that every one of the considerations involved in these historical theories still has relevance.

At the bottom of all of them is an ethical defense of and attack on the inequalities in the distribution of income. This is not confined to labor versus capital; it equally involves the $3500-a-year union man versus the over-$10,000 salaried official, union or corporate. At the bottom of all of these disputes is an aspiration for a standard of living for people generally beyond what the system can provide and beyond what is consistent with other aspirations. The economist can point out some of these basic incompatibilities of desire. But he weakens his case and he loses the audience he ought to persuade if he dogmatically states that the wage and income structure that would eventuate in a relatively competitive order is an optimal one (for society as a whole, for particular workers, or for workers as a whole), and if he blindly regards the existing institutional structure—with or without strong unions—as a good approximation to the competitive regime envisaged in Walrasian general equilibrium.[26]

competition sets on behavior are not narrow. I have seen this hypothesis denied (and defended) by assertion, but I know of no careful documentation and appraisal of its degree of validity.

[26] In my judgment the present symposium revealed how important it is to carry out—within professional circles—a meticulous restatement, in

Yet it will be an empty victory for him if he keeps his audience only by telling them what they wish to hear. And hence the honest economist must stress the limits and uncertainties that surround any extensive programs for bettering the position of labor by collective bargaining. This is in any case what, in its heart of hearts, the labor movement itself increasingly has learned—as may be witnessed by its increasing resort to politics. And that the state itself can—for worse or better—greatly alter economic reality, no one in this century will deny.[27]

---

terms of the modern logical syntax of welfare economics, of the implicit ethical value judgments that lie behind much present-day economic writing on this and other problems. Every economist has the right as a citizen to propagandize; but as a scientist—as a social scientist—he has a duty, according to my old-fashioned creed, to give disciplined attention to the facts of empirical life and logical argumentation.

[27] [*Editor's note:* Professor Clark epitomizes the above argument as follows (with apologies to Hilaire Belloc):

> If workers, low-paid, seek to better their lot
> By grabbing some dough from the rich,
> It makes jobs for more workers—or else it does not;
> I cannot be positive which.]

CHAPTER XVI

Selections from the Discussion

of Samuelson's Paper

[*Editor's note:* Professor Samuelson did not read his paper in full but merely gave an elaboration of its last section dealing with welfare economics. The essence of his paper here discussed will be found in his "Final Comment," chap. xvii.]

BOULDING. I would like to make a comment on this welfare economics approach. If we take some kind of a welfare function, it seems to me it has a shape something like a hat, really.

SAMUELSON. Whose?

BOULDING. Any kind of welfare function exhibits some sort of a maximum, doesn't it?

SAMUELSON. I don't know.

BOULDING. Aren't we talking about maximizing welfare? Here are all the possible variables of the system stretched out in *n*-dimensional space.

SAMUELSON. A roller coaster hat?

BOULDING. The thing that I suspect is that it is something like a pork-pie hat, that the top is pretty flat, but it has sharp edges; that is, it doesn't matter much where you are over a certain range but there are cliffs that you can fall over. That is, society can come a tremendous cropper if it goes beyond a certain critical point.

SAMUELSON. I am not sure of the metric in which this is measured.

BOULDING. Cardinal utility or anything. This can be a rubber utility as well. It doesn't make any difference, does it?

FRIEDMAN. Sure.

SAMUELSON. I have no objection to that.

FRIEDMAN. If you are talking about cliffs, it certainly does.

BOULDING. The thing I feel about welfare economics is that all it is doing is building a little fence around the top of the hill here, you see, and saying you shouldn't go outside that. We don't know where the top is, and that is why we have a Bergson function which, in fact, you can't have. We can draw a little fence around it with all the points inside.

SAMUELSON. If anyone has led a revolt against marginalism—by which one means local conditions—I have uniformly in all my published writings done so. Chamberlin's problem, by the way, is a good case of roller coasters there, because where you have indivisibility—

CHAMBERLIN. I don't have any indivisibility. That isn't a part of my case.

SAMUELSON. Case of differentiated product. Why then any problem for pure competition? Why not a million products, each one produced infinitesimally? Yours is a problem that "things get worse before they get better" and it requires "total conditions"—not a very good name by the way for it—but it requires nonlocal, nonderivative conditions.

CHAMBERLIN. There aren't any indivisibilities. They don't figure in my system at all.

BOULDING. If I get back to my point, though, the thing I am asking, you see, is: Are there certain states of society that you cannot go beyond without disaster in some sense? And I suspect we don't really have much to say about that; and yet that is, it seems to me, a much more critical question than this question of whether you ought to have a little more of this or a little more of that. And welfare economics really says very little about it. I don't think economics can say much about it, you see; and I certainly feel that all we have said about the labor movement here has been no more than walking around a little on the plateau and that the real question is how near the cliff are you?

Now, I would argue, of course, that the cliff that our particular society is about to walk over has very little to do with economic problems. It is a breakdown of our world political system, and the labor movement does not have much to do with that.

Actually, from the point of view of internal problems, I suspect very strongly that the labor movement is an excellent insurance against internal disorder. You see, that is perhaps its greatest significance.

SAMUELSON. I could quite agree.

BOULDING. All these other things are small in comparison with that. The thing the labor movement gives us is this sociological sense of identification of the worker with something that is an integral part of his society which otherwise he may not have.[1] And that is a tremendous safeguard against revolution, to put it bluntly.

WRIGHT. It may also be an insurance against growth too. That is the trouble. That is what I was developing in this paper of mine, that you have an eternal conflict of standards. You have these quite legitimate and desirable union aims, if you take them in isolation, the sense of identity and participation, a world free from rivalry and coercion, and all that sort of thing. Of course, I think it is extremely naïve to suppose that unions would ever give us a world free from rivalry. But let that pass. But all of these noneconomic aims of unions, which I think are the significant part of unions, every darn one of them, has the effect of cutting down on the growth

---

[1] *Comment by Wright:* While conceding a great deal of merit to this point of view, I must protest the implication found in much recent literature that the union is the only organization a "laborer" can find to join.

of the national income, it seems to me, and on the introduction of change. Also, I think, they tend to have serious effects on opportunity because the watchword of the union movement is the routinization of promotion.

I have been very much concerned to notice the National Labor Relations Board ruling that an employer has to give the union all the figures on just how much he pays everybody. The first thing that a union does, it seems to me, is to want to bring everybody down to definite specific classifications. Bill Jones is thirty-five years old and has been in the place five years. Therefore, he rates so and so, and so on up. Now this system gives no regard to the exceptional man. There is no chance for the free lance. That element of spontaneity in social life on which, I think, freedom and technological creativity alike depend is struck at. That is what, I think, is the trouble with England. The people with new ideas don't get a chance.

BOULDING. The trouble in England goes far deeper than the growth of the labor movement or the existence of the labor movement; and to some extent any objectionable elements in the labor movement are a reflection of the nature of the whole society, for it is a pretty good generalization about trade unionism that it is very much like the society in which it exists. If you have racketeering unions, there are racketeering employers; and if you have a society which has lost this—whatever it is—*élan* or something, then the labor movement will reflect that also. But I don't think you can point to the labor movement and say this is the thing which freezes up your change.

SAMUELSON. It may contribute.

WRIGHT. It certainly contributes an immensely powerful institutional organization for the ossification of society.

FRIEDMAN. I would like to change the topic for a moment and go back to the welfare problem. It seems to me this kind of welfare analysis that Professor Samuelson is describing leaves you in the position of the end justifying the means. Of course, you can only have one ultimate end; and I am not arguing that people have more than one ultimate end; but, in many ways, it seems to me that the ultimate end, really, has to be the *process* by which agreement is reached and the means used. It seems to me that those who have defended the competitive system have done so not solely because they figure some kind of a sum of utilities can be maximized in this way, but much more because it seemed to them to be the system which was consistent with the maximum degree of individual responsibility, with the maximum reliance upon persuasion and discussion as a means of reconciling conflict.

SAMUELSON. By the way, in my own work, I generalize this welfare function completely beyond the goods and services which people are awarded in market baskets to the process by which they arrive in economic life at the goods and services, and give end content to the different processes by which you arrive at this.[2]

FRIEDMAN. Once you have done that, it of course becomes so general that in order to get any results out of it we have to do so by discussing the particular specific ends.

SAMUELSON. This is a language; it isn't theorems.

WRIGHT. I would like to make some low-brow remarks on the subject of welfare economics. I am not a mathematician. This is the way it strikes me. I can well understand that there might be societies in which people would be happier than in our society and in which they might have higher spiritual quality or in which they had better tastes or different forms of social organization which in some way produced happier men. I do not see how in the name of heaven we can prove scientifically that merely redistributing income will make people happier. I can assume some hypothetical optimum—that is, that there may be some more optimum solution—but how do

---

[2] *Comment by Wright:* Unquestionably such a procedure can cover the whole problem by definition—but can it have specific content?

you know what it is? One could just as *scientifically* argue that the total of happiness would be increased by redistributing incomes from blonds to brunettes as that it would be increased by redistributing from rich to poor.

SAMUELSON. We are absolutely at one. I am a complete positivist as far as the role of the economist in specifying what the nature of the welfare function is.

WRIGHT. Then you are not justified in dynamiting society in order to get something which we can't prove scientifically as economists. If this thing is just something you happen to like, maybe it is right if you convince enough people that it is so. Why, then, they can—

SAMUELSON. This is the basic problem of politics, of how you form compromise value judgments and implement them.

WRIGHT. I would appeal to growth and opportunity as justifying a rather highly concentrated distribution of wealth, at any given time, plus a good deal of turnover over time.

SAMUELSON. Much more perhaps than under *laissez faire* of the nefarious past.

FRIEDMAN. You see the difficulty. When you use this completely formal welfare economics language you seem to be saying—or people will interpret you as saying—that you can't justify anything as being "right" compared to something else as "wrong"; that it "all depends."

SAMUELSON. I don't say that at all.

FRIEDMAN. It seems to me the real role of the economist is much less to justify anything than to see wherein it is that people are making silly statements.

SAMUELSON. Movements involving general social loss for example: rent control, for example, I don't know whether rent control is one, but it may be a case of general social loss that any boob could recognize as such.

FRIEDMAN. The difficulty with that statement is that boobs don't recognize it as such. They represent it as the opposite, and they seem inevitably to be able to find an argument from this generalized approach to welfare economics with its major emphasis on the possibility that all kinds of strange things may yield all kinds of strange results. It sounds to me as if what you are saying is that you can't do any damage.

SAMUELSON. No, it does not at all. I have written repeatedly on this subject. I don't think what I have written has been widely read, but at no point have I ever written *without* trying to debunk the pretension of welfare economics. I just point out its extremely humble function in clarifying certain issues that are not avoidable in contemporary discussions but which are kicked around and obscured and not understood. But if I have erred in this respect in the literature, gone too far, I would like to have it pointed out and change it.

KNIGHT. There is an almost complete coincidence of dates between Mill's *Political Economy* and the Marx-Engels *Communist Manifesto*. That seems to me to dramatize one point. The history of the nineteenth century strongly suggests that a free society is most efficient in making people dislike that kind of society. It is the most efficient producer of discontent that world political evolution has so far produced. Yet society, to be "successful"—if you can use that word about it—politically, ought to make people like that kind of society, and liberal society seems to do exactly the opposite.

HABERLER. Maybe any kind of society makes you dissatisfied with it.

KNIGHT. The nineteenth century seems to take the prize, even over other forms. And Hitler, on the contrary—and judging from what little we know, Stalin too—has so far temporarily been quite successful in making people like the kind of society they have.

FRIEDMAN. Or in concealing the evidences of dislike.

KNIGHT. We don't know too much, of course.

WRIGHT. Maybe Dr. Johnson's remark is appropriate, that equality of opportunity is a self-defeating goal because the more nearly you attain it the more unfavorable the implications to those who don't achieve the maximum and, therefore, the greater the unhappiness. And he said that it would be much better to restrict the chances of people to about what they could do, and to have everybody stay in that state of life to which it had "pleased God to call them." That I think is the ideal that our modern society is feeling its way back to by the most extraordinary double talk. I don't happen to believe in that type of society. Dr. Johnson's idea was that it would be a happier society because then fewer people would suffer from frustrated ambition. You see—that if everybody wanted to be President of the United States, and there could only be, perhaps, six Presidents of the United States in one lifetime, out of one hundred-odd million Americans, all the rest of them, 129,999,999 Americans would be frustrated, you see, and that it would be better, therefore, only to allow maybe ten people the chance to be President of the United States. There is a good deal in that from a purely "scientific" point of view. Maximum opportunity may create maximum dissatisfaction.

KNIGHT. Freedom of opportunity implies the possibility of being defeated—yet perhaps not being defeated is one of the most important human wants.

WRIGHT. The thing that bothers me most about the whole business is that it would seem that one of the most universal and least admirable attributes of the human race is jealousy. And a society makes progress, at least, if you define progress as increased output, to the extent that it is willing to tolerate individual achievement and individual experimentation—which means tolerating differences in salary, in wealth, in authority, etc.—and to the extent that it allows a relative irrationality or, that is to say, nonroutinized opportunity for people to get to do what they want to do, and to be what they want to be. To be a good businessman, for example, by getting to be a good businessman—and you can't put being a good businessman down into elaborate formal examinations.

The great virtue, as I see it, of the *laissez-faire* economists and the whole *laissez-faire* gospel was that they preached a tolerance toward achievement, which is very important. This allowed a degree of decentralized leadership and high achievement and made jealousy not respectable.

Now, the effect of the union movement and of welfare economics is to make jealousy respectable and to encourage everybody to gang up on the fellow who is doing a little bit better.

KNIGHT. But so much of that is due to the paid agitator.

SAMUELSON. Why does he get such a resonant response in the people?

KNIGHT. Why do they pay him for it? It is a vicious circle, of course.

BOULDING. You can't avoid the development of the skills of organization. That is something we have to face in our social development. One of the things that develops along with everything else is the ability to organize. I think myself that the growth of the labor movement is to be explained very largely in those terms. It isn't a question of demand. It is a question of supply. The supply curve of organizations, as it were, has been moving very rapidly to the right.

KNIGHT. Success succeeds.

BOULDING. Look at John L. Lewis. I don't think the labor movement in this country is egalitarian. It is extremely imbued with our whole general pattern.

KNIGHT. Look at Lewis's salary and Petrillo's.

BOULDING. And they like it.

CLARK. Can you think of any kind of organization for great society in this century where we won't jolly well have to tolerate a lot of difference of authority in one form or another—John L. Lewis's form or another?

BOULDING. I like John L. very much because I regard the national state as a much greater threat to everybody and everything than the labor movement, and anybody who would get up and spit in its eye is one of my pals. If you are looking at your checks and balances, an independent labor movement is a strong check against the power of the state.

KNIGHT. That is so wrong. That kind of an independent labor movement is just what is going to give you the omnipotent state.

WRIGHT. The fact of great authority is not so important as the means by which it is attained; and while the labor movement permits of great concentration of authority—for example, John L. Lewis—its emphasis on the means of getting this concentration in a mature union is on some sort of seniority, something like that, which has the effect of inducing a narrow conformist mentality. In other words, I think that the society which does not allow for the young screwball is likely to be held back. It has got to have enough decentralization and room for experimentation in it.

And the thing is that you have a democratic gospel: "Equality." You say this fellow has got eyes, nose, and mouth just like me. What is he doing getting five times as much as I do? And then the union says, "Well, it is better to avoid fights; we will just let everybody go up at the same rate." You see it in academic life, all the pressure for automatic salary plans and that sort of thing.

The effect of it is to hold down imaginative achievement. It is a very curious and ironical thing that the left-wing policy, which is advertised as a policy for the young and the underdog, is in its actual effects so much of the time really a policy aimed against the nonconformist adventurer—the very man whom theoretically it ought to admire the most. . . .

FRIEDMAN. I want to raise a question that I started raising earlier. Why do we have this interest in the proportion of wages in the grand total, why do we have a lot of discussion about what supposedly determines this proportion? I don't know what it is.

SAMUELSON. The real interest of most people is in the personal distribution of income, and they rather simple-mindedly confuse some fractional share alleged to be constant over time, because of something that Bowley measured, as a rough index of something desirable or undesirable about the personal distribution of income.

FRIEDMAN. I think that is right. If that is the case, there is plenty of empirical evidence that there is only a tenuous connection between these two and that we can infer practically nothing concerning the personal distribution of income from the functional.

SAMUELSON. Many people are interested, and properly from their viewpoints, in all of this only as it relates to the personal distribution of income both in its absolute and relative aspects.

BOULDING. I give another answer to that question. In fact, I think I have a couple of answers. I am interested in knowing the empirical facts as to whether this distribution is fairly stable over long periods and, if so, why. I am not sure I know the answer. It is an extremely important question from the point of view of, shall we say, the long-run stability of capitalism if this proportionate distribution is fairly stable.

FRIEDMAN. Why?

BOULDING. Suppose we take the extreme Marxian case. Suppose that every increase in the national product goes to nonlabor income. Wages are fixed at the subsistence level and any increase in productivity goes to nonlabor. Now empirical fact shows that in our society Marx isn't right—but it is very important to know *why* he isn't right. It is important to know whether there are circumstances under which he might be right or societies about which he might be right, as I suspect there may very well be.

I am interested in it from another point of view. It is also an empirical fact that proportional distribution shows a marked shift in time of depression toward labor income and away from nonlabor income. Now, that is a very interesting empirical fact. It is interesting to us why that is so, and I don't think that the marginal productivity theory gives us any kind of answer to that question at all.

In the depression of 1933, I think the proportional distribution was something like 74 per cent to labor income as against 63 today and something like that before.

CLARK. Is that in nonlabor incomes or profits, dividends?

BOULDING. Labor income, the wages item.

CLARK. You get a decidedly different proportional behavior according as the nonwage remainder includes the profits of business or its distributed earnings. They were maintaining dividends out of capital for a while.[3]

BOULDING. I think that all these things are interesting, actually; and it is interesting to know if there are any causal factors here and which way they operate.

CLARK. There is another proportion which I think would be significant within this proportion, and that is the ratio of wages of organized labor to the profits of the employers of the same organized labor.

BOULDING. There are all kinds of breakdowns.

CLARK. I think in a breakdown pertinent to collective bargaining problems, wages would show a much larger ratio to the other shares than they do for the economy as a whole where "nonlabor income" includes large amounts going to working farmers, small traders, and so on.

WRIGHT. This stability of the ratio between labor and nonlabor income is really a hopeful thing for capitalism or the reverse: hopeful in the sense that it shows the Marxian doctrine of increasing misery has to be taken with a huge grain, or huge grains, of salt; pessimistic in the sense that here you have a lot of people being filled full of a notion that their

[3] *Comment by Clark:* I believe that at or about the time when labor income was 74 per cent of the whole, aggregate industrial net earnings were a minus quantity.

relative income should be increased and will be increased by a large margin. And here you have something that indicates that this process is probably going to be futile. It seems to me that the second argument is for a more explosive situation.

KNIGHT. Why should labor's fraction increase when the investment per laborer is increasing enormously or even remaining constant?

BOULDING. I don't think the ordinary rank and file man ever thinks of proportional distribution.

KNIGHT. That is the answer. People don't care about the facts and don't know anything about them. It is not a fair comparison to say the proportions. What happens to the proportions when the proportion of capital to labor in the economy is increasing?

CLARK. One key factor in the predominant state of mind of organized labor is an enormous overestimate of the amount of profits relative to wages. This builds partly on the fact that the wage bill is likely to be not more than 25 per cent of the total gross sales of an industry, which, of course, is a misleading comparison.

KNIGHT. But the laborers are simply being taught that misunderstanding in the universities in every other department except economics, and even by half the economists. That is staggering. Carl Becker, one of our best historians, said that, of course, since the industrial revolution, property produces a greater part of the product, and so it gets a greater part of the product.

SAMUELSON. If the labor people really regard the salaries of the executives, say in the over-$10,000 class, as something to be plundered in the same sense as property return is to be plundered, it boils down to a fairly simple kind of a leveling rather than a classification on the basis of productivity factors.

FRIEDMAN. The recent increase in the proportion of national income attributable to labor may be largely due to changes in taxes, so that you save a lot of money if instead of paying yourself dividends you pay yourself salaries. I shouldn't be surprised if that accounted for a significant part of the change.

SAMUELSON. The corporation itself has been growing in the American scene. In the old comparisons—

BOULDING. It hasn't since 1929. The income of unincorporated businesses is up to what is nearly 20 per cent of national income now against something like 13 per cent then. So there is distinct evidence that the importance of the corporation is declining.

CHAMBERLIN. Wouldn't it be extraordinary if labor income did anything else but stay fairly close to a fairly constant percentage? In other words, suppose it rose from 50 per cent to 95 per cent. Wouldn't that require extraordinary explanations as to why it should fluctuate so widely?

KNIGHT. If the labor fraction were to increase one fourth, capital would have to disappear.

CLARK. Of course, a stable fraction isn't very meaningful in a society changing from a society predominantly of farmers and small tradesmen. They are a minority portion of the whole.

WRIGHT. If we could shift to a more specific topic for a short while, I would like to get the sense of this body before we adjourn. Do we believe that raising money wages in a depression will increase employment or decrease employment? I would just like to know as a matter of curiosity. Here are eight economists. Do we think that raising money wages in a depression will increase employment or decrease employment?

FRIEDMAN. Raising money-wage rates?

WRIGHT. Yes.

FRIEDMAN. How do you raise them?

WRIGHT. Union action or minimum wages. Will that increase employment or decrease employment?

FRIEDMAN. And you do nothing else, keep the monetary system the same?

HABERLER. You have to say what you mean by that exactly.

FRIEDMAN. I will answer you, decrease employment. I can conceive of your doing other things at the same time but, insofar as there are no offsetting independent influences, I will answer, raising money-wage rates in depression will decrease employment.

SAMUELSON. Let me state this. There was an 8 million postwar unemployment prediction made in Washington, and I don't know what harm that did on the tax front. I think not very much. But it has been said to me that it did encourage the New Deal government to let unions raise wages; and then it has been further said to me, "And perhaps that is why the full 8 million unemployed didn't develop." Now, my guess is— I did not know how to refute that.

FRIEDMAN. Suppose you had to answer Wright's question with a straight yes or no answer. What would you say, an increase or decrease of unemployment? At the bottom of the depression, assuming no effect whatsoever on the monetary policy.

SAMUELSON. How can it not have an effect?

BOULDING. It will always have an effect on velocity.

FRIEDMAN. No change in the conditions under which the monetary authorities are ready to create new money, no change in the fiscal side, in the level of taxation, in the level of transfer payment, or anything else.

SAMUELSON. Is it at the bottom of the depression?

FRIEDMAN. At a time when there are 10 million unemployed, 8 million unemployed.

SAMUELSON. I would not be sure of its effect then. With overcapacity all around, investment rather low and inelastic, and depending upon the state of liquidity of business, it would be possible at the expense of profits, that is, nonlabor income— this might set off many effects that would cause more employment. I couldn't be sure.

WRIGHT. It might not even be at the expense of the profits. It might be merely at the expense of cash balances; that is, you could conceivably, if you had higher money wages, encourage business to encroach on its—

FRIEDMAN. I don't see how the higher money-wage rates themselves induce them to do it.

SAMUELSON. I could construct a model in which employment would go up and profits would go up, real profits.

FRIEDMAN. If you had to predict one way or the other, what would you predict?

BOULDING. The real trouble is the things you have to introduce into a model, the effects on distribution policy, on liquidity policy. Here is a very simple model. Suppose the increase in wage rates does not result in any change in employment. What would happen?

FRIEDMAN. But the question is whether it will.

BOULDING. Suppose it does not. What would happen? If we may come out with the answer, this is one way to start. In the first place, it is likely that there would be a shift in the money stock toward household balances. I think I would rather expect that. Business paying at a higher wage—the money balances of businesses being drawn down—and household balances rising. Now that, however, will be pretty temporary, I am pretty sure. Another result is the money comes back into business. The business inventories are depleted as a result of this, especially industries of goods. If business has a policy of maintaining inventories, then I would expect this to increase employment. We regard the price system as rather sticky, of course, as I think in depressions it is reasonable to, with all supplies elastic. The simplest theory of enterprise you can assume is what I call the theory of homeostasis, following Mr. Noyes, that is, the theory of homeostasis of the balance sheet. We assume that what the enterprise wants to do is to maintain the structure of its balance sheets (that is essentially Mr. Noyes' theory of consumer choice). Now, as a matter of fact, that isn't a bad approximation; and if you assume that the liquidity preferences aren't changed, then you would certainly expect a rise in wage rates to raise output during a depression.[4]

FRIEDMAN. You see what the trouble is. The trouble is that we are really talking different languages. We started out with a rise in wage rates produced by union action. That would mean a rise in particular wage rates, rise in relative wage rates.

BOULDING. Suppose that you passed a law—you could perfectly well do it—saying that every man you employed this week had to be employed next week at a wage rate 10 per cent higher and if you didn't do that you would be put in jail.

FRIEDMAN. Including the employer?

BOULDING. No, because he doesn't get wages.

SAMUELSON. Peron did something like that. He declared a universal wage increase.

BOULDING. You can do this. We haven't exploited this method of control. I think we ought to develop the analysis of this kind of thing.

CLARK. We followed a somewhat different route in 1933—increased wages with shorter hours—and some queer movements resulted.

BOULDING. Didn't Blum do something like this? Anyway, we could at least hypothesize that all wage rates rise by 10 per cent for everybody, if you like, who has a Social Security number. Well, as I say, you could very well draw up a model in which employment rose as a result of this, and it would be a fairly plausible one. On the other hand, of course, it does depend on the reactions which a thing like this sets off, on what people's preferences are, and on how it disturbs the balance sheet the people wish to maintain.

WRIGHT. My instinct would be that it would decrease employment. However, I can see models in which such a manda-

---

[4] *Comment by Wright:* I should dissent not so much from Dr. Boulding's logic as his assumptions of fact.

Comment by Boulding: Professor Wright asked for logic. I should dissent from his instinct.

tory money-wage increase might induce dishoarding, might induce some increase in consumption, and might produce more investment; but there would always be the likelihood of an adverse effect on marginal profit. Therefore, I think the best answer is the one Haberler gives, that since ultimately any such possible favorable reactions would come through a change in MV, there are lots of other ways of changing MV which don't involve the negative possibilities on profit expectations; and, therefore, since all that your money-wage increase amounts to is at best a possible hypothetical shift in MV, it would be better to induce that shift by other institutional means, deficit financing or something like that; and you would in that way miss the effects on cost and on the marginal efficiency of capital which the wage increase would imply.

CHAPTER XVII

Final Comments by Participants

[*Editor's note:* After the session was completed several of the participants sent in final statements of their position and comments on the other papers. These final summaries are given herewith.]

J. M. Clark: Comment on Professor Friedman's Position

PERHAPS the most uncompromising disagreement revealed by the conference is that between Professor Friedman's views and my own. I have tried, in revising the body of my paper, to clarify my position on some of the controverted points, but some major matters remain. We agree that the power of unions to affect wage levels has been much exaggerated, but I attach more importance than he does to the amount they have been able to accomplish, beyond what would have taken place in any case. We agree that the efforts of unions to get more gains than economic forces permit have harmful results; but in assessing these results, he appears to attribute to union policies more responsibility for unemployment than I would, and less for inflation. I even go part-way with him in relating sound economic wage adjustments to a competitive ideal, though we part company where he assumes that it is feasible to create a competitive labor market and leave the adjustments to the market's automatic and unguided action.

Our most far-reaching difference would seem to center in the question whether our entire economy, including the labor market, can and should be made thoroughly and unmitigatedly competitive. In the body of my paper I have taken the position that this would lead to too-low wages. The employer would have an inevitable advantage, equal competition between employers and individual workers being inconsistent with the modern type of production. Elsewhere I have taken the position that human nature is not suited to a world in which there is nothing between separate individuals and households, and the overwhelming, impersonal state, with every man's hand against every other's in a universal competitive struggle.[1] More basic than man's competitive urge is his need to belong to a group, on which he can fall back, and whose sustaining attitude sets limits on the competitive struggle. In meeting this need, unions seem to have an inevitable place to fill, and one that cannot be dismissed by proposing to strip them of all powers that have a monopolistic character.

Professor Friedman is opposed even to considering what an economically correct wage would be—that should be left to market forces, presumably after the market has been made thoroughly competitive, though he seems equally intolerant of such analysis under existing conditions, which are far from competitive. The reason seems to lie in the claim that such analysis is either a pious wish or a first step toward direct controls of wages. In this idiom, piety is obviously taken as synonymous with futility, for reasons which it might be inexpedient to analyze.[2] It is true that there is an attitude to be

[1] Cf. my *Alternative to Serfdom* (U. of Chicago Press, 1944), pp. 18-19, 25, 49-52; and chap. iii.

[2] *Comment by Friedman:* Deficiencies in my exposition are doubtless responsible for making the difference between Professor Clark and myself on this point seem greater than it is. I have no objection to the determination of what the economically correct wage would be. If this could be done it would provide a real basis for judging how far we now are from this standard and what the effect of union as well as enterprise

found in Washington which cannot see any departure from a standard of real or supposed economic correctness without trying to correct it; but this attitude seems to be directed toward business—chiefly big business—and not toward labor. If we come to direct wage controls (which means also price controls) it will presumably be because inflation has driven us to it.

The feasibility of his own program is supported by reasoning to the effect that if organized labor realizes how little economic power it really possesses, then mild measures will be sufficient to take its excess powers away.[3] Logically, such realization of ineffectualness might make the unions' resistance milder, but it is not evident how it would reduce the scope of the changes required to make the labor market thoroughly competitive. This would call for changes which labor would, quite sincerely, regard as meaning the destruction of unions—and would resist accordingly. Milder measures may have their uses, but they would not do what Professor Friedman appears to be calling for.

Are Unions "Monopolies"?

It may be true, as Professor Haberler suggests, that no very good purpose is served by attaching the "monopoly" label to unions—or to businesses, for that matter—and it is certainly

---

monopoly has been. My objection is rather to the specification of principles of "good" behavior for participants in bargaining without consideration of the forces that would or could lead to conformity with these principles. It seems to me a pious wish to hope that the participants will voluntarily be "good" if being "good" conflicts with what they regard as their primary interests. And the only simple way I can see of enforcing the principles is by government wage fixing or its equivalent.

[3] *Comment by Friedman:* My position does not depend in any way on whether organized labor does or does not realize the limitations of its power. I have deliberately avoided the problem of "political feasibility." My position is rather that competitive forces are sufficiently strong and ubiquitous to need little positive assistance to be extremely effective; and

true that useful analysis of market situations must be in much more specific rather than such general terms. But the general terms still have some prima-facie value as designating broad categories of situations. "Competition" refers to a situation in which the seller is controlled, or limited, by the buyer's option to trade with rival sellers (if they offer better terms). If this option is excluded, monopoly exists; and in the typical collective bargaining situation, the option is effectually excluded. This describes a fact, irrespective of whether the seller uses his opportunity to maximize his income in the fashion described in customary theoretical models. (This last is probably very rarely done by business "monopolies.") As to terminology, there is a certain inconsistency in the prevalent usage of freely designating as "monopoly" many conditions well short of the above criterion, if they occur in business, but sedulously avoiding application of the term to unions, no matter how clearly it may be warranted. Is it not more honest to say, "We have different policies toward monopoly in business and in labor," than to say, "We are opposed to monopoly; when we find a kind we do not want to oppose, we will call it by a different name"?

As to the extent to which monopoly power is used, there are considerations on both sides. With unions, a policy aiming at "more, without limit" has a considerable degree of public approval and is fortified by a well-developed theory that higher wages increase the effective demand for labor; and neither of these factors is matched in the case of business. On the other hand, the seller of labor has to face a buyer who can do a good deal more effective bargaining than most buyers of commodities. And when an industry curtails output in connection with an increase of price, it automatically gets rid of its "variable costs" for labor and materials, for the output that is no longer produced; while a union in a corresponding situation faces a much more complex set of reactions and adjustments. If it wants to

___

that the absence of deliberate interference by the state with their operation is the major need.

exclude surplus workers, it must plan ahead and limit membership and eligibility for work; and this may incur a sacrifice of good will. And the union is unlikely to connect this necessity with any particular wage increase, or even with a policy of wage increases. Thus simple generalities are inadequate.

The Question of Marginal Productivity

Marginal productivity has come into the discussions largely in connection with the question whether, if wages move in more or less stable proportion to average productivity, they may fail to agree with the movements of marginal productivity. The same principle, viewed from the other end, appears to be involved in the point made by Professor Wright, that wages might be so high as to cut into the marginal profit necessary to expansion of employment, even if average profit was sufficient. To deal adequately with the issues involved would call for a treatise, both theoretical and realistic, on the meaning and behavior of marginal productivity and its relations to the Keynesian "marginal efficiency of capital" and to the willingness and ability to pay wages. This treatise has not been written, and obviously cannot be written for this occasion, but a few notes may be pertinent, beyond the very general caveat, already made, that the market manages to absorb methods of wage payment which cannot possibly agree with any precisely determined marginal productivity.

In the first place, while changes in marginal productivity need not accord precisely with changes in average productivity, they need not disagree markedly either, and there are prima-facie grounds for supposing that they may keep close enough together to be within the very wide latitude of tolerance suggested for application of the average productivity wage standard. The most noted attempt at measurement is the Cobb-Douglas formula, representing product as a function of labor and capital in the form $P = L^m C^{1-m}$. It is a property of this formula that the shares marginally imputed to the factors would absorb constant fractions of the product, no matter how the quantities of the factors and of the product might vary. If the exponent of labor is two-thirds, the share marginally imputed to labor would always be two-thirds of total product. This, of course, is merely suggestive, though interesting. In its original and more meaningful form, it represented the historical trends of totals for American manufacturing for a twenty-year period, but not the cyclical movements within those trends. Such a historical trend need not agree with the functions that would be effective in the market at any one moment, for various reasons, including Professor Wright's race between innovation and imputation.

These currently effective functions represent "expectations" —a misleading term for what one is willing to risk on a more or less uncertain prospect. The field includes prosperous and unprosperous industries; within each industry it includes enterprises in all states of profit and loss, expansion and decline; and within single enterprises it includes successful and unsuccessful experiments in the combination of factors. If an industry is making too many losses—that is, paying more for the factors than they produce—it may reduce its payments for the factors, or it may raise its selling prices, thus raising the marginal products of all the factors it uses. Industry as a whole may, under some conditions, be able to make a similar adjustment of prices. Enterprises that pioneer in successful innovation create spots where marginal products exceed marginal costs, temporarily; and these include profitable enterprises and some that are successfully reducing losses. It is innovations that enable capital— the relatively increasing factor—to maintain its imputed share of the total product. Otherwise, its marginal product would presumably decline abruptly with increasing funds seeking investment, and its imputed percentage share of total product would decline.

Not all discrepancies between wages and marginal product

need to be rectified by equating wages to marginal products. When a plant is working below capacity, a 5 per cent increase in direct labor and materials would increase product approximately 5 per cent. Then if direct labor and materials received their full short-run marginal product, they would absorb the whole, and there would be nothing left for any other shares, including indirect labor. If this happened, it would not be through increasing wages, but through reducing selling prices to short-run marginal costs, and this could only be temporary since, in this case, marginal cost would be below average cost. This kind of short-run marginal product is not a basis for fixing wage rates.

The opposite case has been mentioned by Professor Wright, where an increase of wages might absorb the marginal profit, though average profit was still adequate. This means that marginal cost would be above average cost, implying that the plant would be working beyond its efficient capacity. This again would be essentially a temporary condition. Or it might be because industry is employing the last, least efficient 5 per cent of the working population, in which case the appropriate adjustment would seem to be a differential wage for the less efficient workers.[4] In either case it does not seem appropriate that wages in general should be kept down to the level of this kind of low marginal productivity; and it occurs in time of extra-strong demand, when the difficulty is likely to be solved by an increase of prices. Or if not, and if production is somewhat restricted, this means restriction of the peak of a boom, which has often been urged as desirable, and which is at least not a self-evident evil.

The kind of marginal productivity that is relevant to the setting of basic wage rates is not derived from the short-run situation either of boom or depression, but a much longer-run

[4] *Comment by Wright:* Is it not somewhat sweeping to assume that marginal cost only lies above average when the "last 5 per cent" is being employed?

adjustment, necessarily inaccurate and subject to the uncertainties of a long-term commitment. It relates to the kind of competition between labor and capital which is implicit in the redesigning of productive establishments, and deciding what proportion between labor and capital is most economical—or will be most economical during the lifetime of the establishment, at the relative costs that prevail, or that are expected to prevail during the pertinent period. Such judgments as this cannot be expected to be precise, and the demand for labor is probably more affected by expansion or contraction of business in general, in which demand for labor and for capital move together instead of competing with one another. Some combinations of labor and capital are clearly uneconomical under existing wage-price structures and with existing technical knowledge; but within the limits thus set, there must be considerable latitude within which there is no clearly determined answer, and trial and error is in order.

The indicated conclusion is that, while wages can affect the total effective demand for labor, the nature of the effect is far from simple; and while marginal productivity plays a part in determining the response to the demands of labor for wage changes, it is not the only factor that enters in, nor does it set limits that are sharp and definite.

Comments by Dr. Boulding on the Discussion of His Paper

I have left my paper pretty much in the same form as that in which it was presented to the Institute, in order to give the reader a clear idea of what was being discussed. I confess that the violence of the opposition somewhat surprised me, perhaps because I have been living with this set of ideas now long enough for them to become friends. Professors, like dogs, are wont to bark at strangers, and it may be that I underestimate the strangeness of my little pets.

The opposition centered around two features: the "widow's cruse" theory of profits on the one hand and the apparent conflict with Walrasian equilibrium theory on the other. In a sense these represent two aspects of a single difficulty. The economist is accustomed to think of distribution as determined essentially by the price system, and the price system as determined by the physical production functions on the one hand, relating quantities of input to quantities of output, and the demand or utility functions on the other hand, describing the tastes of consumers. This does not seem to leave any room for the kind of determination by strictly "financial" decisions which forms the essential element in my system. If the prices of factors of production, along with all other prices, are determined at the point where there are no excess demands or supplies, the distribution of income then seems to be determined uniquely by the distribution of ownership of the factors, and there seems to be no place for the kind of indeterminacy involved in the "widow's cruse."

The resolution of this apparent paradox lies in the recognition that dividends and interest are not payments in exchange but are essentially transfer payments, analogous, say, to the transfer payments of government. The purchase of labor is an exchange: money (the wage) is subtracted and the product of the labor is added to the balance-sheet totals of the employer. The rent of physical capital, including land, likewise represents a "cost"—i.e., an asset transformation, the money rent being transformed into a corresponding value of product. If the value of the product is greater than its cost—i.e., if in the exchange or production transformations which constitute enterprise the total value of assets grows—profits are made. Dividends and interest, however, represent a direct subtraction from the asset totals—i.e., from the net worth—without any corresponding additions. This is why, of course, accountants have been extremely unwilling to follow the economists' practice of regarding interest and some "normal" profit as a "cost," although for purposes of price theory it is highly convenient to do so.

All that the Walrasian system determines is a set of equilibrium prices and quantities transformed—equilibrium in the sense that there are no excess demands or supplies. There are any number of such sets of prices, however, consistent with various systems of transfer payments. What my system does not adequately deal with, I must admit, is the problem of the effects of disequilibria in the price-wage structure on the macroeconomic aggregates. This defect it shares with all "Keynesian" type systems, and it is the main reason why such systems tend to break down as the economy approaches full employment.

In saying that dividend and interest payments are essentially "transfer" payments, I do not imply any judgment on their moral necessity. It is tempting, of course, to draw the inference that they are not paid "for" anything in the sense that wages are paid "for" the product of labor, and hence to derive a quasi-Marxian or at least Hobsonian system of "surplus value" or unearned income. Such an inference, however, is unjustified. The ethical critique of any institution depends very largely on what are its practicable alternatives, and although profits may not be paid "for" any specific service, they may well be a general price that we pay for a reasonably uncoercive and technologically progressive society.

Nevertheless, there is a reasonable inference that this price should be as small as possible. How big it should be depends on how great an incentive is necessary to stimulate the desired amount of investment (accumulation) and technical change. I assume here that we should not accumulate merely to provide full employment—that once the desired amount of investment is determined, any increase in product necessary to secure full employment should be represented by consumption.

It may well be that the incentives to progress depend not so much on the total of profit, nor on the proportionate distribution of profit and wages, as on the distribution of profit itself as between the innovator and the noninnovator. This is a corner of the problem which is still somewhat dark.

I may conclude with some general observations on the whole meeting. In the unlikely event of a good trade unionist ever getting to read these papers and discussions he would certainly be impressed by what is at worst an unfriendly and at best a querulous attitude toward the labor movement. Whatever its sociological virtues, we seem to be saying, the labor movement is an economic nuisance, if not a positive danger. This attitude is, I think, an honest one: we are not the hired propagandists of the N.A.M., and have no personal axe to grind, even though there are some signs among us of the inflation-generated discontent of the white-collar worker. In considerable degree, however, this attitude arises out of the nature of our specialized skills as economists, and out of the nature of the abstraction which is economics. We are specialists in exchange, in the price system, and in the market. The labor movement is part of the expression of that hatred of the market which has dominated the history of the West in the past hundred years, and which reaches its supreme expression in socialism. But the market is our baby: we cannot help loving it a little. Hence, even though Samuelson can show that almost any degree of interference with the market can be justified by an appropriate Bergson welfare function,[5] we can hardly help having a welfare function of our own which gives the market mechanism itself a high priority. We must beware, however, of giving our private welfare functions any sanctity of erudite authority.

Supplementary Discussion by Paul A. Samuelson

Except for the few clearly marked addenda to my paper, I have left it in its original form so that any reader can see what

---

[5] *Comment by Wright:* But *only* to the man who holds that particular function.

may have given rise to various parts of the discussion. I feel that I benefited much from the oral discussion; and had I talked less and listened more, I might have benefited even more. But some issues perhaps still seem to hang in air, and so a few final comments on welfare economics may therefore be in order.

Take for example the marginal productivity theory. In its simplest form it is a theory of price formation in a world of complete certainty, perfect competition, and continuously substitutable production functions subject to special laws of returns. To the degree that any or all of these conditions are not met, we can question the empirical relevance of the doctrine. But even if its extreme conditions could be perfectly realized, what does it tell us? And what are its ethical or normative attributes?

The operational meaning of the last question is as follows: From outside of economics give an economist a detailed set of norms or ethical judgments; identify the given configuration of economic goods and services enjoyed by different individuals as determined by marginal productivity in the market place; finally, use the outside norms to determine how the market result compares with all other technically feasible results. What will the verdict be? The odds are a billion to one that it will have to be as follows:

The competitive configuration rates higher than many alternative configurations, and it also rates lower than many other alternative configurations.

This is of course not saying much; and unless more can be said, no one would be much interested in the pricing mechanism. Under suitable conditions of returns and tastes, this much more can be said, and essentially only this much more:

There does not *exist an alternative configuration that makes* every *individual better off than he would have been in the ideal competitive configuration.*

What is the significance of this limited statement in a world where more than a single Robinson Crusoe exists? It tells us this:

> *By means of a discoverable system of ideal "lump-sum" additions or subtractions from each person's market-determined income, we can utilize the device of a pricing system to arrive at a true unique optimum position (defined in terms of any single outside-prescribed set of ethical norms that respect individuals' appraisal of their own autonomous well-being and that tell us how we are to evaluate the deserts of different individuals).*[6]

As a supplement to the above remarks, I am reproducing a diagram that I put on the blackboard during the Institute in an attempt to clarify the oral discussion. I cannot claim that it succeeded at all in this purpose, but its interest to readers may justify the short space it occupies. For simplicity, assume that there are but two individuals or classes, called wage earners and *non*wage earners or by any other convenient names. If the total of natural resources is limited and if technology is far from perfect, then everybody cannot have as much of all goods and services as he wishes. In fact, if we may speak loosely of the utility of each of the two individuals, it is clear that no matter

[6] Sometimes it is said, "If the original distribution of wealth has been judged ethically optimal, then the resulting competitive solution will be ethically optimal." As a loose and rough approximation, this is an admissible statement. But we must remember that there can be no *prior* knowledge of what the ethical worth of the distribution of ownership of resources is until we already know what will be the market-determined pricing of the services of the wealth items. On careful logical examination, it turns out that the kernel of truth in the above quotation rests in a rough identification of transfers of titles to incomes with lump-sum transfers. Put in this way, the quoted doctrine is immediately revealed to be only a rough approximation: e.g., giving me a 99 per cent ownership of the receipts from Bing Crosby's voice would definitely alter and distort the uses to which he would put that voice, and could not be a lump-sum transfer, strictly speaking; those familiar with the Pigou doctrines of "external effects" will realize why this is.

what the form of economic organization only certain combinations of their two utilities are possible. Any point on the figure shows the utility for each of the two individuals, i.e., U_n and U_w. The first thing that strikes the eye is that there is an unattainable region which present technology and resources do not permit us to reach. No act of politics or economic reorganization will en-

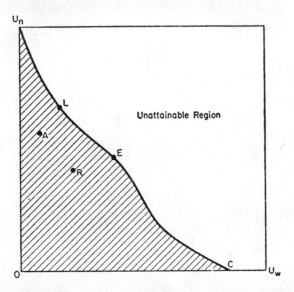

able us to get outside the heavy utility possibility frontier. But of course, by bad economic organization or luck, we can easily end up somewhere *inside* the utility possibility frontier.

Now what is the significance of a system of pricing in a perfectly competitive regime (where the technological laws of returns and of tastes just happen to be appropriate for perfect competition and *laissez faire*)? Under these ideal conditions, we can say: the community will end up *on* the frontier—say at the point marked *L*—and not somewhere inside it. This is the true content of Smith's Invisible Hand doctrine, and just about its only content. I should add that this same result can conceptually be achieved *without* the use of a market mechanism:

as a practical administrative device, the price mechanism has much to be said for it, but this should not obscure the logical point that the final configuration can be defined and reached purely by considering the production functions and taste patterns of the individuals.[7]

Everyone agrees that in actuality the world is not at the ideal *laissez-faire* point. Presumably it is actually somewhere else, inside the frontier, say at *A*. Since we have no need to work with numerical utility, it is not a completely meaningful question to ask "how far inside" we are because of market imperfections; but from the discussion it will be clear that Professor Chamberlin would regard the realistic importance of union deviations from competitive conditions as being substantively more important than would Professor Friedman.

Two further points in the diagram require attention. It is not clear whether the ideal *laissez-faire* point would make every class better off than is actually the case at *A*. If we defined our groups very narrowly it is only too easy to believe that *somebody* would benefit on balance from market imperfection; nonetheless, I have drawn the *A* point southwest of the *L* point so that everyone is worse off. Some of the discussion raised the

---

[7] In a single-family Robinson Crusoe regime, the point marked *C* would be the counterpart of the *L* point. Crusoe might reach this point by calculation that did or did not involve internal prices. If he did use pricing, there is no need for this to involve "imputation" in the usual sense of the word—i.e., marginal productivity identification of the shares of factors through use of the Euler theorem as in the Clark-Walras models, or more generally through Wieser-Walras simultaneous equation. Indeed, in an entirely possible Crusoe world, constant returns to scale might be absent, so that the above would be impossible or residually tautological: yet all of Crusoe's decisions—whether to work or dance an extra hour, whether to sow a hillside with wheat or hyacinths or leave it fallow—could be optimally made, both with or without prices.

I am reserving for a later paper the related important question of the ethical valuation of the freedoms and restraints imposed by competitive trading as ethical ends for their own sake and independently of questions of economic efficiency.

question of a "Robin Hood" interference which would actually benefit one person at the expense of another. The movement from A to R represents such a case. The more you are interested in U_w and the less in U_n, the more you would applaud such a move if it were the only alternative. But the more you favored U_n, the more opposite your verdict would be.

However, even if you thought that the "general interest" required favoring U_w, you might argue that "Robin Hood" was an inefficient way of doing this; that instead one should move directly from L to E by a utopian tax program, or ameliorate the imperfections of the market and move in a couple of steps from A to E. Note that E makes everybody better off than R does.

I don't suppose many would argue that it is better to be at R than E if these were the only choices. But this hardly justifies the conclusion often met with in the writings of economists: Let the competitive market determine its prices without interference, correcting the result by means of political tax decisions. Such a prescription is to be judged at the tactical level: you would rather end up at E than R, but you may not end up at E; and then you would certainly prefer ending up at R to ending up at A. Where to move from A and in what order of precedence is not dependent upon economics: all that economists can do is to point out the "dead-weight harm" that many policies may involve, meaning by this last term "being inside the utility frontier."

There may be other ways of formulating the basic problem of welfare economics than the above—ways that are easier to understand and more interesting to read. But whether couched in the dogmatism of the so-called old welfare economics or the woolliness of the so-called new welfare economics, or in the hateful trappings of mathematical symbols, such ways must in all logic boil down to the same essence.

Because space is short, I can only indicate four dicta that seem inconsistent with the above analysis:

(1) "The relations that pricing would bring about are of little or no importance for welfare."

(2) "A configuration reached by perfect competition is necessarily an ideal one."

(3) "A configuration reached by perfect competition is a 'best obtainable compromise' in some sense."

(4) "Any group not satisfied with the interpersonal distribution of competitive income should not use deviations from competitive conditions to improve the situation; it should instead turn to politics (discussion, persuasion, taxation, transfer expenditure) in its attempts to change the market-determined income structure."

The fallaciousness of (1) and (2) are obvious. There is no particular logical basis for (4) and it must rest its case on a particular diagnosis of tactics and strategy that economics has no particular competence to appraise. To save (3) from being wrong, we must insert implicit premises which make it an empty truism, or posit a special empirical hypothesis concerning politics, ethics and administration. If you are extremely skeptical concerning the feasibility of any favorable movements away from L, you may rationally favor (3)—not as a point in any sense representing "justice" (an extraeconomic word) but as constituting "expediency."

We must never lose sight of this fact: What is best under one set of norms need not be best under another set of norms. This raises the basic question of all politics: How do divergent norms become reconciled? Does there result some compromise set of norms which is to be the acceptable basis for policy judgments?

The discussion in this volume again and again has reminded me of a passage in Dicey's classic work on the rise and fall of nineteenth century English individualism: ". . . the assumption that democracy in its best form can become a government which at any rate tries to look, not to the interest of a class, even though the class be made up of the greater number and the poorest among the inhabitants of England, but to the interests of the whole nation." [8]

What is this Rousseau-like "general will," this "interest of the whole nation"? Until given content, the concept tells us nothing: when given content, we can examine it to see whether it does represent a superconsensus of norms. The cardinal sin is to leave it a mystical undefined concept, and then without realizing it, give it the concrete content of, say, the 1928 market place.

[8] A. V. Dicey, *Law and Opinion in England* (2nd ed.; Macmillan, 1914), p. xc.

CHAPTER XVIII

Concluding Summary

BY DAVID McCORD WRIGHT

IN winding up the report of this institute it is worth while to point out the wide area of agreement shown on practical problems by all the participants:

(1) All participants, except possibly Dr. Friedman,[1] agree that there are important sociological and noneconomic reasons for having unions.

(2) But we all further agree that labor power like corporate power must be subject to restraints for the public welfare.

(3) We all further agree that the welfare of individual labor groups is not necessarily identical with the welfare of the country as a whole, or of labor as a whole.

(4) The participants all feel that the present expectations of many labor groups as to what should be considered a "normal" pattern of wage increases (for example the 10 per cent

---

[1] *Comment by Friedman:* I do not feel competent to judge whether "unions" perform useful sociological and noneconomic functions. But all such alleged functions seem clearly capable of being performed either by unions that are restricted to the employees of a single employer, or by other social or political organizations. And I agree with Professor Chamberlin (see chap. viii), though for somewhat different reasons, that unions restricted to the indicated scope cannot be regarded as having any harmful economic effects. Hence, I see no conflict between sociological, or noneconomic considerations, and economic considerations; the former, if they argue for unions, argue for "company" unions; the latter, if they argue against unions, argue against noncompany unions.

per annum pattern) are far in excess of any reasonable expectations that can be formed as to the future rate of growth of the economy's productive capacity.

(5) We all agree that many of the fringe-end benefits and pension plans now being demanded could, if pushed much further, prove far more harmful to the growth of the economy than simple wage increases.

(6) It was generally conceded that many unions, by "featherbedding" and other practices, create an atmosphere of slackness and sabotage, thus seriously retarding the efficiency of the fields concerned.

These results are the important results. The remainder of this section represents the writer's personal reaction to some of the more detailed arguments.

One of the outstanding qualities of modern social thought is an unwillingness to recognize the need for a *balancing* of social alternatives. We are unwilling to recognize that there is always a certain amount of inconsistency among the various aims we seek, and that more of A—say job security—may mean less of B—say individual opportunity or rising living standards. Of course, there will always be disputes as to where to draw the line. But the really explosive element in the modern situation is the refusal to admit of *any* need for compromise. We want a complete, simultaneous realization of *all* conceivable social standards. But since in the nature of things many of the standards are somewhat contradictory, and simultaneous attainment is impossible, it follows that *no government or social system of any kind could satisfy at the same time all the standards which many intellectuals, labor leaders, and theologians are now insisting upon.* There cannot be unity or internal peace in this country until this need for balancing aims is recognized.[2]

[2] For example, pensions are *ceteris paribus* a good thing. Pensions funded, as in the case of the academic profession, so that one can move

We find this problem particularly in the case of "welfare economics." To many people, equality per se is a desirable goal. But we must remember that, given the unequal distribution of biological genes referred to by Dr. Samuelson,[3] an equal chance for unequals must lead to unequal results. Even if the runners all start at the same tape, only one, or two (if there is a tie), are likely to come in first.

Now of course the runners do not all start at the same tape in our society; hence some of the participants have spoken of the popularity of "Robin Hood" or "Jesse James" activity, and I agree with them that this is a question which cannot be pushed to one side. The welfare-redistributive point is so important that I should like to make a systematic statement of the problem as I see it.[4]

First of all, no one, I submit, can dispute that even the purely competitive adjustment is always capable of improvement, from the point of view of the ethical norms or "welfare functions" of some individuals or groups, through redistribution, etc.

To grant that much, however, does not get us very far. For, as is now generally conceded, it is obviously impossible to satisfy *all* of these particular "welfare functions" at the same time. The problem of social organization, therefore, under any system, *is* the problem of reconciling or judging between conflicting claims and values. We do not say much in pointing out

without losing one's deposit are especially good. But pensions which are lost by shifting help greatly to immobilize labor and to create in middle-aged men a feeling of confinement. Since writing this, I have received a bulletin from one of the regional offices of the Bureau of Labor Statistics, U. S. Department of Labor (released Feb. 18, 1951), which ends with the following significant statement: "The great extension of pension plans, seniority, and similar job rights raises special problems in the transfer of workers from nondefense to defense jobs."

[3] In a portion of the discussion not reported here.

[4] To save space for others I confine myself to this point only. My comments on other points will be found in the discussions and notes.

that, whatever solution or method of solution we adopt, *some-one* will always be dissatisfied. Nor is the fact that you can't please everyone a valid scientific reason for abandoning the competitive market—or for that matter any other system of social organization. Neither the union movement, nor any other movement, can derive any conclusive sanction from such a one-sided mode of analysis.

If modern welfare economics, to be sure, did give us an *objective, universally applicable, scientific* standard which enabled us to by-pass the problem of reconciling claims, and told us exactly, by scientific law, who "ought" to get what, then, indeed, we would have a powerful engine for testing, or quite possibly discarding, the results of any actual market. But such an objective, universally valid standard is precisely what a large number of modern welfare economists say that their analysis cannot give.[5] For the relative intensity of subjective individual wants is not capable of precise, neutral, scientific

[5] See for example Professor Samuelson's remarks, this volume, pp. 111, 112, 348. I have summarized my own views as follows: "As originally worked out, mathematical welfare economics included a more or less explicit general assumption that people had substantially similar tastes and capacities for enjoyment. On that basis it was possible to prove 'scientifically' that subsidizing certain industries and penalizing others, taking money from Peter and paying Paul, if done according to certain rules, would give greater total 'satisfaction.' But it was soon found out that we cannot *scientifically* compare the 'satisfactions' of particular individuals. For since people have different tastes, money, and everything else, may mean different things subjectively to one person than to another. About all that is left of the theory now, therefore, as a scientific proposition, is that if one man is made better off, without anyone else being worse off, total 'welfare' has (probably) increased. But, still worse, in full employment we cannot subsidize Peter without taxing Paul directly or by inflation. So the theory further reduces itself merely to a statement that if the national output grows in such a way as to permit a gain to both Paul and Peter at neither's expense, it will (probably) be a good thing—and we scarcely needed welfare analysis to guess that." "Toward Coherent Anti-Trust," *Virginia Law Review* (October, 1949), p. 668.

comparison. And on a more practical level, even if one grants, for example, that Professor Samuelson's point *"E"* may possibly exist, the writer does not see how we can ever in *fact* know where *"E"* is, or whether or not we have actually reached it.[6]

We are thus obliged always to go beyond science, or economics, or mere individual prejudice, if we wish to discuss distribution. We must begin, first, by trying to reach some sort of consensus of opinion on ethical values. And these ethical values relate not merely to the *results* which are reached, but also the *process* by which we reach them.

Yet among the ethical norms prized in a democracy we place a high value on persuasion or noncoercion. And, as Professor Knight has argued here, a relatively competitive market may often give tolerable approximation to such an ideal. On the other hand, however, we also have another ethical prejudice, supplementing the standard of noncoercion: namely, one in favor of giving people a "fair" chance, and against the indefinite accumulation of hereditary advantage. Welfare economics may thus be of value in reminding us that under our mores some sort of compromise balance must be struck between these ethical norms. I cannot see that it tells us much more. Certainly it gives us no precise, conclusive, universal rules. Concerning the problem of a balance, however, I want to say two principal things:

First of all, granted a desire for some redistribution to give a "fair chance," this redistribution should, I submit, be a systematic, relatively noncoercive one reached by the deliberate

---

[6] Regarding welfare analysis in general, cf. the following: "The position is still very weak. Individuals must still be economic men, and goods and jobs perfectly divisible. Goods must not give rise to external economies or diseconomies of consumption. External economies and diseconomies of production must also be absent. Situations must not occur which make the fulfillment both of equilibrium and the 'optimum' conditions impossible." I. M. D. Little, *A Critique of Welfare Economics* (Oxford University Press, 1950), p. 257.

political judgment of the community. The redistributions achieved by the un-co-ordinated, shortsighted, and ofttimes violent acts of particular groups may do far more harm than good. There is *no* guarantee whatever that they will actually benefit the people who should most be helped, and, as we have seen in this discussion, a great many reasons why they often might not. Having set up a system of "competitive co-operation"—for that is what our system is—the "Robin Hood" privilege should be the carefully guarded and limited prerogative of the state *only*.

My second point is more specific. Equality is a good thing, but so are rising living standards and greater opportunity. As Mr. Boulding has shown in some of his articles, a profit or income tax *can* affect incentive adversely (and hence growth). More important, as I have shown in my *Democracy and Progress*,[7] an income tax is not so much a tax on the rich as on those who are *getting* rich. It is often more of a discriminatory and unfair burden upon the *new* man than upon the old man. Merely making a large income doesn't mean one has a large fortune. Thus in levying taxes, while it is "fair" to make the receivers of large incomes pay "more," we must be careful lest in doing so we (1) hold back growth and (2) discriminate unduly against the rags-to-riches opportunities of our *poorer* citizens. A tax structure running from, say, 10 per cent to 40 per cent makes sense to me.[8] One running from, say, 10 per cent to 90 per cent seems undemocratic, and a definite discouragement to growth and opportunity.

On the question of opportunity there is another point to be remembered. While the state, through "free" services—health, education, etc.—can do much to give poorer citizens a better chance, mere training or mere health is not enough. Equally important is the chance to *use* one's health or training after one re-

[7] (Macmillan, 1949.)
[8] With proper carry-over adjustments, etc.

ceives it. It is not enough to be trained as a scientist if no further opportunity is given to make or, more likely, to use new discoveries. It is not enough to be trained as a doctor if a state-imposed medical code renders the doctor an automaton. It is not enough to be an inventor if one's invention is sabotaged by a security-conscious union. Growth comes through change; change and opportunity require spontaneity and incentive; spontaneity and incentive require differential rewards and a great deal of un-co-ordinated competition.[9] Thus again we come up against the impossibility of satisfying all our aims at once, and the need to determine how far we want to satisfy one at the expense of others.

[9] On these points see my *Democracy and Progress, op. cit.; Capitalism* (McGraw-Hill, 1951).

Index

Wages (Cont.)
and production, volume of, 37,
71-72
real. *See* Real wages
scientific approach to, 103-104
subsistence, 302-303. *See also* Subsistence theory of wages;
Wages, competitive
and competition, 316
and marginal productivity
theory, 302-303
theories, 1-3, 278-279, 312-314,
341-342
general evaluation of, 341
historical phases of, 2-3
and shares of national income,
341
survey of, 314-341. *See also* Indeterminacy theory; Marginal
productivity theory; Pur-
chasing power theory; Subsistence theory; Wage fund
doctrine
"Wages fund," 132
Walker, F., 317
Walras, Léon, 141, 156, 159, 160,
162, 166, 167, 301, 305, 321,
327, 331, 336, 341, 369, 370,
375
Wants, comparability of, 112

Wealth, national. *See* Income, na-
tional; Production, volume of
Wealth of Nations, 313
Webb, Beatrice, 115, 247
Webb, Sidney, 115, 247
Welfare economics, 111-112, 193,
372-378, 381-385. *See also,*
Ethics
evaluation of, 343-345, 347-349,
351
and individuality, 351
Welfare functions, 112, 343-344,
347-348, 381-382. *See also*
Ethics
Bergson, 371
defined, 381
Welfare state, 230, 241
Whitehead, A. N., 271
"Widow's cruse," 132, 139, 141,
149-150, 152, 155, 166, 167,
369
Wieser, F. von, 304, 327, 375
Wieser-Walras simultaneous equation,
375
Wright, D. McC., 121, 273, 340,
385
papers, 260-277, 278-291, 379-
385
discussion of, 7, 16, 292-311,
337, 339, 340, 365, 366, 367